DEVELOPER'S GUIDE TO MICROSOFT® PRISM 4

DEVELOPER'S GUIDE TO
Microsoft® Prism 4

Building Modular MVVM Applications
using Windows® Presentation Foundation
and Microsoft Silverlight®

Bob Brumfield
Geoff Cox
David Hill
Brian Noyes
Michael Puleio
Karl Shifflett

ISBN: 9780735656109

Contents

The Team
Who Brought You
This Guide

Vision	David Hill
Authors	Bob Brumfield, Geoff Cox, David Hill, Brian Noyes, Michael Puleio, and Karl Shifflett
Reviewers	Larry Brader, Mani Krishnaswami, Diego Poza, Fernando Simonazzi, and Blaine Wastell
Documentation Lead	Nelly Delgado
Editors	Tina Burden and Sharon Smith
Graphic Artist	Katie Niemer

The Prism 4 Development Team

The Microsoft patterns & practices team involves both experts and the broader community in its projects. The authors drove this book's direction and developed its content, but they want to acknowledge the individuals who contributed to Prism in various ways.

Program Management	Karl Shifflett and Blaine Wastell (Microsoft Corporation)
Architecture / Development	Bob Brumfield, David Hill, and Michael Puleio (Microsoft Corporation); Fernando Simonazzi (Clarius Consulting); Brian Noyes (Software Insight); Geoff Cox and Matias Bonaventura (Southworks SRL)
Testing	Larry Brader (Microsoft Corporation); Mani Krishnaswami, Meenakshi Krishnamoorthi, Rathi Velusamy, Ravindra Varman, Sangeetha Manickam, and Sanghamitra Chilla (Infosys Technologies Ltd)
Documentation	Nelly Delgado (Microsoft Corporation); Diego Poza (Southworks SRL)
Sustained Engineering	Fernando Antivero (Southworks SRL)
Editing / Production	Tina Burden (TinaTech, Inc.); Sharon Smith and Katie Niemer (Modeled Computation); John Hubbard (Eson); Ted Neveln (Ballard Indexing Services); Tom Draper and Patrick Lanfear (Twist Creative LLC)

Release Management Advisory Council

Richard Burte (ChannelCatalyst.com, Inc.)
Bill Wilder of Fidelity Investments, Clifford Tiltman of Morgan Stanley, Rob Eisenberg of Blue Spire, Norman Headlam, Ward Bell of IdeaBlade, Paul Jackson of CM Group Ltd., John Papa of Microsoft, Julian Dominguez of Clarius Consulting, Ted Neveln of Ballard Indexing Services, Glenn Block of Microsoft, Michael Kenyon of IHS, Inc., Terry Young of PEER Group, Jason Beres of Infragistics, Peter Lindes of The Church of Jesus Christ of Latter-day Saints, Mark Tucker of Neudesic, LLC, David Platt of Rolling Thunder Computing, Steve Gentile of Strategic Data Systems, Markus Egger of EPS Software Corp. & CODE Magazine, Ryan Cromwell of Strategic Data Systems, Todd Neal of McKesson Corp, Dipesh Patel of Fidelity Investments, David Poll of Microsoft Corporation, Ezequiel Jabid of Southworks SRL

Community

Attendees at patterns & practices symposium, PDC, TechReady, and TechEd conferences who provided informal feedback; Prism users who provided feedback on CodePlex, through our blogs, surveys, and via email.

Thank you!

Foreword

What comes after "Hello, World?"

WPF and Silverlight developers are blessed with an abundance of excellent books, videos, and online articles from which to learn how to build a single screen application. These resources teach data binding, dependency properties, resources, styles, effects, control templating, and many other fundamentals of XAML platform programming. There's no lack of tutorials on Model-View-ViewModel (MVVM), the justly popular and predominant pattern for structuring an individual screen. But they stop short of the guidance you need to deliver a non-trivial application in full.

Your first screen goes well. You add a second screen and a third. Because you started your solution with the built-in "Navigation Application Template," adding new screens feels like hanging shirts on a closet rod. You are on a roll. Until the harsh reality of real application requirements sets in.

As it happens, your application has 30 screens not three. There's no room on that closet rod for 30 screens. Some screens are modal pop-ups; you don't navigate to a pop-up. Screens become interdependent such that user activity in one screen triggers changes that propagate throughout the UI. Some screens are optional; others are visible only to authorized users. Some screens are permanent, while other screens can be opened and closed at will. You discover that navigating back to a previously displayed screen creates a new instance. That's not what you expected and, to your horror, the prior instance is gone along with the user's unsaved changes.

You realize that the out-of-the-box navigation is useless to you. You are resigned to ripping it out and starting over. You consider building your own UI framework, but decide to survey the scene first. Surely someone has been down this road before. Surely someone has published guidance and code to cope with the scale, variety, and complexity of your real world application.

Someone has. The Microsoft Prism Library, code samples, and the book that you're reading now are the culmination of a five year quest to consolidate the best advice and techniques from experts and practitioners in the field.

Prism covers all of the scenarios just mentioned and many more. You'll find guidance and supporting code for:

- Partitioning the application into modules, those semi-autonomous islands of functionality that should be developed and maintained independently.

- Mechanisms for loading modules asynchronously or on-demand so that applications start quickly.
- A publish/subscribe apparatus, the event aggregator, for passing messages among components that cannot and should not connect directly.
- Dynamically composing a complex screen, such as a dashboard, from several simpler views.
- Creating pages using View-First, ViewModel-First, or a controller that makes them and coordinates them.
- Initializing views with parameters or context information as when launching an editor that targets a selected customer.
- Guidelines and examples of automated tests for views and view models that depend upon asynchronous data sources.

Many developers will see in Prism an all-in-one solution from a single trusted source. They have neither the time nor inclination to scrutinize each component, compare it with competitors, and assemble a custom framework from a buffet of alternatives. They fear the "Franken-framework" of mismatched parts from multiple vendors. For this audience, Prism is a safe and reliable choice. I don't know of a solution as comprehensive, well documented, or well supported. The design is sound. The code is solid and tested. Great applications are built exclusively with Prism and yours can be one of them.

Other developers look at Prism a little differently. They see Prism as a compendium of patterns and strategies for building WPF and Silverlight UIs. The shipped software is a confederation of optional components. They might embrace Prism modularity but prefer someone else's alternative to **DelegateCommands**. They could choose a third party injection container instead of MEF or Unity. They might use a region only in the shell or not use regions at all. For this audience, Prism is a source of inspiration and advice. It's a storehouse of code to use, ignore, or replace as they see fit.

One of Prism's great and hard won achievements is that it supports both perspectives equally. It's a coherent framework of cooperating components that work seamlessly together. Yet each part stands on its own, ready to collaborate, without depending on any of the others.

Whether you adopt it whole or in part, I urge you to read this book, study the Quick-Starts, and explore the reference implementations. That's the best way to master Prism itself. Better still, you'll become a more capable programmer, equipped to anticipate real-world UI architectural challenges and solve them effectively.

Ward Bell
VP Technology, IdeaBlade (www.ideablade.com)
Silverlight MVP

Foreword

Building WPF and Silverlight applications can be challenging, especially for those new to the technology. Building clean, maintainable, extensible, testable, loosely coupled ones—with no idea where to start—is close to impossible. In late 2007, I was privileged to get a call from Glenn Block at Microsoft asking if I was interested in working with the Microsoft patterns & practices team on a project that would become the first release of Prism, which was released as the Composite Application Guidance for WPF in June 2008.

I had been working with WPF on complex customer applications, trying to figure out the best practices and patterns on my own. This was a fantastic opportunity to provide some guidance and feedback to the team on what mattered, what worked, and what didn't, in real customer apps that I had worked on. I had worked with various patterns & practices teams before as an external advisor, but this was my first opportunity to come in as a consultant and participate as an integral part of the team.

It turned out to be a wonderful experience for me. The team included some of the most intelligent, creative, and fun individuals I have had a chance to work with in this industry. The maturity of the team's development process, the effort that they put into collecting community input and keeping the community involved throughout the development process, and their collective design and coding prowess and professionalism made it clear from the start that the right people were working on guiding the .NET development community on the right way to build apps. I learned a ton in the process and hopefully contributed something that helped make Prism a better product. So, naturally I was delighted when I got the chance to work closely with the team again on the release of Prism 4.

Prism 4 offers many things to many people. One of the biggest misconceptions is that because it offers so much, it is too big or too complicated for smaller apps. One of the early design goals of Prism was to keep the concerns of Prism separated in the same way Prism helps you separate your own application's concerns in the presentation layer. I think the team did a great job of doing that, and you can easily use just commands, or just events, or just modularity, or just UI composition or some combination of the above in ways that are minimally intrusive to the rest of your application code. Add to that the new Model-View-ViewModel (MVVM) pattern guidance, Managed Extensibility Framework (MEF) integration, and navigation functionality of Prism 4, and you have a great set of tools in a toolkit that can help you develop apps of any size.

If you are writing a small app, there are some great tools and techniques in here that will help you to keep your app from becoming a maintenance liability. If you are developing a large application with a complex UI, you need something like Prism 4 to keep you from being overwhelmed by the complexity and the volume of code that can result from not basing your app on well-defined design patterns and thoroughly tested code to help you implement those patterns.

This book is another new feature of Prism 4. Previous releases provided great documentation in a standard Help format, consisting of many short topics with links to related topics. And while that format is essential when you are writing code and need to look up little bits and pieces to keep you moving forward, there was a very important phase of just getting up to speed on Prism and learning the concepts that was being neglected. You couldn't read a book, end-to-end, or chapter by chapter to learn the concepts and see some code to make those concepts clear, because no such book existed (much as I tried to find the time to write that book myself).

The structure of a good book on a programming technology is inherently different from good help topics. This book is structured so that you can read it from cover to cover or just refer to the topics that interest you, without having to be at your computer as you do so. To supplement the book, the help documentation online has additional material, including hands-on labs and advanced information about the reference implementations and QuickStarts. Because the book is available in print and e-book form, you can take it with you on a plane or to the beach, so that when you do sit down to write your Prism code, you are immediately productive and past the "What is it and how do I use it" phase. You can then refer to the online help, hands-on labs, QuickStart topics, and so on when you are at your computer and using Visual Studio.

Additionally, with this book you get the collective knowledge of the entire team, not just the perspective of a single or small group of authors. All of the Prism developers and designers collaborated and contributed to the content you will find in this book. If one person wrote a portion, several others reviewed, commented, and improved it. However, you are primarily getting the content from the developers who wrote the features, which is a rare opportunity. Customers often ask me: "Where is the best place to start learning about Prism, and how can I use it?" In the past, I had to point them to a fragmented collection of articles, podcasts, and blog posts. Now I have a simple and easy answer, and I can point them one place – right here to this book.

Brian Noyes
Chief Architect, IDesign Inc. (www.idesign.net)
Silverlight MVP

1   Introduction

Prism provides guidance designed to help you more easily design and build rich, flexible, and easy-to-maintain Windows Presentation Foundation (WPF) desktop applications, Rich Internet Applications (RIAs) built with the Microsoft® Silverlight® browser plug-in, and Windows Phone 7 applications. Prism uses design patterns that embody important architectural design principles, such as separation of concerns and loose coupling. These patterns help you to design and build applications by using loosely coupled components that can evolve independently but that can be easily and seamlessly integrated into the overall application. These types of applications are known as composite applications.

> **Note:** *Prism was the code name for the guidance formally known as the **Composite Application Guidance for WPF and Silverlight**. For brevity and conciseness, and due to customer demand, this guidance is now referred to simply as **Prism**.*

Prism is intended for software developers who are building WPF or Silverlight applications that typically feature multiple screens, rich user interaction, and data visualization, and that embody significant presentation and business logic. These applications typically interact with multiple back-end systems and services and, using a layered architecture, may be physically deployed across multiple tiers. It is expected that the applications will evolve significantly over their lifetimes in response to new requirements and business opportunities. In short, these applications are built to last and built for change. Applications that do not demand these characteristics may not benefit from using Prism.

Prism includes reference implementations, QuickStarts, reusable library code (the Prism Library), and extensive documentation. This version of Prism targets the Microsoft .NET Framework version 4 and Silverlight version 4, and includes new guidance related to the Model-View-ViewModel (MVVM) pattern, navigation, and the Managed Extensibility Framework (MEF). Because Prism is built on the .NET Framework 4 (which includes WPF) and Silverlight 4, familiarity with these technologies is useful for evaluating and adopting Prism.

It should be noted that, while Prism is not difficult to learn, developers must be ready and willing to embrace patterns and practices that may be new to them. Management understanding and commitment is crucial, and the project deadline must accommodate an investment of time up front for learning these patterns and practices.

Why Use Prism?

Designing and building rich WPF or Silverlight client applications that are flexible and easy to maintain can be challenging. This section describes some of the common challenges you might encounter when building WPF or Silverlight client applications, and describes how Prism helps you to address those challenges.

CLIENT APPLICATION DEVELOPMENT CHALLENGES

Typically, developers of client applications face quite a few challenges. Application requirements can change over time. New business opportunities and challenges may present themselves, new technologies may become available, or even ongoing customer feedback during the development cycle may significantly affect the requirements of the application. Therefore, it is important to build the application so that it is flexible and can be easily modified or extended over time. Designing for this type of flexibility can be hard to accomplish. It requires an architecture that allows individual parts of the application to be independently developed and tested, and then modified or updated later, in isolation, without affecting the rest of the application.

Most enterprise applications are sufficiently complex that they require more than one developer—maybe even a large team of developers that includes user interface (UI) designers and localizers, in addition to developers. It can be a significant challenge to decide how to design the application so that multiple developers or subteams can work effectively on different pieces of the application independently, while still ensuring that the pieces come together seamlessly when integrated into the application.

Designing and building applications in a monolithic style can result in applications that are very difficult and inefficient to maintain. Here, *monolithic* refers to an application in which the components are very tightly coupled and there is no clear separation between them. Typically, applications designed and built this way can cause problems for the developer. It may be difficult to add new features or replace existing features, it may be difficult to resolve bugs without breaking other portions of the application, and the application may be difficult to test and deploy. Also, a monolithic design affects the ability of developers and designers to work together efficiently.

THE COMPOSITE APPROACH

An effective remedy for these challenges is to partition the application into a number of discrete, loosely coupled, semi-independent components that can then be easily integrated into an application shell to form a coherent solution. Applications designed and built this way are known as composite applications.

Composite applications provide many benefits, including the following:

- They allow modules to be individually developed, tested, and deployed by different individuals or subteams. They also allow them to be modified or extended with new functionality more easily, thereby allowing the application to be more easily extended and maintained. Note that even single-person projects can benefit from this modular approach because the resulting applications are easier to test and maintain.

- They provide a common shell composed of UI components from various modules that interact in a loosely coupled way. This reduces the contention that arises from multiple developers adding new functionality to the UI, and it promotes a unified appearance.

- They promote reuse and a clean separation of concerns between the application's horizontal capabilities, such as logging and authentication, and its vertical capabilities, such as business functionality that is specific to the application. This also allows you to more easily manage the dependencies and interactions between application components.

- They help maintain a separation of roles by allowing different individuals or sub-teams to focus on a specific task or piece of functionality according to their focus or expertise. In particular, they provide a cleaner separation between the UI and the business logic of the application—this means that the UI designer can focus on creating a richer user experience.

Composite applications are highly suited to a range of client application scenarios. For example, a composite application is ideal for creating a rich end-user experience over disparate back-end systems. The following illustration shows an example of this type of a composite application.

Composite application with multiple back-end systems

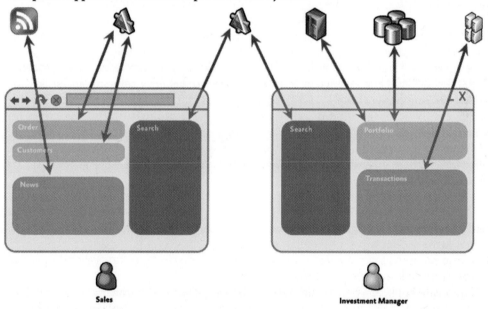

In this type of application, the user can be presented with a rich and flexible user experience that provides a task-oriented focus over functionality that spans multiple back-end systems, services, and data stores, where each is represented by one or more dedicated modules. The clean separation between the application logic and the UI allows the application to provide a consistent and differentiated appearance across all constituent modules.

Additionally, a composite application can be useful when there are independently evolving components in the UI that heavily integrate with each other and that are typically maintained by separate teams. The following illustration shows a screen shot of this type of application. The highlighted areas represent independent components that are integrated into the UI.

Stock Trader Reference Implementation composite application

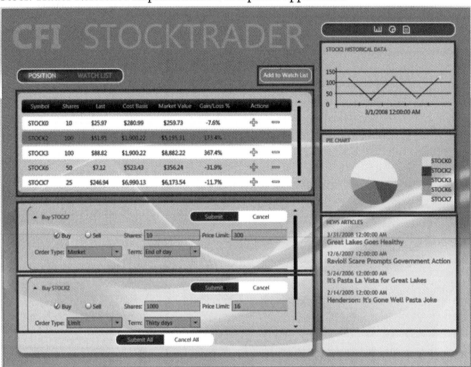

In this case, the composite application allows the UI to be composed dynamically. This delivers a flexible user experience. For example, it can allow new functionality to be dynamically added to the application at run time, which enables rich end-user customization and extensibility.

CHALLENGES NOT ADDRESSED BY PRISM

Although Prism helps you to address many of the challenges you might face when building WPF or Silverlight applications, there are many other challenges that you might face, depending on your application scenario and requirements. For example, Prism does not directly address the following topics:

- Occasional connectivity and data synchronization
- Service and messaging infrastructure design
- Authentication and authorization

- Application performance
- Application versioning
- Error handling and fault tolerance

Getting Started with Prism

This section describes how to install and start exploring Prism. You can download Prism from MSDN.

PREREQUISITES

Prism assumes that you have hands-on experience with WPF or Silverlight. There are a few important tools and concepts that Prism uses heavily, and you should become familiar with them. They include the following:

- **XAML (Extensible Application Markup Language)**. This is the language used to declaratively define and initialize the user interface in WPF and Silverlight applications.
- **Data binding**. This is how UI elements are connected to components and data in WPF and Silverlight.
- **Resources**. These are used to create and manage styles, data templates, and control templates in WPF and Silverlight.
- **Commands**. These are used to connect user gestures and input to controls.
- **User controls**. These are components that provide custom behavior or custom appearance.
- **Dependency properties**. These are extensions to the common language runtime (CLR) property system to enable property setting and monitoring in support of data binding, routed commands, and events.
- **Behaviors.** Behaviors are objects that encapsulate interactive functionality that can be easily applied to controls in the user interface.

INSTALLING PRISM

This section describes how to install Prism. It involves the following three steps:

1. Install system requirements.

2. Extract the Prism source code, binaries, and documentation.

3. Register the Prism binaries.

Step 1: Install System Requirements

Prism was designed to run on the Windows® 7, Windows Vista®, or Windows Server® 2008 operating systems. This version has been smoke tested on Windows XP Professional and Windows Server 2003, but it has not been exhaustively tested. WPF applications built using this guidance require the .NET Framework 4, and Silverlight applications require Silverlight 4.

Before you can use the Prism Library, you need to install the following:
- Microsoft .NET Framework 4 (installed with the Microsoft Visual Studio® 2010 development system)
- Microsoft Visual Studio 2010 Professional, Premium, or Ultimate editions

Note: *You can also use Visual Studio 2010 Express Edition and the Prism Library to develop Prism applications.*

If you are developing Silverlight applications, you need to install the following:
- Microsoft Silverlight 4 Tools for Visual Studio 2010 (required for Silverlight development; this includes the developer Silverlight runtime)

Note: *Although the Silverlight Tools for Visual Studio 2010 are not required, all WPF and Silverlight developers should download and use the latest version of the Silverlight Tools for Visual Studio 2010.*
The WPF and Silverlight Designer for Visual Studio is updated, together with the Silverlight developer runtime and software development kit (SDK), which are included in the download. These updates include new features and bug fixes.

You should also consider installing the following optional tools:
- Microsoft Expression Blend® 4 design software. A professional design tool for creating compelling user experiences and applications for WPF and Silverlight.
- Windows Phone Developer Tools SDK. For Windows Phone 7 development.

Note: *For more information about using Prism on Windows Phone 7, see the Windows Phone 7 Developer Guide community site on CodePlex.*

Step 2: Extract the Prism Source Code, Binaries, and Documentation
To install the Prism assets, right-click the Prismv4.exe file, and then click **Run as administrator**. This will extract the source code, binaries, and documentation into the folder of your choice.

Step 3: Register the Prism Binaries
Registering the Prism Library with Visual Studio is not required, but doing so simplifies the task of referencing the Prism Library assemblies in your projects. If you choose to register the binaries, they will be listed in the Visual Studio **Add References** dialog box when you add a reference. If you choose not to register the binaries, you will need to manually set a file reference to the Prism Library binaries in your projects. The Prism Library signed assemblies will be placed in the following folders:
- {prism}\Bin\Desktop
- {prism}\Bin\Silverlight
- {prism}\Bin\Phone

To register the Prism Library binaries, run the RegisterPrismBinaries.bat batch file located in the folder where you extracted Prism. This batch file creates a temporary .reg file with the information required to register the Desktop, Silverlight, and Phone folders containing the binaries, and then uses it to update the registry. Because updating the registry is a privileged operation, a User Account Control (UAC) prompt will appear if you do not have elevated privileges.

> **Note:** *At most, one copy of the binaries can be registered using the script. If multiple copies of the Prism Library are registered, only the binaries for the last registered copy will be available in Visual Studio.*

EXPLORING PRISM

Now that you have successfully installed Prism, it's time to see what it includes. This section provides a brief overview of the various elements included in Prism, including the Prism Library, documentation, and the various QuickStarts and reference implementations.

What's New in This Release

This release of Prism has been updated to target WPF 4 and Silverlight 4, and it contains several areas of new and significantly updated guidance, including the following:

- **Managed Extensibility Framework (MEF)**. Prism now includes guidance on using MEF to manage dependencies and to maintain loose coupling between components. The use of MEF is explored in Chapter 3, "Managing Dependencies Between Components."

- **The Model-View-View Model (MVVM) pattern**. Previous versions of Prism have provided extensive guidance on the use of separated presentation patterns. This guidance has now been updated to focus on the MVVM pattern. Chapter 5 provides an overview of the MVVM pattern and describes how to implement it. Chapter 6 covers more advanced MVVM scenarios.

- **Navigation**. Prism now provides guidance on implementing navigation within your WPF or Silverlight application. This guidance covers both state-based navigation, which is used when you update the visual state of a single view, and view-switching navigation, which is used when navigating between views. Both approaches are covered in depth in Chapter 8, "Navigation."

Prism now also provides signed binary versions of the Prism Library assemblies. These assemblies are provided as a convenience for developers who want to use the Prism Library without modification in their own applications. In addition, all Visual Studio projects (for the Prism Library as well as the reference implementations and QuickStarts) have also been migrated to use Visual Studio 2010 and Silverlight 4.

What's Included

Prism consists of the following:

- **Prism Library source code**. The source code for the Prism Library assemblies, including the core Prism functionality, plus Unity and MEF extensions, which provide additional components for using Prism with the Unity Application Block (Unity) and the Managed Extensibility Framework.

- **Prism binary assemblies**. Signed binary versions of the Prism Library assemblies. These assemblies are located in the bin folder and are provided as a convenient way for developers to use the Prism Library. The Prism binaries can be rebuilt and can be registered with Visual Studio by using the provided script files. The binary assemblies also include the Unity Application Block and the Service Locator assemblies.

- **Reference implementations**. Comprehensive sample applications that illustrate how Prism can be used to implement real-world application scenarios. The reference implementations are intentionally incomplete, but they illustrate how many of the patterns in Prism can work together within a single application. Prism provides two reference implementations: the Stock Trader Reference Implementation (Stock Trader RI) and the MVVM Reference Implementation (MVVM RI).

- **QuickStarts**. Prism includes the source code for several small, focused sample applications that illustrate the MVVM pattern, navigation, UI composition, modularity, commanding, event aggregation, and multi-targeting.

- **Documentation**. The Prism 4 documentation provides an overview of the goals and concepts behind Prism and detailed guidance on using each of the capabilities and design patterns provided by Prism. The next section provides a chapter-by-chapter overview of the topics covered.

Exploring the Documentation

The Prism documentation spans a wide range of topics, including an overview of common development challenges and the composite application approach, an overview of the Prism Library and the design patterns that it implements, as well as step-by-step instructions for using the Prism Library during development. The documentation is intended to appeal to a broad technical audience to help readers understand and use Prism within their own applications. The documentation includes the following:

- **Chapter 2, "Initializing Prism Applications."** This chapter discusses what needs to happen to get a modular Prism application up and running.

- **Chapter 3, "Managing Dependencies Between Components."** Applications based on the Prism Library rely on a dependency injection container. Although Prism has the ability to work with nearly any dependency injection container, the Prism Library provides two default options for dependency injection containers: Unity or MEF. This chapter discusses the different capabilities and what you need to think about when working with a dependency injection container.

- **Chapter 4, "Modular Application Development."** This chapter discusses the core concepts, key decisions, and core scenarios that you will encounter when you create a modular client application with Prism.

- **Chapter 5, "Implementing the MVVM Pattern."** Using the MVVM pattern, you separate the UI of your application and the underlying presentation and business logic into three separate classes: the view, model, and view model. This chapter discusses the core concepts behind the MVVM pattern and describes how to use Prism to implement the pattern in your application.

- **Chapter 6, "Advanced MVVM Scenarios."** This chapter provides guidance on implementing more advanced scenarios by using the MVVM pattern, including how to implement composite commands (commands that represent a group of commands), and how to handle asynchronous web service and user interactions. This chapter also provides guidance on using a dependency injection container, such as Unity or MEF, to handle the construction, connection, and configuration of the MVVM classes.

- **Chapter 7, "Composing the User Interface."** Regions are placeholders that allow a developer to specify where views will be displayed in the application's UI. In Prism, there are two approaches to displaying views in a region: view discovery and view injection. This chapter describes how to work with regions and the UI. It also includes information to help UI designers to understand composite applications.

- **Chapter 8, "Navigation."** Navigation is the process by which an application coordinates changes to its UI as a result of a user's interaction with the application or internal application state changes. This chapter provides guidance on implementing state-based navigation, where the state of the UI in a view is updated to reflect navigation, and view-switching navigation, where a new view is created and displayed in a region.

- **Chapter 9, "Communicating Between Loosely Coupled Components."** This chapter discusses the various options for communicating between components in different modules, using commanding, the event aggregator, region context, and shared services.

- **Chapter 10, "Sharing Code Between Silverlight and WPF."** Multi-targeted code is used to target two different platforms with largely the same code base. In this topic, the targeted technologies are WPF and Silverlight. This chapter helps you understand what multi-targeting is and its advantages and disadvantages. Prism provides the Project Linker tool to help you to automatically create and maintain links from a source project to a target project to share code that is common between Silverlight and WPF.

- **Chapter 11, "Deploying Prism Applications."** This chapter addresses deployment considerations for Prism WPF and Silverlight applications.

- **Appendix A, "Glossary."** This appendix provides a concise summary of the terms, concepts, design patterns, and capabilities provided by Prism.

- **Appendix B, "Patterns in the Prism Library."** This appendix describes the software design patterns applied in the Prism Library and the Stock Trader RI. This topic primarily targets architects and developers who want to become familiar with the patterns used to address the challenges in building composite applications.

- **Appendix C, "Prism Library."** This appendix provides an overview of the Prism Library.

The following topics are included with the Prism download and on MSDN:

- **Appendix D, "Upgrading from Previous Versions."** This appendix discusses what you need to know if you are upgrading from previous versions of Prism.

- **Appendix E, "Extending Prism."** This appendix discusses how you can extend Prism modularity, behaviors, and navigation.

- **Appendix F, "Reference Implementations."** This appendix describes the reference implementations included with Prism. For more information, see the section "Exploring the Reference Implementations."

- **Appendix G, "QuickStarts."** Prism includes the source code for several Quick-Starts that demonstrate key concepts. For more information, see the next section, "Exploring the QuickStarts."

- **Appendix H, "Prism Hands-On Labs."** The hands-on labs demonstrate how to build a simple composite application, step-by-step, in WPF and Silverlight. This appendix primarily targets developers who want to understand the basic concepts of the Prism Library. It also includes a deployment hands-on lab for publishing and updating a Prism WPF application with ClickOnce.

Exploring the QuickStarts

The QuickStarts are small, focused applications that illustrate specific Prism-related concepts. QuickStarts are an ideal starting point if you want to gain an understanding of a key concept and you are comfortable learning new techniques by examining source code. Prism includes the following QuickStarts:

- **Modularity QuickStarts for WPF and Modularity QuickStarts for Silverlight**. These QuickStarts demonstrate how to build WPF and Silverlight applications composed of modules. The modules can be statically loaded if the shell contains a reference to the module's assembly, or dynamically loaded if modules are dynamically discovered and loaded at run time. The QuickStarts demonstrate using the Unity container and MEF.

- **Basic MVVM QuickStart and MVVM QuickStart**. The Basic MVVM QuickStart demonstrates how to build a very simple application that implements the MVVM presentation pattern. The MVVM QuickStart demonstrates how to build an application that implements the MVVM presentation pattern, showing some of the more common challenges that developers can face, such as validation, UI interactions, and data templates.

- **UI Composition QuickStart**. This QuickStart demonstrates how to build WPF and Silverlight UIs composed of different views that are dynamically loaded into regions and that interact with each other in a decoupled way. It illustrates how to use both the view discovery and view injection approaches for UI composition.

- **State-Based Navigation QuickStart**. This QuickStart demonstrates an approach to defining the navigation of a simple application. It uses the Silverlight Visual State Manager (VSM) to define the different states that the application has, and defines animations for both the states and the transitions between states.

- **View-Switching Navigation QuickStart**. This QuickStart demonstrates how to use the Prism Region Navigation API. The QuickStart shows multiple navigation scenarios, including navigating to a view in a region, navigating to a view in a region contained in another view (nested navigation), navigation journal support, just-in-time view creation, passing contextual information when navigating to a view, views and view models participating in navigation, and using navigation as part of an application built through modularity and UI composition.
- **Commanding QuickStart**. This QuickStart demonstrates how to build a WPF or Silverlight UI that uses commands provided by the Prism Library to handle UI actions in a decoupled way.
- **Event Aggregation QuickStart**. This QuickStart demonstrates how to build a WPF or Silverlight application that uses the Event Aggregator service. You can use this service to establish loosely coupled communications between components in your application.
- **Multi-Targeting QuickStart**. This QuickStart demonstrates the structure of a project created to multi-target WPF and Silverlight environments. It provides a desktop experience (on WPF) and a Rich Internet Application (RIA) experience (on Silverlight).

Exploring the Reference Implementations

The Prism reference implementations are example applications based on real-world challenges customers are facing. When you look at these applications, look at them as a reference for building applications with the Prism Library. The Prism reference implementations include:

- **Stock Trader Reference Implementation**. The Stock Trader RI is a composite application that demonstrates an implementation of the baseline architecture using the Prism Library.
- **MVVM Reference Implementation**. The MVVM RI demonstrates complex challenges that developers face when they use the MVVM pattern to create applications.

UPGRADING FROM EARLIER RELEASES

If you are upgrading from a previous release of this guidance, you should review "Upgrading from Previous Releases" in Appendix D to understand the major differences between this and the previous releases.

If you are upgrading from the Composite UI Application Block (which targeted Windows Forms) to the Prism Library, you should review "Upgrading from the Composite UI Application Block" in Appendix D so that you understand how the concepts in the Composite UI Application Block map to the Prism Library. This appendix is available on MSDN.

An Overview of Prism

This section describes some of the design goals behind Prism and contains a brief summary of Prism's key concepts. It then provides an overview of the first few steps required to create a basic Prism application.

PRISM DESIGN GOALS

Prism is designed around the core architectural design principles of separation of concerns and loose coupling. This allows Prism to provide many benefits, including the following:

- **Reuse**. Prism promotes reuse by allowing components and services to be easily developed, tested and integrated into one or more applications. At the component level, Prism facilitates the reuse of unit-tested components that can be easily discovered and integrated at run time through dependency injection. At the application level, Prism supports the use of modules that encapsulate application-level capabilities and can be reused across applications.

- **Extensibility**. Prism helps you create applications that are easy to extend by managing component dependencies, thereby allowing you to build components that can be easily integrated or replaced with alternative implementations at run time, and by providing you with the ability to decompose an application into modules that can be independently updated and deployed. Many of the components in the Prism Library itself can also be extended or replaced.

- **Flexibility**. Prism helps you create flexible applications that you can update easily as new capabilities are developed and integrated. Prism also lets you use common services and components to develop WPF and Silverlight applications, allowing the applications to be deployed and consumed in the most appropriate way. It also allows applications to provide different experiences based on role or configuration.

- **Team Development**. Prism promotes team development by allowing separate teams to develop and even deploy different parts of the application independently. Prism helps to minimize cross-team dependencies and allows teams to focus on different functional areas (such as UI design, business logic implementation, and infrastructure code development) or on different business-level functional areas (such as profile, sales, inventory, or logistics).

- **Quality**. Prism can help to increase the quality of applications by allowing common services and components to be fully tested and made available to the development teams. In addition, by providing fully tested implementations of common design patterns and the guidance needed to fully take advantage of them, Prism allows development teams to focus on their application requirements instead of implementing and testing infrastructure code.

It is important to note that Prism was designed so that you can use any of Prism's capabilities and design patterns individually, or all of them together, depending on your requirements and your application scenario. Prism was designed so that it could be incrementally adopted, allowing you to use the capabilities and design patterns that make sense for your particular application without requiring major structural changes.

Finally, because software testing should be considered a first-class development activity and tightly integrated into the development process, Prism provides extensive support for various types of software testing, thereby allowing you to design and build applications that are easy to test. Prism itself was developed with testing in mind. It was developed to meet multiple strict quality gates to ensure that it meets Microsoft security standards and will function correctly on multiple operating systems, with multiple versions of Visual Studio, and with multiple programming languages. Unit tests were run after each check-in. In addition, the Prism library was tested against several additional quality gates, as listed in the following table.

Test	Description
Acceptance testing	Validates the application functionality using user scenarios to drive the test requirements. Tests can be executed manually or automated.
Application building exercises	Team members build applications that consume the deliverable software.
Black box testing	Manual acceptance tests performed from the user point of view.
Cross-browser testing	All automated tests are run on multiple browsers.
Cross-platform testing	All automated tests are run on multiple platforms.
Globalization testing	All automated tests are run on multiple languages.
Performance testing	Measures how fast a particular aspect of a system performs under prescribed load levels.
Security review	Internal Microsoft security audit standards that cover thread models, identifying attack factors and running the code though security analysis tools.
Stress testing	Measures stability of the system under extreme loads; specifically designed to identify issues such as memory leaks and threading issues.
White box testing	In-depth source code analysis validating the coding standards, structure, and how the code maps to the overall architecture.

The Prism Library source code includes unit and UI automation tests, as shown in the following table. You can use these as an educational resource, or you can run the tests against the Prism Library itself. This allows you to customize, re-compile, test, and deploy a modified version of the Prism Library using similar quality gates as the Prism team.

Test	Description
UI automation tests	Limited range of acceptance testing; these drive the application from the user perspective.
Unit tests	Validate the implementation of a class.

PRISM KEY CONCEPTS

Prism provides capabilities and design patterns that may be unfamiliar to you, especially if you are new to design patterns and composite application development. This section provides a brief overview of the main concepts behind Prism and defines some of the terminology that you will see used throughout the documentation and code.

- **Modules**. Modules are packages of functionality that can be independently developed, tested, and (optionally) deployed. In many situations, modules are developed and maintained by separate teams. A typical Prism application is built from multiple modules. Modules can be used to represent specific business-related functionality (for example, profile management) and encapsulate all the views, services, and data models required to implement that functionality. Modules can also be used to encapsulate common application infrastructure or services (for example, logging and exception management services) that can be reused across multiple applications.

- **Module catalog**. In a composite application, modules must be discovered and loaded at run time by the host application. In Prism, a module catalog is used to specify which modules are to be loaded, when they will be loaded, and in the order in which they will be loaded. The module catalog is used by the **ModuleManager** and **ModuleLoader** components, which are responsible for downloading the modules if they are remote, loading the module's assemblies into the application domain, and initializing the module. Prism allows the module catalog to be specified in different ways, including programmatically in code, declaratively in XAML, or in a configuration file. You can also implement a custom module catalog if you need to.

- **Shell**. The shell is the host application into which modules are loaded. The shell defines the overall layout and structure of the application, but it is typically unaware of the exact modules that it will host. It usually implements common application services and infrastructure, but most of the application's functionality and content is implemented within the modules. The shell also provides the top-level window or visual element that will then host the different UI components provided by the loaded modules.

- **Views**. Views are UI controls that encapsulate the UI for a particular feature or functional area of the application. Views are used in conjunction with the MVVM or Model-View-Presenter (MVP) patterns, which are used to provide a clean separation of concerns between the UI and the application's presentation logic and data. Views are used to encapsulate the UI and define user interaction behavior, thereby allowing the view to be updated or replaced independently of the underlying application functionality. Views use data binding to interact with view model and presenter classes.

- **View models and presenters**. View models are classes that encapsulate the application's presentation logic and state. They are part of the MVVM pattern. View models encapsulate much of the application's functionality. Presenters are similar to view models in that they encapsulate the presentation logic and state. They are used as part of the MVP pattern. Both view models and presenters define the properties, commands, and events to which controls in the view can data-bind.

- **Models**. Model classes encapsulate the application data and business logic. They are used as part of the MVVM or MVP patterns. Models encapsulate data and any associated validation and business rules to ensure data consistency and integrity.

- **Commands**. Commands are used to encapsulate application functionality in a way that allows them to be defined and tested independently of the application's UI. They can be defined as command objects or as command methods in the view model or presenter. Prism provides the **DelegateCommand** class and the **Composite Command** class. The latter is used to represent a collection of commands which are all invoked together.

- **Regions**. Regions are logical placeholders defined within the application's UI (in the shell or within views) into which views are displayed. Regions allow the layout of the application's UI to be updated without requiring changes to the application logic. Many common controls can be used as regions, allowing views to be automatically displayed within a control, such as a **ContentControl**, **ItemsControl**, **ListBox**, or **TabControl**. Views can be displayed within a region programmatically or automatically. Prism also provides support for implementing navigation with regions. Regions can be located by other components through the **RegionManager** component, which uses **RegionAdapter** and **RegionBehavior** components to coordinate the display of views within specific regions.

- **Navigation**. Navigation is defined as the process by which an application coordinates changes to its UI as a result of a user's interaction with the application or internal application state changes. Prism supports two styles of navigation: state-based navigation, in which the state of an existing view is updated to implement simple navigation scenarios, and view-switching navigation, in which new views are created and old views are replaced within the application's UI. View-switching navigation uses a Uniform Resource Identifier (URI)–based navigation mechanism in conjunction with Prism regions to allow flexible navigation schemes to be implemented.

- **Event aggregator**. Components in a composite application often need to communicate with other components and services in the application in a loosely coupled way. To support this, Prism provides the **EventAggregator** component, which implements a pub-sub event mechanism, thereby allowing components to publish events and allowing other components to subscribe to those events without either of them requiring a reference to the other. The **EventAggregator** is often used to allow components defined in different modules to communicate with each other.

- **Dependency injection container**. The Dependency Injection (DI) pattern is used throughout Prism to allow the dependencies between components to be managed. Dependency injection allows component dependencies to be fulfilled at run time, and it supports extensibility and testability. Prism is designed to work with Unity or MEF, or with any other dependency injection containers by using the **ServiceLocator**.

- **Services**. Services are components that encapsulate non-UI related functionality, such as logging, exception management, and data access. Services can be defined by the application or within a module. Services are often registered with the dependency injection container so that they can be located or constructed as required and used by other components that depend on them.

- **Controllers**. Controllers are classes that are used to coordinate the construction and initialization of views that are to be displayed in a region within the application's UI. Controllers encapsulate the presentation logic that determines which views are to be displayed. The controller uses Prism's view-switching navigation mechanism, which provides an extensible URI-based navigation mechanism to coordinate the construction and placement of views within regions. The Application Controller pattern defines an abstraction that maps to this responsibility.

- **Bootstrapper**. The **Bootstrapper** component is used by the application to initialize the various Prism components and services. It is used to initialize the dependency injection container to register any application-level components and services with it. It is also used to configure and initialize the module catalog and the shell's view and view model or presenter.

- **Multi-targeting**. Prism supports the development of applications that can target both WPF and Silverlight. By using a separated presentation pattern, such as the MVVM or MVP patterns, you can separate the UI of your application from its presentation and business logic. View model, presenter, and model classes can be reused in both WPF and Silverlight versions of the same application. WPF-specific and Silverlight-specific views can then be defined in a way that encapsulates the UI for each.

Prism is designed so that you can use any of the preceding capabilities and design patterns individually, or all of them together, depending on your requirements and your application scenario. You can use the MVVM pattern, modularity, regions, commands, or events in any combination without having to use all of them. Of course, if you want to take full advantage of the benefits that separation of concerns and loose coupling offer, you will typically use many of Prism's capabilities and design patterns in conjunction with each other. The following diagram shows a typical Prism application architecture and illustrates how all the capabilities of Prism can work together within a multi-module composite application.

Typical composite application architecture with the Prism Library

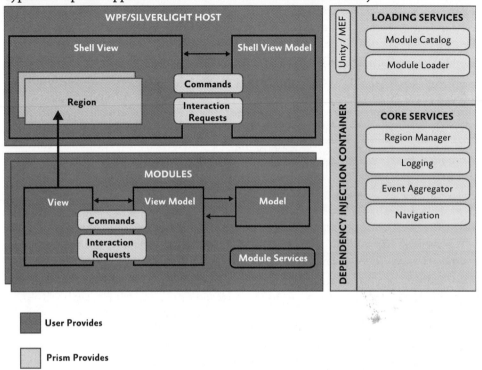

Most Prism applications consist of a shell application that defines regions for display-ing top-level views and shared services that can be accessed by the loaded modules. The shell defines a suitable catalog to specify which modules are to be loaded at startup time or on demand, as appropriate. A dependency injection container is also defined, which allows component dependencies to be fulfilled at run time. Shared services and compo-nents are registered with the container by the **Bootstrapper** when the application starts.

Individual modules encapsulate a portion of the overall application's functionality and—using a separated presentation pattern such as MVVM—define views, view models, models, and service components. When the modules are loaded, views defined within the modules are displayed within the regions defined by the shell. After initialization com-pletes, the user navigates within the application by using state-based or view-switching navigation to coordinate the visual update or display of new views within the application's regions.

USING PRISM
Now that you have seen the major capabilities and design patterns that Prism supports, it is time to see how easily you can start to use Prism to develop a new application. This section provides an overview of the first few steps required to create a basic Prism ap-plication. You can extend this basic application to take advantage of the additional capa-bilities and design patterns provided by Prism, as required by your scenario.

Note: *Although the Prism Library can be easily used to build new composite WPF or Silverlight applications (or applications that target both), you can also use Prism with existing applications so that they can take advantage of one or more Prism capabilities or design patterns.*

Typically, a Prism application consists of a shell project and multiple module projects. The following illustration shows common activities that you will need to complete when you use the Prism Library to develop a composite application.

Activities for creating a composite application

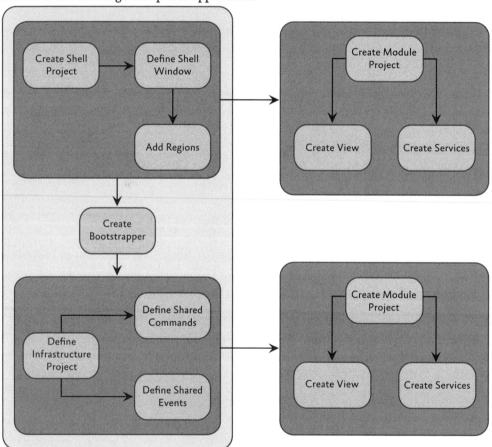

To fully realize the benefits of loose coupling and separation of concerns architectural design principles, a Prism application uses most or all of the Prism capabilities and design patterns described previously in this chapter. However, this example describes only the steps required to create a basic Prism application that consists of a single module which defines a single view.

Prism Library References
Most of your projects will need to reference the Prism Library assemblies. Prism provides signed binary versions of the Prism Library assemblies and a script that allows you to register them with Visual Studio so that you can use the Visual Studio **Add References** *dialog box to add references to them. If you decide not to register the binaries, you will need to manually add references to the Prism Library binaries to your projects. You can also include the Prism Library projects in your solution and then use project references to them. The latter has the advantage of being able to use features such as Go To Definition to step down into the Prism types, as well as being able to build and sign the Prism Library assemblies with your own strong name or certificate as part of your build process.*

Defining the Shell

The application shell provides the basic layout for the application. This layout is defined by using regions that modules can use to place views. Views, like shells, can use regions to define discoverable areas that content can be added to, as shown in the following illustration. Shells typically set the appearance for the entire application and contain the styles that are used throughout the application.

Shells, views, and regions

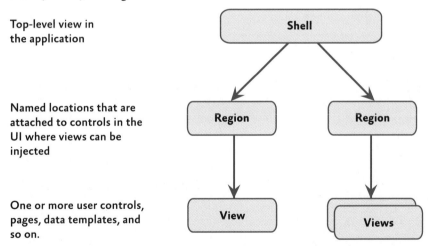

Creating the Bootstrapper

The bootstrapper is the glue that connects the application with the Prism Library services and the Unity or MEF containers. Each application creates an application-specific bootstrapper, which typically inherits from either **UnityBootstrapper** or **MefBootstrapper**, as shown in the following illustration. You will need to decide the approach you want to use to populate the module catalog. Minimally, each application will provide a module catalog and a shell.

By default, the bootstrapper uses the .NET Framework **Trace** class to log events. Most applications will supply their own logging service, such as Enterprise Library logging. Applications can supply their logging service in their bootstrapper.

By default, the **UnityBootstrapper** and **MefBootstrapper** enable the Prism Library services. These can be disabled or replaced in your application-specific bootstrapper. The following diagram shows how an application connects to the Prism Library

Connecting to the Prism Library

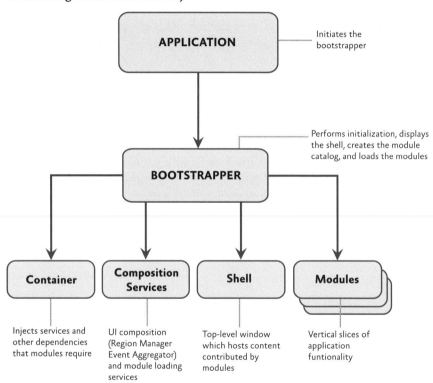

Creating a Module

A module contains the views and services specific to a piece of the application's functionality. In many development scenarios, modules are contained in separate assemblies and developed by separate teams. A module is denoted by a class that implements the **IModule** interface. During initialization, modules register their views and services and may add one or more views to the shell. Depending on the module discovery approach that you use, you may need to apply attributes to your module classes or define dependencies between your modules.

Adding a Module View to the Shell

Modules place content in the shell's regions. During initialization, modules use the **RegionManager** to locate regions in the shell and add one or more views to those regions or register one or more view types to be created within those regions. The **Region Manager** is responsible for keeping track of regions throughout the application and is a core service initialized by the bootstrapper.

More Information

For more information about Prism concepts, see the remaining chapters in this guide.

To download Prism binaries, source code, and documentation, see "Prism" on MSDN at http://www.microsoft.com/Prism.

If you have comments on this guide, visit the Prism community site at http://www.codeplex.com/Prism.

Additional Prism content is provided in the following appendixes on MSDN:

- Appendix D, "Upgrading from Previous Versions" on MSDN:
  http://msdn.microsoft.com/en-us/library/ff921073(PandP.40).aspx.

- Appendix E, "Extending Prism" on MSDN:
  http://msdn.microsoft.com/en-us/library/gg430866(PandP.40).aspx.

- Appendix F, "Reference Implementations" on MSDN:
  http://msdn.microsoft.com/en-us/library/gg405483(PandP.40).aspx.

- Appendix G, "QuickStarts" on MSDN:
  http://msdn.microsoft.com/en-us/library/gg430879(PandP.40).aspx.

- Appendix H, "Prism Hands-On Labs" on MSDN:
  http://msdn.microsoft.com/en-us/library/gg405475(PandP.40).aspx.

Prism assumes that you have hands-on experience with WPF or Silverlight. If you need general information about WPF and Silverlight, see the following resources:

- Windows Presentation Foundation on MSDN:
  http://msdn.microsoft.com/en-us/library/ms754130.aspx.

- MacDonald, Matthew. *Pro WPF in C# 2010: Windows Presentation Foundation in .NET 4*, Apress, 2010.

- Nathan, Adam. *WPF 4 Unleashed*. Sams Publishing, 2010.

- Bugnion, Laurent. *Silverlight 4 Unleashed*, Sams Publishing, 2010.

- Brown, Pete. *Silverlight 4 in Action*, Manning Publications, 2010.

  If you need general information about Silverlight, see the following resources:
- Microsoft Silverlight Home Page:
  http://www.microsoft.com/silverlight/.

- Microsoft Silverlight Resources:
  http://www.microsoft.com/silverlight/resources/default.aspx.

- Microsoft Silverlight Community:
  http://silverlight.net/default.aspx.

- Silverlight Documentation on MSDN:
  http://msdn.microsoft.com/en-us/library/cc838158(vs.95).aspx.
- Silverlight Books:
  http://www.silverlightbooks.net/.
- Project Rosetta:
  http://visitmix.com/labs/rosetta/.

For more information about UAC, see "What is User Account Control":
http://windows.microsoft.com/en-US/windows7/What-is-User-Account-Control.
For more information about the Unity Application Block, see "Unity Application Block" on MSDN:
http://www.msdn.com/unity.
For more information about the Managed Extensibility Framework, see "Managed Extensibility Framework" on MSDN:
http://msdn.microsoft.com/en-us/library/dd460648.aspx.
For more information about the Common Service Locator, see "CommonService Locator" on CodePlex:
http://commonservicelocator.codeplex.com/.
For additional tools and resources, see the following:

- Microsoft Silverlight 4 Tools for Visual Studio 2010:
  http://go.microsoft.com/fwlink/?LinkID=177428.
- Microsoft Expression Blend 4:
  http://www.microsoft.com/expression/products/Blend_Overview.aspx.
- Windows Phone Developer Tools SDK:
  http://go.microsoft.com/fwlink/?LinkId=185968.
- Windows Phone 7 Developer Guide community site on CodePlex:
  http://wp7guide.codeplex.com.

For a list of the new features, assets, and API changes, see "What's New in Prism 4.0" on MSDN:
http://msdn.microsoft.com/en-us/library/gg430871(PandP.40).aspx.
To access web resources more easily, see the online version of the bibliography on MSDN:
http://msdn.microsoft.com/en-us/library/gg405487(PandP.40).aspx.

COMMUNITY

Prism's community site is **http://www.codeplex.com/Prism**. On this community site, you can post questions, provide feedback, or connect with other users to share ideas. Community members can also help Microsoft plan and test future offerings and download additional content, such as extensions and training material.

2   Initializing Prism Applications

This chapter explains what needs to happen to get a Prism application up and running. A Prism application requires registration and configuration during the application startup process—this is known as *bootstrapping* the application.

What Is a Bootstrapper?

A bootstrapper is a class that is responsible for the initialization of an application built using the Prism Library. By using a bootstrapper, you have more control of how the Prism Library components are connected to your application.

The Prism Library includes a default abstract **Bootstrapper** base class that can be specialized for use with any container. Many of the methods in the bootstrapper classes are virtual methods. You can override these methods as appropriate in your custom bootstrapper implementation. The following diagram illustrates the stages of the bootstrapping process.

Basic stages of the bootstrapping process

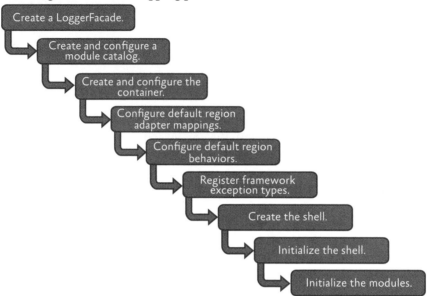

The Prism Library provides some additional base classes, derived from **Bootstrapper**, that have default implementations that are appropriate for most applications. The only stages left for your application bootstrapper to implement are creating and initializing the shell.

DEPENDENCY INJECTION

Applications built with the Prism Library rely on dependency injection provided by a container. The library provides assemblies that work with the Unity Application Block (Unity) or Managed Extensibility Framework (MEF), and it allows you to use other dependency injection containers. Part of the bootstrapping process is to configure this container and register types with the container.

The Prism Library includes the **UnityBootstrapper** and **MefBootstrapper** classes, which implement most of the functionality necessary to use either Unity or MEF as the dependency injection container in your application. In addition to the stages shown in the previous illustration, each bootstrapper adds some steps specific to its container.

CREATING THE SHELL

In a traditional Windows Presentation Foundation (WPF) application, a startup Uniform Resource Identifier (URI) is specified in the App.xaml file that launches the main window. In a Silverlight application, the **RootVisual** property on the application is set in the code-behind file used by the App.xaml file.

In an application created with the Prism Library, it is the bootstrapper's responsibility to create the shell or the main window. This is because the shell relies on services, such as the Region Manager, that need to be registered before the shell can be displayed.

Key Decisions

After you decide to use the Prism Library in your application, there are a number of additional decisions that you need to make:

- You will need to decide whether you are using MEF, Unity, or another container for your dependency injection container. This will determine which provided bootstrapper class you should use and whether you need to create a bootstrapper for another container.

- You should think about the application-specific services you want in your application. These will need to be registered with the container.

- You should determine whether the built-in logging service is adequate for your needs or if you need to create another logging service.

- You should decide how modules will be discovered by the application. Options include explicit code declarations, code attributes on the modules discovered via directory scanning, configuration, or XAML.

   The rest of this chapter provides more information about the bootstrapping process.

Core Scenarios

Creating a startup sequence is an important part of building your Prism application. This section describes how to create a bootstrapper and customize it to create the shell, configure the dependency injection container, register application level services, and how to load and initialize the modules.

CREATING A BOOTSTRAPPER FOR YOUR APPLICATION

If you choose to use either Unity or MEF as your dependency injection container, creating a simple bootstrapper for your application is easy. You will need to create a new class that derives from either **MefBootstrapper** or **UnityBootstrapper**, and then implement the **CreateShell** method. Optionally, you can override the **InitializeShell** method for shell-specific initialization.

Implementing the CreateShell Method

The **CreateShell** method allows a developer to specify the top-level window for a Prism application. Typically, the shell is the **MainWindow** or **MainPage**. You implement the **CreateShell** method by returning an instance of your application's shell class. In a Prism application, you can create the shell object or resolve it from the container, depending on your application's requirements.

   The following code example illustrates the use of the **ServiceLocator** to resolve the shell object.

```C#
protected override DependencyObject CreateShell()
{
    return ServiceLocator.Current.GetInstance<Shell>();
}
```

Note: *You will often see the* **ServiceLocator** *being used to resolve instances of types instead of the specific dependency injection container. The* **ServiceLocator** *is implemented by calling the container; therefore, it is a good choice for container-agnostic code. You can also directly reference and use the container instead of using the* **Service Locator***.*

Implementing the InitializeShell Method

After you create a shell, you may need to run initialization steps to ensure that the shell is ready to be displayed. Depending on whether you are writing a WPF or Silverlight application, the **InitializeShell** method implementations will vary. For Silverlight applications, you set the shell as the application's visual root, as shown in the following example.

```C#
protected override void InitializeShell()
{
    Application.Current.RootVisual = Shell;
}
```

For WPF applications, you create the shell application object and set it as the application's main window, as shown in the following code (from the Modularity QuickStarts for WPF).

```C#
protected override void InitializeShell()
{
    Application.Current.MainWindow = Shell;
    Application.Current.MainWindow.Show();
}
```

The base implementation of **InitializeShell** does nothing. You do not need to call the base class implementation.

CREATING AND CONFIGURING THE MODULE CATALOG

If you are building a module application, you will need to create and configure a module catalog. Prism uses a concrete **IModuleCatalog** instance to keep track of which modules are available to the application, which modules may need to be downloaded, and where the modules reside.

The **Bootstrapper** provides a protected **ModuleCatalog** property to reference the catalog, as well as a base implementation of the virtual **CreateModuleCatalog** method. The base implementation returns a new **ModuleCatalog**; however, this method can be overridden to provide a different **IModuleCatalog** instance instead, as shown in the following code (from the **QuickStartBootstrapper** in the Modularity with MEF for Silverlight QuickStart).

```C#
protected override IModuleCatalog CreateModuleCatalog()
{
    // When using MEF, the existing Prism ModuleCatalog is still
    // the place to configure modules via configuration files.
    return ModuleCatalog.CreateFromXaml(new Uri(
                "/ModularityWithMef.Silverlight;component/ModulesCatalog.xaml",
                UriKind.Relative));
}
```

In both the **UnityBootstrapper** and **MefBootstrapper** classes, the **Run** method calls the **CreateModuleCatalog** method and then uses the returned value to set the class's **ModuleCatalog** property. If you override this method, it is not necessary to call the base class's implementation because you will replace the functionality it provides. For more information about modularity, see Chapter 4, "Modular Application Development."

CREATING AND CONFIGURING THE CONTAINER

Containers play a key role in an application created with the Prism Library. Both the Prism Library and the applications built on top of it depend on a container for injecting required dependencies and services. During the container configuration phase, several core services are registered. In addition to these core services, you may have application-specific services that provide additional functionality as it relates to composition.

Core Services

The following table lists the core non-application specific services in the Prism Library.

Service interface	Description
IModuleManager	Defines the interface for the service that will retrieve and initialize the application's modules.
IModuleCatalog	Contains the metadata about the modules in the application. The Prism Library provides several different catalogs.
IModuleInitializer	Initializes the modules.
IRegionManager	Registers and retrieves regions, which are visual containers for layout.
IEventAggregator	Provides loose coupling of events between publishers and subscribers.
ILoggerFacade	Provides a wrapper for a logging mechanism, so that you can choose your own logging mechanism. The Stock Trader Reference Implementation (Stock Trader RI) uses the Enterprise Library Logging Application Block, via the **Enterprise LibraryLoggerAdapter** class, as an example of how you can use your own logger. The logging service is registered with the container by the bootstrapper's **Run** method, using the value returned by the **CreateLogger** method. Registering another logger with the container will not work; instead override the **Create Logger** method on the bootstrapper.
IServiceLocator	Allows the Prism Library to access the container. If you want to customize or extend the library, this may be useful.

Application-Specific Services

The following table lists the application-specific services used in the Stock Trader RI. You can use the RI as an example to understand the types of services that your application might provide.

Services in the Stock Trader RI	Description
IMarketFeedService	Provides real-time (mocked) market data. The **PositionSummary PresentationModel** updates the position screen based on notifications it receives from this service.
IMarketHistoryService	Provides historical market data used for displaying the trend line for the selected fund.
IAccountPositionService	Provides the list of funds in the portfolio.
IOrdersService	Persists submitted buy/sell orders.
INewsFeedService	Provides a list of news items for the selected fund.
IWatchListService	Handles when new watch items are added to the watch list.

There are two **Bootstrapper**-derived classes available in Prism: the **UnityBootstrapper** and the **MefBootstrapper**. Creating and configuring the different containers involves similar concepts that are implemented differently.

Creating and Configuring the Container in the UnityBootstrapper

The **UnityBootstrapper** class's **CreateContainer** method simply creates and returns a new instance of a **UnityContainer**. In most cases, you will not need to change this functionality. However, the method is virtual, and therefore provides that flexibility.

After the container is created, you will probably need to configure it for your application. The **ConfigureContainer** implementation in the **UnityBootstrapper** registers a number of core Prism services by default, as shown in the next code example.

Note: *An example of this is when a module registers module-level services in its* **Initialize** *method.*

```
C# UnityBootstrapper.cs
protected virtual void ConfigureContainer()
{
    ...
    if (useDefaultConfiguration)
    {
    RegisterTypeIfMissing(typeof(IServiceLocator), typeof(UnityServiceLocatorAdapter),
true);
    RegisterTypeIfMissing(typeof(IModuleInitializer), typeof(ModuleInitializer),
true);
    RegisterTypeIfMissing(typeof(IModuleManager), typeof(ModuleManager), true);
    RegisterTypeIfMissing(typeof(RegionAdapterMappings),
typeof(RegionAdapterMappings), true);
```

```
    RegisterTypeIfMissing(typeof(IRegionManager), typeof(RegionManager), true);
    RegisterTypeIfMissing(typeof(IEventAggregator), typeof(EventAggregator), true);
    RegisterTypeIfMissing(typeof(IRegionViewRegistry), typeof(RegionViewRegistry),
true);
    RegisterTypeIfMissing(typeof(IRegionBehaviorFactory),
typeof(RegionBehaviorFactory), true);
    }
}
```

The bootstrapper's **RegisterTypeIfMissing** method determines whether a service has been registered already—it will not register it twice. This allows you to override the default registration through configuration. You can also turn off default registration of any services. To do this, use the overloaded **Bootstrapper.Run** method, passing in **false**. You can also override the **ConfigureContainer** method and disable services that you do not want to use, such as the event aggregator.

Note: *If you turn off the default registration, you will need to manually register required services.*

To extend the default behavior of **ConfigureContainer**, simply add an override to your application's bootstrapper, and optionally call the base implementation, as shown in the following code (from the **QuickStartBootstrapper** in the Modularity for WPF (with Unity) QuickStart). This implementation calls the base class's implementation, registers the **ModuleTracker** type as the concrete implementation of **IModuleTracker**, and registers the **callbackLogger** as a singleton instance of **CallbackLogger** with Unity.

```
C#
protected override void ConfigureContainer()
{
    base.ConfigureContainer();

    this.RegisterTypeIfMissing(typeof(IModuleTracker), typeof(ModuleTracker), true);
    this.Container.RegisterInstance<CallbackLogger>(this.callbackLogger);
}
```

Creating and Configuring the Container in the MefBootstrapper

The **MefBootstrapper** class's **CreateContainer** method does several things. First, it creates an **AssemblyCatalog** and a **CatalogExportProvider**. The **CatalogExportProvider** allows the **MefExtensions** assembly to provide default exports for a number of Prism types, and still allows you to override the default type registration. Then **CreateContainer**, using the **CatalogExportProvider**, creates and returns a new instance of a **CompositionContainer**. In most cases, you will not need to change this functionality. However, the method is virtual, and therefore provides that flexibility.

Note: *In Silverlight, because of security restrictions, it is not possible to retrieve an assembly by using a type. Instead, Prism uses another method that uses the **Assembly. GetCallingAssembly** method.*

After the container is created, it needs to be configured for your application. The **ConfigureContainer** implementation in the **MefBootstrapper** registers a number of core Prism services by default, as shown in the following code example. If you override this method, consider carefully whether you should invoke the base class's implementation to register the core Prism services or provide these services in your implementation.

```C#
protected virtual void ConfigureContainer()
{
    this.RegisterBootstrapperProvidedTypes();
}

protected virtual void RegisterBootstrapperProvidedTypes()
{
    this.Container.ComposeExportedValue<ILoggerFacade>(this.Logger);
    this.Container.ComposeExportedValue<IModuleCatalog>(this.ModuleCatalog);
    this.Container.ComposeExportedValue<IServiceLocator>(new
MefServiceLocatorAdapter(this.Container));
    this.Container.ComposeExportedValue<AggregateCatalog>(this.AggregateCatalog);
}
```

Note: *In the* **MefBootstrapper***, the core services of Prism are added to the container as singletons so they can be located throughout the application via the container.*

In addition to providing the **CreateContainer** and **ConfigureContainer** methods, the **MefBootstrapper** provides two methods to create and configure the **AggregateCatalog** used by MEF. The **CreateAggregateCatalog** method simply creates and returns an **AggregateCatalog** object. Like the other methods in the **MefBootstrapper**, **Create AggregateCatalog** is virtual and can be overridden if necessary.

The **ConfigureAggregateCatalog** method allows you to add type registrations to the **AggregateCatalog** imperatively. For example, the **QuickStartBootstrapper** from the Modularity with MEF for Silverlight QuickStart explicitly adds ModuleA and ModuleC to the **AggregateCatalog**, as shown in the following code.

```C#
protected override void ConfigureAggregateCatalog()
{
    base.ConfigureAggregateCatalog();
    // Add this assembly to export ModuleTracker
    this.AggregateCatalog.Catalogs.Add(
            new AssemblyCatalog(typeof(QuickStartBootstrapper).Assembly));
    // Module A is referenced in the project and directly in code.
    this.AggregateCatalog.Catalogs.Add(
            new AssemblyCatalog(typeof(ModuleA.ModuleA).Assembly));
```

```
    // Module C is referenced in the project and directly in code.
    this.AggregateCatalog.Catalogs.Add(
            new AssemblyCatalog(typeof(ModuleC.ModuleC).Assembly));
}
```

More Information

For more information about MEF, **AggregateCatalog**, and **AssemblyCatalog**, see "Managed Extensibility Framework Overview" on MSDN:

http://msdn.microsoft.com/en-us/library/dd460648.aspx.

For more information about the Unity Application Block, see "Unity Application Block" on MSDN:

http://www.msdn.com/unity.

To access web resources more easily, see the online version of the bibliography on MSDN:

http://msdn.microsoft.com/en-us/library/gg405487(PandP.40).aspx.

3 Managing Dependencies Between Components

Applications based on the Prism Library are composite applications that may consist of many loosely coupled types and services. They need to interact to contribute content and receive notifications based on user actions. Because they are loosely coupled, they need a way to interact and communicate with one another to deliver the required business functionality.

To tie together these various pieces, applications based on the Prism Library rely on a dependency injection container. Dependency injection containers reduce the dependency coupling between objects by providing a facility to create instances of classes and manage their lifetimes based on the container's configuration. As an object is created, the container injects any dependencies that the object has into it. If those dependencies have not yet been created, the container creates and resolves the dependencies first. In some cases, the container itself is resolved as a dependency. For example, when they use the Unity Application Block (Unity) as the container, modules have the container injected so that they can register their views and services with that container.

There are several advantages of using a container:

- A container removes the need for a component to locate its dependencies or manage their lifetimes.
- A container allows swapping of implemented dependencies without affecting the component.
- A container facilitates testability by allowing dependencies to be mocked.
- A container increases maintainability by allowing new components to be easily added to the system.

In the context of an application based on the Prism Library, there are specific advantages to using a container:

- A container injects module dependencies into the module when it is loaded.
- A container is used for registering and resolving view models and views.
- A container can create the view models and inject the view.
- A container injects the composition services, such as the region manager and the event aggregator.

- A container is used for registering module-specific services (services that have module-specific functionality).

Note: *Some samples in the Prism guidance rely on the Unity Application Block (Unity) as the container. Other code samples—for example, the Modularity QuickStarts—use Managed Extensibility Framework (MEF). The Prism Library itself is not container-specific, and you can use its services and patterns with other containers, such as Castle Windsor, StructureMap, and Spring.NET.*

Key Decision: Choosing a Dependency Injection Container

The Prism Library provides two options for dependency injection containers: Unity or MEF. Prism is extensible, however. With a little bit of work, you can use other containers in your application. Both Unity and MEF provide the same basic functionality for dependency injection, even though they work very differently. Some of the capabilities provided by both containers include the following:

- They both register types with the container.
- They both register instances with the container.
- They both imperatively create instances of registered types.
- They both inject instances of registered types into constructors.
- They both inject instances of registered types into properties.
- They both have declarative attributes for marking types and dependencies that need to be managed.
- They both resolve dependencies in an object graph.

Unity provides several capabilities that MEF does not:

- It resolves concrete types without registration.
- It resolves open generics.
- It uses interception to capture calls to objects and add additional functionality to the target object.

MEF provides several capabilities that Unity does not:

- It discovers assemblies in a directory.
- It uses .xap file download and assembly discovery.
- It recomposes properties and collections as new types are discovered.
- It automatically exports derived types.
- It is deployed with the .NET Framework.

The containers have differences in capabilities and work differently, but the Prism Library will work with either container and provide similar functionality. When considering which container to use, keep in mind the preceding capabilities and determine which fits your scenario better.

CONSIDERATIONS FOR USING THE CONTAINER

You should think about the following before using a container.

- Consider whether it is appropriate to use the container to register and resolve components:
  - The performance impact of registering with the container and resolving instances from it might not be acceptable in your scenario. For example, if you need to create 10,000 polygons to draw a surface within the local scope of a rendering method, the cost of resolving all of those polygon instances through the container might have a significant performance cost because of the container's use of reflection for creating each entity.
  - If there are many or deep dependencies, the cost of creating components can increase significantly.
  - If the component does not have any dependencies or is not a dependency for other types, it may not make sense to put it in the container.
  - If the component has a single set of dependencies that are integral to the type and will never change, it may not make sense to put it in the container.
- Consider whether a component's lifetime should be registered as a singleton or instance:
  - If the component is a global service that acts as a resource manager for a single resource, such as a logging service, you may want to register it as a singleton.
  - If the component provides shared state to multiple consumers, you may want to register it as a singleton.
  - If a new instance of the object that is being injected must be injected each time a dependent object needs one, register it as a non-singleton. For example, each view probably needs a new instance of a view model.
- Consider whether you want to configure the container through code or configuration:
  - If you want to centrally manage all the different services, configure the container through configuration.
  - If you want to conditionally register specific services, configure the container through code.
  - If you have module-level services, consider configuring the container through code so that those services are registered only if the module is loaded.

Note: *Some containers, such as MEF, cannot be configured via a configuration file and must be configured via code.*

Core Scenarios

Containers are used for two primary purposes: registering types and objects and resolving them.

REGISTERING TYPES AND OBJECTS

Before you can inject dependencies into an object, the types of the dependencies need to be registered with the container. Registering a type typically involves passing the container an interface and a concrete type that implements that interface. There are two primary means for registering types and objects: through code or through configuration. The specific means vary from container to container.

Typically, there are two ways of registering types and objects in the container through code:

- You can register a type or a mapping with the container. At the appropriate time, the container will build an instance of the type you specify.

- You can register an existing object instance in the container as a singleton. The container will return a reference to the existing object.

Registering Types with the Unity Container

During initialization, a type can register other types, such as views and services. Registration allows their dependencies to be provided through the container and allows them to be accessed from other types. To do this, the type will need to have the container injected into the module constructor. The following code shows how the **OrderModule** type in the Commanding QuickStart registers a type.

```
C# OrderModule.cs
public class OrderModule : IModule
{
    public void Initialize()
    {
        this.container.RegisterType<IOrdersRepository, OrdersRepository>(new
ContainerControlledLifetimeManager());

        ...
    }
    ...
}
```

Depending on which container you use, registration can also be performed outside the code through configuration. For an example of this, see "Registering Modules using a Configuration File" in Chapter 4, "Modular Application Development."

Note: *The advantage of registering in code rather than in configuration is that the registration happens only if the module loads.*

Registering Types with MEF

MEF uses an attribute-based system for registering types with the container. As a result, adding type registration to the container is simple. It requires the addition of the **[Export]** attribute to a type, as shown in the following code example.

```C#
[Export(typeof(ILoggerFacade))]
public class CallbackLogger: ILoggerFacade
{
}
```

Another option when you use MEF is to create an instance of a class, and then register that instance with the container. The **QuickStartBootstrapper** in the Modularity for Silverlight with MEF QuickStart shows an example of this in the **ConfigureContainer** method, as shown in the following code.

```C#
protected override void ConfigureContainer()
{
    base.ConfigureContainer();

    // Because we created the CallbackLogger and it needs to
    // be used immediately, we compose it to satisfy any imports it has.
    this.Container.ComposeExportedValue<CallbackLogger>(this.callbackLogger);
}
```

Note: *When you use MEF as your container, we recommend that you use attributes to register types.*

RESOLVING TYPES AND OBJECTS

After a type is registered, it can be resolved or injected as a dependency. When a type is being resolved and the container needs to create a new instance, it injects the dependencies into the new instance.

In general, when a type is resolved, one of three things happens:

- If the type has not been registered, the container throws an exception.

  Note: *Some containers, including Unity, allow you to resolve a concrete type that has not been registered.*

- If the type has been registered as a singleton, the container returns the singleton instance. If this is the first time the type was called for, the container creates it and holds on to it for future calls.

- If the type has not been registered as a singleton, the container returns a new instance.

Note: *By default, types registered with MEF are singletons, and the container holds a reference to the object. In Unity, new instances of objects are returned by default, and the container does not maintain a reference to the object.*

Resolving Instances with Unity

The following code example from the Commanding QuickStart shows where the **Orders EditorView** and **OrdersToolBar** views are resolved from the container to associate them with the corresponding regions.

```csharp
C# OrderModule.cs
public class OrderModule : IModule
{
    public void Initialize()
    {
        this.container.RegisterType<IOrdersRepository, OrdersRepository>(new
ContainerControlledLifetimeManager());

        // Show the Orders Editor view in the shell's main region.
        this.regionManager.RegisterViewWithRegion("MainRegion",
                            () => this.container.Resolve<OrdersEditorView>());

        // Show the Orders Toolbar view in the shell's toolbar region.
        this.regionManager.RegisterViewWithRegion("GlobalCommandsRegion",
                            () => this.container.Resolve<OrdersToolBar>());
    }
    ...
}
```

The **OrdersEditorPresentationModel** constructor contains the following dependencies (the orders repository and the orders command proxy), which are injected when it is resolved.

```csharp
C# OrdersEditorPresentationModel.cs
public OrdersEditorPresentationModel( IOrdersRepository ordersRepository,
OrdersCommandProxy commandProxy )
{
    this.ordersRepository = ordersRepository;
    this.commandProxy    = commandProxy;

    // Create dummy order data.
    this.PopulateOrders();

    // Initialize a CollectionView for the underlying Orders collection.
#if SILVERLIGHT
```

```
        this.Orders = new PagedCollectionView( _orders );
#else
        this.Orders = new ListCollectionView( _orders );
#endif
        // Track the current selection.
        this.Orders.CurrentChanged += SelectedOrderChanged;
        this.Orders.MoveCurrentTo(null);
}
```

In addition to the constructor injection shown in the preceding code, Unity also allows for property injection. Any properties that have a **[Dependency]** attribute applied are automatically resolved and injected when the object is resolved.

Resolving Instances with MEF

The following code example shows how the **Bootstrapper** in the Modularity for Silverlight with MEF QuickStart obtains an instance of the shell. Instead of requesting a concrete type, the code could request an instance of an interface.

```C#
protected override DependencyObject CreateShell()
{
    return this.Container.GetExportedValue<Shell>();
}
```

In any class that is resolved by MEF, you can also use constructor injection, as shown in the following code example from ModuleA in the Modularity for Silverlight with MEF QuickStart. ModuleA has an **ILoggerFacade** and an **IModuleTracker** injected.

```C#
[ImportingConstructor]
public ModuleA(ILoggerFacade logger, IModuleTracker moduleTracker)
{
    if (logger == null)
    {
        throw new ArgumentNullException("logger");
    }
    if (moduleTracker == null)
    {
        throw new ArgumentNullException("moduleTracker");
    }
    this.logger = logger;
    this.moduleTracker = moduleTracker;
    this.moduleTracker.RecordModuleConstructed(WellKnownModuleNames.ModuleA);
}
```

Another option is to use property injection, as shown in the **ModuleTracker** class from the Modularity for Silverlight with MEF QuickStart. The **ModuleTracker** class has an instance of the **ILoggerFacade** injected.

```C#
[Export(typeof(IModuleTracker))]
public class ModuleTracker : IModuleTracker
{
    // Due to Silverlight/MEF restrictions, this must be public.
    [Import] public ILoggerFacade Logger;
}
```

Note: *In Silverlight, imported properties and fields must be public.*

Using Dependency Injection Containers and Services in Prism

Dependency injection containers, often referred to as just *containers*, are used to satisfy dependencies between components. Satisfying these dependencies typically involves registration and resolution. The Prism Library provides support for the Unity container and for MEF, but it is not container-specific. Because the library accesses the container through the **IServiceLocator** interface, the container can be replaced. To do this, your container must implement the **IServiceLocator** interface. Usually, if you are replacing the container, you will also need to provide your own container-specific bootstrapper. The **IServiceLocator** interface is defined in the Common Service Locator Library. This is an open source effort to provide an abstraction over Inversion of Control (IoC) containers, such as dependency injection containers, and service locators. The objective of using this library is to take advantage of IoC and Service Location without tying them to a specific implementation.

The Prism Library provides the **UnityServiceLocatorAdapter** and the **MefService LocatorAdapter**. Both adapters implement the **IServiceLocator** interface by extending the **ServiceLocatorImplBase** type. The following illustration shows the class hierarchy.

The Common Service Locator implementations in Prism

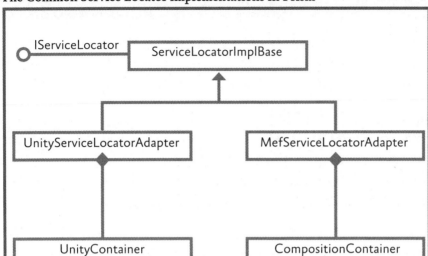

Although the Prism Library does not reference or rely on a specific container, it is typical for an application to rely on one. This means that while it is reasonable for a specific application to refer to the container, the Prism Library does not refer to the container directly. For example, the Stock Trader RI and several of the QuickStarts included with Prism rely on Unity as the container. Other samples and QuickStarts rely on MEF.

Using IServiceLocator

The following code shows the **IServiceLocator** interface.

```C#
public interface IServiceLocator : IServiceProvider
{
    object GetInstance(Type serviceType);
    object GetInstance(Type serviceType, string key);
    IEnumerable<object> GetAllInstances(Type serviceType);
    TService GetInstance<TService>();
    TService GetInstance<TService>(string key);
    IEnumerable<TService> GetAllInstances<TService>();
}
```

The Service Locator is extended in the Prism Library with the extension methods shown in the following code. You can see that **IServiceLocator** is used for resolving only, which means that it is used to obtain an instance; it is not used for registration.

C# ServiceLocatorExtensions
```csharp
public static class ServiceLocatorExtensions
{
    public static object TryResolve(this IServiceLocator locator, Type type)
    {
        try
        {
            return locator.GetInstance(type);
        }
        catch (ActivationException)
        {
            return null;
        }
    }

    public static T TryResolve<T>(this IServiceLocator locator) where T: class
    {
        return locator.TryResolve(typeof(T)) as T;
    }
}
```

The **TryResolve** extension method—which the Unity container does not support—returns an instance of the type to be resolved if it has been registered; otherwise, it returns **null**.

The **ModuleInitializer** uses **IServiceLocator** to resolve the module during module loading, as shown in the following code examples.

C# ModuleInitializer.cs - Initialize()
```csharp
IModule moduleInstance = null;
try
{
    moduleInstance = this.CreateModule(moduleInfo);
    moduleInstance.Initialize();
}
...
```

C# ModuleInitializer.cs - CreateModule()
```csharp
protected virtual IModule CreateModule(string typeName)
{
    Type moduleType = Type.GetType(typeName);
    if (moduleType == null)
    {
        throw new ModuleInitializeException(string.Format(CultureInfo.CurrentCulture,
Properties.Resources.FailedToGetType, typeName));
    }

    return (IModule)this.serviceLocator.GetInstance(moduleType);
}
```

Considerations for Using IServiceLocator

IServiceLocator is not meant to be the general-purpose container. Containers have different usage semantics, which often determines why that container is chosen. Bearing this in mind, the Stock Trader RI uses the dependency injection container directly instead of using the **IServiceLocator**.

In the following situations, it may be appropriate for you to use the **IServiceLocator**:

- You are an independent software vendor (ISV) designing a third-party service that needs to support multiple containers.

- You are designing a service to be used in an organization that uses multiple containers.

More Information

For more information about containers, see the following:

- "Unity Application Block" on MSDN:
  http://www.msdn.com/unity.

- Unity community site on CodePlex:
  http://www.codeplex.com/unity.

- "Managed Extensibility Framework Overview" on MSDN:
  http://msdn.microsoft.com/en-us/library/dd460648.aspx.

- MEF community site on CodePlex:
  http://mef.codeplex.com/.

- "Inversion of Control Containers and the Dependency Injection pattern" on Martin Fowler's website:
  http://www.martinfowler.com/articles/injection.html.

- "Design Patterns: Dependency Injection" in *MSDN Magazine*:
  http://msdn.microsoft.com/en-us/magazine/cc163739.aspx.

- "Loosen Up: Tame Your Software Dependencies for More Flexible Apps" in *MSDN Magazine*:
  http://msdn.microsoft.com/en-us/magazine/cc337885.aspx.

- Castle Project:
  http://www.castleproject.org/container/index.html.

- StructureMap:
  http://structuremap.sourceforge.net/Default.htm.

- Spring.NET:
  http://www.springframework.net/.

To access web resources more easily, see the online version of the bibliography on MSDN: http://msdn.microsoft.com/en-us/library/gg405487(PandP.40).aspx.

4   Modular Application Development

A modular application is an application that is divided into a set of functional units (named modules) that can be integrated into a larger application. A client module encapsulates a portion of the application's overall functionality and typically represents a set of related concerns. It can include a collection of related components, such as application features including user interface and business logic, or pieces of application infrastructure, such as application-level services for logging or authenticating users. Modules are independent of one another but can communicate with each other in a loosely coupled fashion. Modular applications can make it easier for you to develop, test, deploy, and extend your application.

For example, consider a personal banking application. The user can access a variety of functions—such as transferring money between accounts, paying bills, and updating personal information—from a single user interface (UI). However, behind the scenes, each of these functions is encapsulated within a discrete module. These modules communicate with each other and with back-end systems, such as database servers and web services. Application services integrate the various components within each of the different modules and handle the communication with the user. The user sees an integrated view that looks like a single application.

The following illustration shows a design of a modular application with multiple modules.

Module composition

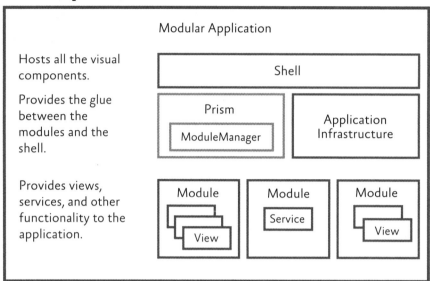

Benefits of Building Modular Applications

You are probably already building a well-architected application by using assemblies, interfaces, and classes, and employing good object-oriented design principles. Even so, unless you take great care, your application design may still be *monolithic* (meaning that all the functionality is implemented in a tightly coupled way within the application), which can make the application difficult to develop, test, extend, and maintain.

The modular application approach, on the other hand, can help you to identify the large-scale functional areas of your application and allow you to develop and test that functionality independently. This can make development and testing easier, and it can also make your application more flexible and easier to extend in the future. The benefit of the modular approach is that it can make your overall application architecture more flexible and maintainable because it allows you to break your application into manageable pieces. Each piece encapsulates specific functionality, and each piece is integrated through clear but loosely coupled communication channels.

PRISM'S SUPPORT FOR MODULAR APPLICATION DEVELOPMENT

Prism provides support for modular application development and for run-time module management within your application. Using Prism's modular development functionality can save you time because you don't have to implement and test your own modularity framework. Prism supports the following modular application development features:

- A module catalog for registering named modules and each module's location. You can create the module catalog in the following ways:
    - By defining modules in code or Extensible Application Markup Language (XAML)
    - For Windows Presentation Foundation (WPF): By discovering modules in a directory so that you can load all your modules without explicitly defining them in a centralized catalog
    - For WPF: By defining modules in a configuration file
- Declarative metadata attributes for modules to support initialization mode and dependencies.
- Integration with dependency injection containers to support loose coupling between modules.
- For module loading:
    - Dependency management, including duplicate and cycle detection to ensure that modules are loaded in the correct order and only loaded and initialized once.
    - On-demand and background downloading of modules to minimize application startup time. The remaining modules can be loaded and initialized in the background or when they are required.

Core Concepts

This section introduces the core concepts related to modularity in Prism, including the **IModule** interface, the module loading process, the module catalog, communicating between modules, and dependency injection containers.

IMODULE: THE BUILDING BLOCK OF MODULAR APPLICATIONS

A module is a logical collection of functionality and resources that is packaged so that it can be separately developed, tested, deployed, and integrated into an application. A package can be one or more assemblies, either as a loose collection or bundled together in a .xap file. Each module has a central class that is responsible for initializing the module and integrating its functionality into the application. That class implements the **IModule** interface.

> *The presence of a class that implements the **IModule** interface is enough to identify the package as a module.*

The **IModule** interface has a single method, named **Initialize**, within which you can implement whatever logic is required to initialize and integrate the module's functionality into the application. Depending on the purpose of the module, it can register views into composite user interfaces, make additional services available to the application, or extend the application's functionality. The following code shows the minimum implementation for a module.

```csharp
C#
public class MyModule : IModule
{
    public void Initialize()
    {
        // Do something here.
    }
}
```

Note: *Instead of using the initialization mechanism provided by the* **IModule** *interface, the Stock Trader RI uses a declarative, attribute-based approach for registering views, services, and types.*

MODULE LIFETIME

The module loading process in Prism includes the following:

1. **Registering/discovering modules**. The modules to be loaded at run time for a particular application are defined in a module catalog. The catalog contains information about the modules, their location, and the order in which they are to be loaded.

2. **Loading modules**. The assemblies that contain the modules are loaded into memory. This phase may require the module to be downloaded from the web or otherwise retrieved from some remote location or local directory.

3. **Initializing modules**. The modules are then initialized. This means creating instances of the module class, and then calling the **Initialize** method on them via the **IModule** interface.

The following figure shows the module loading process.

Module loading process

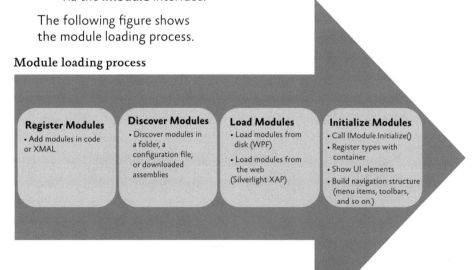

MODULE CATALOG

The **ModuleCatalog** class holds information about the modules that can be used by the application. The catalog is essentially a collection of **ModuleInfo** classes. Each module is described in a **ModuleInfo** class that records the name, type, and location, among other attributes of the module. The typical approaches to filling the **ModuleCatalog** with **ModuleInfo** instances are:

- Registering modules in code
- Registering modules in XAML
- Registering modules in a configuration file (WPF only)
- Discovering modules in a local directory on disk (WPF only)

The registration and discovery mechanism you should use depends on what your application needs. Using a configuration file or XAML file allows your application to not require references to the modules. Using a directory can allow an application to discover modules without having to specify them in a file.

CONTROLLING WHEN TO LOAD A MODULE

Prism applications can initialize modules as soon as possible, known as *when available*, or when the application needs them, known as *on-demand*. For Silverlight applications, modules can be downloaded with the application or in the background after the application starts. Consider the following guidelines for loading modules:

- Modules required for the application to run must be downloaded with the application and initialized when the application runs.
- Modules containing features that are almost always used in typical usage of the application can be downloaded in the background and initialized when they become available.
- Modules containing features that are rarely used (or are support modules that other modules optionally depend upon) can be downloaded in the background and initialized on-demand.

Consider how you are partitioning your application, common usage scenarios, application start-up time, and the number and size of downloads to determine how to configure your module for downloading and initialization.

INTEGRATING MODULES WITH THE APPLICATION

Prism provides the following classes to bootstrap your application: the **UnityBootstrapper** or the **MefBootstrapper**. These classes can be used to create and configure the module manager to discover and load modules. In a few lines of code, you can override a configuration method to register modules specified in a XAML file, a configuration file, or a directory location.

Use the module **Initialize** method to integrate the module with the rest of the application. The way you do this varies, depending on the structure of your application and the content of the module. The following are common things to do to integrate your module into your application:

- Add the module's views to the application's navigation structure. This is a common practice if you are building composite UI applications by using view discovery or view injection.
- Subscribe to application-level events or services.
- Register shared services with the application's dependency injection container.

COMMUNICATION BETWEEN MODULES

Even though modules should have loose coupling between each other, it is common for modules to communicate with each other. There are several loosely coupled communication patterns, each with its own strengths. Typically, combinations of these patterns are used to create a communication solution. The following are some of these patterns:

- **Loosely coupled events**. A module can broadcast that a certain event has occurred. Other modules can subscribe to that event so that they will be notified when the event occurs. Loosely coupled events are a lightweight manner of setting up communication between two modules, and are easily implemented. However, a design that relies too heavily on events can become hard to maintain, especially if many events have to be orchestrated to fulfill a single task. In that case, it might be better to consider a shared service.
- **Shared services**. A shared service is a class that can be accessed through a common interface. Typically, shared services are found in a shared assembly and provide system-wide services, such as authentication, logging, or configuration.
- **Shared resources**. If you do not want modules to directly communicate with each other, you can also have them communicate indirectly through a shared resource, such as a database or a set of web services.

DEPENDENCY INJECTION AND MODULAR APPLICATIONS

Containers like the Unity Application Block (Unity) and Managed Extensibility Framework (MEF) allow you to easily use Inversion of Control (IoC) and Dependency Injection, which are powerful design patterns that help to compose components in a loosely coupled fashion. Dependency injection allows components to obtain references to the other components that they depend on without requiring those references to be hard coded. This promotes better code reuse and improved flexibility. Dependency injection is very useful when building a loosely coupled, modular application. Prism is designed to be agnostic about the dependency injection container used to compose components within an application. The choice of container is up to you and will largely depend on your application requirements and preferences. However, there are two principal dependency injection frameworks from Microsoft to consider: Unity and MEF.

The patterns & practices Unity Application Block provides a full-featured dependency injection container. It supports property-based and constructor-based injection and policy injection, which allow you to transparently inject behavior and policy between components. It also supports a host of other features that are typical of dependency injection containers.

MEF (which is now part of .NET Framework 4 and Silverlight 4) provides support for building extensible .NET applications by supporting dependency injection–based component composition, and it provides other features that support modular application development. It allows an application to discover components at run time and then integrate those components into the application in a loosely-coupled way. MEF is a great extensibility and composition framework. It includes assembly and type discovery, type dependency resolution, dependency injection, and some assembly and .xap download capabilities. Prism enables you to take advantage of these MEF features, as well as the following:

- Associating module types to their .xap location
- Registering modules via XAML and code attributes for both WPF and Silverlight
- Registering modules via configuration files and directory scans (WPF only)
- Tracking state as the module is loaded
- Using custom declarative metadata for modules (MEF only)

Both the Unity and MEF dependency injection containers work seamlessly with Prism.

Key Decisions

The first decision you will make is whether you want to develop a modular solution. There are numerous benefits of building modular applications as discussed in the previous section, but there is a commitment in terms of time and effort that you need to make to reap these benefits. If you decide to develop a modular solution, there are several more things to consider:

- **Determine the framework you will use**. You can create your own modularity framework, or you can use Prism, MEF, or another framework.

- **Determine how to organize your solution**. Approach a modular architecture by defining the boundaries of each module, including which assemblies are part of each module. You can decide to use modularity to ease the development, as well as to have control over how the application will be deployed or if it will support a plug-in or extensible architecture.

- **Determine how to partition your modules**. Modules can be partitioned differently based on requirements: for example, by functional areas, provider modules, development teams, and deployment requirements.

- **Select the core services that the application will provide to all modules**. For example, a core service could be an error reporting service or an authentication and authorization service.

- **If you are using Prism, determine the approach that you will use to register modules in the module catalog**. For WPF, you can register modules in code, XAML, in a configuration file, or you can locate modules in a local directory on disk. For Silverlight, you can register modules in code or XAML.

- **Determine your module communication and dependency strategy**. Modules will need to communicate with each other, and you will need to deal with dependencies between modules.

- **Select your dependency injection container**. Typically, modular systems require dependency injection, Inversion of Control (IoC), or a service locator to enable the loose coupling and dynamic loading and creating of modules. Prism gives you a choice between using the Unity, MEF, or another container and provides libraries for Unity or MEF-based applications.
- **Minimize application startup time**. Think about on-demand and background downloading of modules to minimize application startup time.
- **Determine deployment requirements**. Think about how you intend to deploy your application. This may affect the number of assemblies you put in a .xap file. You might also partition shared libraries, such as the Prism Library, to take advantage of assembly caching in Silverlight.

The next sections provide detailed information to help you with some of these decisions.

Partitioning an Application into Modules

When you develop an application in a modularized fashion, you structure the application into separate client modules that can be individually developed, tested, and deployed. Each module will encapsulate a portion of your application's overall functionality. One of the first design decisions you will have to make is to decide how to partition your application's functionality into discrete modules.

A module should encapsulate a set of related concerns and have a distinct set of responsibilities. A module can represent a vertical slice of the application or a horizontal service layer. The following illustrations show applications segmented into vertical slices and horizontal layers.

An application with modules organized into vertical slices

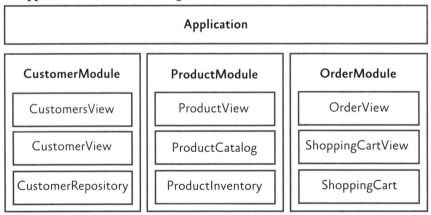

An application with modules organized into horizontal layers

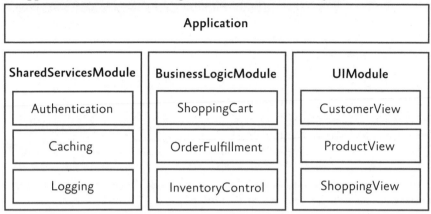

A larger application may have modules organized with vertical slices and horizontal layers.

Some examples of modules include the following:

- A module that contains a specific application feature, such as the News module in the Stock Trader Reference Implementation (Stock Trader RI)

- A module that contains a specific subsystem or functionality for a set of related use cases, such as purchasing, invoicing, or general ledger

- A module that contains infrastructure services, such as logging, caching, and authorization services, or web services

- A module that contains services that invoke line-of-business (LOB) systems, such as Siebel CRM and SAP, in addition to other internal systems

A module should have a minimal set of dependencies on other modules. When a module has a dependency on another module, it should be loosely coupled by using interfaces defined in a shared library instead of concrete types, or by using the **EventAggregator** to communicate with other modules via **EventAggregator** event types.

The goal of modularity is to partition the application in such a way that it remains flexible, maintainable, and stable even as features and technologies are added and removed. The best way to accomplish this is to design your application so that modules are as independent as possible, have well defined interfaces, and are as isolated as possible.

Determining the Ratio of Projects to Modules

There are several ways to create and package modules. The recommended and most common way is to create a single assembly per module. This helps keep logical modules separate and promotes proper encapsulation. It also makes it easier to talk about the assembly as both the module boundary and the way you package and deploy the module. However, nothing prevents a single assembly from containing multiple modules, and in some cases this may be preferred to minimize the number of projects in your solution. For a large application, it is not uncommon to have 10–50 modules. Separating each module into its own project adds a great deal of complexity to the solution and can slow down Visual

Studio performance. It might makes sense to break a module or set of modules into a separate solution to manage this if you choose to follow a one module per assembly Visual Studio project structure.

.xap File and Module Factoring

For Silverlight applications, modules are typically packaged in separate .xap files, although in some cases, you may have more than one module per .xap file. You should consider how many .xap files you need so that you can minimize the number and size of download requests required for the application to start and enable a new feature. If you choose to separate each module into its own project or assembly, you then need to decide whether to put each assembly in its own .xap file for deployment or whether to include multiple assemblies in a single .xap file.

Some factors that influence your choice of whether to include multiple modules in a single .xap file or to separate them include the following:

- **Download size and shared dependencies**. Each .xap file has a small amount of additional size overhead in its manifest and .zip file packaging. Also, if there are common dependencies between the modules and they are not separated into a dependent module or cached library, each .xap file will include those dependent libraries, which could significantly increase the download size.

- **The timing of when multiple modules are needed by the application**. If multiple modules are loaded and used at the same time, such as presenting views at the startup of the application, packaging them in a single .xap file might make the download slightly faster and help ensure that both modules become physically available to the client at the same time. The modularity feature of Prism ensures that modules that indicate dependencies are loaded in the right order. You can use this feature to make sure that there is no improper load order when the modules are split across multiple . xap files. But there is a small amount of performance overhead involved in making two downloads instead of one, even if it is the same total download size.

- **Module versioning**. If different modules will be developed on independent timelines and potentially deployed separately, you will want to put them into separate . xap files so that they can be marked with different versions more cleanly and updated independently.

To avoid downloading the same assemblies more than once in separate .xap files, you can use either of the following approaches:

- Factor shared dependencies into a separate infrastructure module, and have the consuming modules take a dependency on that shared module.

- Use Assembly Library Caching in Silverlight to put the shared types into a shared library that is downloaded once and cached by Silverlight instead of the Prism module downloader.

USING DEPENDENCY INJECTION FOR LOOSE COUPLING

A module may depend on components and services provided by the host application or by other modules. Prism gives you the ability to register dependencies between modules so that they are loaded and initialized in the right order. Prism also supports the initialization of modules when they are loaded into the application. During module initialization, the module can retrieve references to the additional components and services it requires, and/or register any components and services that it contains to make them available to other modules.

Instead of directly instantiating a concrete type, a module should use an independent mechanism to get instances of external interfaces—for example, by using a dependency injection container or factory service. Dependency injection containers such as Unity or MEF allow a type to automatically acquire instances of the interfaces and types it needs through dependency injection. Prism integrates with both Unity and MEF to allow a module to easily use dependency injection.

The following diagram shows the typical sequence of operations when modules are loaded that need to acquire or register references to the components and services.

Example of dependency injection

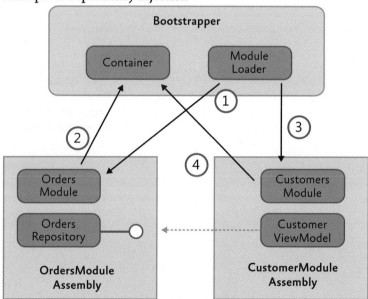

In this example, the **OrdersModule** assembly defines an **OrdersRepository** class (along with other views and classes that implement order functionality). The **Customer Module** assembly defines a **CustomerViewModel** class which depends on the **Orders Repository**, typically based on an interface exposed by the service. The application startup and bootstrapping process contains the following steps:

1. The bootstrapper starts the module initialization process, and the module loader loads and initializes the **OrdersModule**.

2. In the initialization of the **OrdersModule**, it registers the **OrdersRepository** with the container.

3. The module loader then loads the **CustomersModule**. The order of module loading can be specified by the dependencies in the module metadata.

4. The **CustomersModule** constructs an instance of the **CustomerViewModel** by resolving it through the container. The **CustomerViewModel** has a dependency on the **OrdersRepository** (typically based on its interface) and indicates it through constructor or property injection. The container injects that dependency in the construction of the view model based on the type registered by the **OrdersModule**. The net result is an interface reference from the **Customer ViewModel** to the **OrderRepository** without tight coupling between those classes.

Note: *The interface used to expose the* **OrderRespository** *(***IOrderRepository***) could reside in a separate shared services assembly or an orders services assembly that contains only the service interfaces and types required to expose those services. This way, there is no hard dependency between the* **CustomersModule** *and the* **OrdersModule**.

Both modules have an implicit dependency on the dependency injection container. This dependency is injected during module construction in the module loader.

Core Scenarios

This section describes the common scenarios that you will encounter when working with modules in your application. These scenarios include defining a module, registering and discovering modules, loading modules, initializing modules, specifying module dependencies, loading modules on demand, downloading remote modules in the background, and detecting when a module has already been loaded. You can register and discover modules in code, in a XAML or application configuration file, or by scanning a local directory.

DEFINING A MODULE

A module is a logical collection of functionality and resources that is packaged so that it can be separately developed, tested, deployed, and integrated into an application. Each module has a central class that is responsible for initializing the module and integrating its functionality into the application. That class implements the **IModule** interface, as shown in the following code example.

```C#
public class MyModule : IModule
{
    public void Initialize()
    {
        // Initialize module
    }
}
```

The way that you implement the **Initialize** method will depend on the requirements of your application. The module class type, initialization mode, and any module dependencies are defined in the module catalog. For each module in the catalog, the module loader creates an instance of the module class, and then it calls the **Initialize** method. Modules are processed in the order specified in the module catalog. The runtime initialization order is based on when the modules are downloaded and available, and when their dependencies are satisfied.

Depending on the type of module catalog that your application uses, module dependencies can be set either by declarative attributes on the module class itself or within the module catalog file. The following sections provide more information.

REGISTERING AND DISCOVERING MODULES

The modules that an application can load are defined in a module catalog. The Prism Module Loader uses the module catalog to determine which modules are available to be loaded into the application, when to load them, and in which order they are to be loaded.

The module catalog is represented by a class that implements the **IModuleCatalog** interface. The module catalog class is created by the application bootstrapper class during application initialization. Prism provides different implementations of module catalog for you to choose from. You can also populate a module catalog from another data source by calling the **AddModule** method or by deriving from **ModuleCatalog** to create a module catalog with customized behavior.

> **Note:** *Typically, modules in Prism use a dependency injection container and the Common Service Locator to retrieve instances of types that are required for module initialization. Prism supports both the Unity and the MEF containers. Although the overall process of registering, discovering, downloading, and initializing modules is the same, the details can vary based on whether Unity or MEF is being used. The container-specific differences between approaches are explained throughout this chapter.*

Using Code to Register Modules

The most basic module catalog is provided by the **ModuleCatalog** class. You can use this module catalog to programmatically register modules by specifying the module class type. You can also programmatically specify the module name and initialization mode. To register the module directly with the **ModuleCatalog** class, call the **AddModule** method in your application's **Bootstrapper** class. An example is shown in the following code.

```C#
protected override void ConfigureModuleCatalog()
{
    Type moduleCType = typeof(ModuleC);
    ModuleCatalog.AddModule(
      new ModuleInfo()
      {
          ModuleName = moduleCType.Name,
          ModuleType = moduleCType.AssemblyQualifiedName,
      });
}
```

In the preceding example, the shell directly references the modules; therefore, the module class types are defined and can be used in the call to **AddModule**. That is why this example uses **typeof(Module)** to add modules to the catalog.

Note: *If your application has a direct reference to the module type, you can add it by type as shown above; otherwise you need to provide the fully qualified type name and the location of the assembly.*

To see another example of defining the module catalog in code, see StockTrader RIBootstrapper.cs in the Stock Trader Reference Implementation (Stock Trader RI).

Note: *The* **Bootstrapper** *base class provides the* **CreateModuleCatalog** *method to assist in the creation of the* **ModuleCatalog**. *By default, this method creates a* **Module Catalog** *instance, but you can override this method in a derived class to create different types of module catalogs.*

Using a XAML File to Register Modules

You can define a module catalog declaratively by specifying it in a XAML file. The XAML file specifies what kind of module catalog class to create and which modules to add to it. Usually, the .xaml file is added as a resource to your shell project. The module catalog is created by the bootstrapper with a call to the **CreateFromXaml** method. From a technical perspective, this approach is very similar to defining the **ModuleCatalog** in code because the XAML file simply defines a hierarchy of objects to be instantiated.

The following code example shows a XAML file specifying a module catalog.

```
XAML ModularityWithUnity.Silverlight\ModulesCatalog.xaml
<Modularity:ModuleCatalog
 xmlns="http://schemas.microsoft.com/winfx/2006/xaml/presentation"
       xmlns:x="http://schemas.microsoft.com/winfx/2006/xaml"
       xmlns:sys="clr-namespace:System;assembly=mscorlib"
       xmlns:Modularity="clr-
namespace:Microsoft.Practices.Prism.Modularity;assembly=Microsoft.Practices.Prism">
    <Modularity:ModuleInfoGroup Ref="ModuleB.xap" InitializationMode="WhenAvailable">
        <Modularity:ModuleInfo ModuleName="ModuleB" ModuleType="ModuleB.ModuleB,
ModuleB, Version=1.0.0.0, Culture=neutral, PublicKeyToken=null" />
    </Modularity:ModuleInfoGroup>
    <Modularity:ModuleInfoGroup InitializationMode="OnDemand">
        <Modularity:ModuleInfo Ref="ModuleE.xap" ModuleName="ModuleE"
ModuleType="ModuleE.ModuleE, ModuleE, Version=1.0.0.0, Culture=neutral,
PublicKeyToken=null" />
        <Modularity:ModuleInfo Ref="ModuleF.xap" ModuleName="ModuleF"
ModuleType="ModuleF.ModuleF, ModuleF, Version=1.0.0.0, Culture=neutral,
PublicKeyToken=null" >
            <Modularity:ModuleInfo.DependsOn>
                <sys:String>ModuleE</sys:String>
            </Modularity:ModuleInfo.DependsOn>
```

```
          </Modularity:ModuleInfo>
      </Modularity:ModuleInfoGroup>


      <!-- Module info without a group -->
      <Modularity:ModuleInfo Ref="ModuleD.xap" ModuleName="ModuleD"
ModuleType="ModuleD.ModuleD, ModuleD, Version=1.0.0.0, Culture=neutral,
PublicKeyToken=null" />
</Modularity:ModuleCatalog>
```

Note: *A* **ModuleInfoGroup** *provides a convenient way to group modules that are in the same .xap file or assembly, are initialized in the same way, or only have dependencies on modules in the same group.*

Dependencies between modules can be defined within modules in the same **Module InfoGroup**; *however, you cannot define dependencies between modules in different* **ModuleInfoGroup**s.

Putting modules inside module groups is optional. The properties that are set for a group will be applied to all its contained modules. Modules can also be registered without being inside a group.

In your application's **Bootstrapper** class, you need to specify that the XAML file is the source for your **ModuleCatalog**, as shown in the following code.

```C#
protected override IModuleCatalog CreateModuleCatalog()
{
    return ModuleCatalog.CreateFromXaml(new
Uri("/MyProject.Silverlight;component/ModulesCatalog.xaml",
UriKind.Relative));
}
```

Using a Configuration File to Register Modules

In WPF, it is possible to specify the module information in the App.config file. The advantage of this approach is that this file is not compiled into the application. This makes it very easy to add or remove modules at run time without recompiling the application.

The following code example shows a configuration file specifying a module catalog. If you want the module to automatically load, set **startupLoaded="true"**.

```XML ModularityWithUnity.Desktop\app.config
<modules>
  <module assemblyFile="ModularityWithUnity.Desktop.ModuleE.dll"
moduleType="ModularityWithUnity.Desktop.ModuleE, ModularityWithUnity.Desktop.
ModuleE, Version=1.0.0.0, Culture=neutral, PublicKeyToken=null" moduleName="ModuleE"
startupLoaded="false" />
  <module assemblyFile="ModularityWithUnity.Desktop.ModuleF.dll"
moduleType="ModularityWithUnity.Desktop.ModuleF, ModularityWithUnity.Desktop.ModuleF,
```

```
Version=1.0.0.0, Culture=neutral, PublicKeyToken=null" moduleName="ModuleF"
startupLoaded="false">
    <dependencies>
      <dependency moduleName="ModuleE"/>
    </dependencies>
  </module>
</modules>
```

Note: *Even if your assemblies are in the global assembly cache or in the same folder as the application, the* **assemblyFile** *attribute is required. The attribute is used to map the* **moduleType** *to the correct* **IModuleTypeLoader** *to use.*

In your application's **Bootstrapper** class, you need to specify that the configuration file is the source for your **ModuleCatalog**. To do this, you use the **ConfigurationModule Catalog** class, as shown in the following code.

```C#
protected override IModuleCatalog CreateModuleCatalog()
{
    return new ConfigurationModuleCatalog();
}
```

Note: *You can still add modules to a* **ConfigurationModuleCatalog** *in code. You can use this, for example, to make sure that the modules that your application absolutely needs to function are defined in the catalog.*

Note: *Silverlight does not support using configuration files. If you want to use a configuration-style approach for Silverlight, the recommended approach is to create your own* **ModuleCatalog** *that reads the module configuration from a web service on the server.*

Discovering Modules in a Directory

The Prism **DirectoryModuleCatalog** class allows you to specify a local directory as a module catalog in WPF. This module catalog will scan the specified folder and search for assemblies that define the modules for your application. To use this approach, you will need to use declarative attributes on your module classes to specify the module name and any dependencies that they have. The following code example shows a module catalog that is populated by discovering assemblies in a directory.

```C#
protected override IModuleCatalog CreateModuleCatalog()
{
    return new DirectoryModuleCatalog() {ModulePath = @".\Modules"};
}
```

Note: *This functionality is not supported in Silverlight because the Silverlight security model does not allow you to load assemblies from the file system.*

LOADING MODULES

After the **ModuleCatalog** is populated, the modules are ready to be loaded and initialized. Module loading means that the module assembly is transferred from disk into memory. If the assembly is not present on disk, it might have to be retrieved first. An example of this is using Silverlight .xap files to download assemblies from the web. The **ModuleManager** is responsible for coordinating the loading and initialization process.

INITIALIZING MODULES

After the modules load, they are initialized. This means an instance of the module class is created and its **Initialize** method is called. The module should be integrated with the application during initialization. Consider the following possibilities for module initialization:

- **Register the module's views with the application**. If your module is participating in user interface (UI) composition by using view discovery or view injection, your module will need to associate its views or view models with the appropriate region name. This allows views to show up dynamically on menus, toolbars, or other visual regions within the application.

- **Subscribe to application level events or services**. Often, applications expose application-specific services and/or events that your module is interested in. Use the **Initialize** method to add the module's functionality to those application-level events and services. For example, the application might raise an event when it is shutting down and your module might need to react to that event.

  It is also possible that your module must provide some data to an application level service. For example, if you have created a **MenuService** (responsible for adding and removing menu items), you would use the module's **Initialize** method to add the correct menu items.

  Note: *Module instance lifetime is short-lived by default. After the **Initialize** method is called during the loading process, the reference to the module instance is released. If you do not establish a strong reference chain to the module instance, it will be garbage collected.*

  This behavior may be problematic to debug if you subscribe to events that hold a weak reference to your module, because your module will disappear when the garbage collector runs.

- **Register types with a dependency injection container**. If you are using a dependency injection pattern such as Unity or MEF, the module may register types for the application or other modules to use. It may also ask the container to resolve an instance of a type it needs.

SPECIFYING MODULE DEPENDENCIES

Modules may depend on other modules. If Module A depends on Module B, Module B must be initialized before Module A. The **ModuleManager** keeps track of these dependencies and initializes the modules accordingly. Depending on how you defined your module catalog, you can define your module dependencies in code, in a configuration file, or in XAML.

Specifying Dependencies in Code

For WPF applications that register modules in code or discover modules by directory, Prism provides declarative attributes to use when creating a module, as shown in the following code example.

```
C# (when using Unity)
[Module(ModuleName = "ModuleA")]
[ModuleDependency("ModuleD")]
public class ModuleA: IModule
{
    ...
}
```

Specifying Dependencies in XAML

The following XAML shows where Module F depends on Module E.

```
XAML ModulesCatalog.xaml
<Modularity:ModuleInfo Ref="ModuleF.xap" ModuleName="ModuleF" ModuleType="ModuleF.
ModuleF, ModuleF, Version=1.0.0.0, Culture=neutral, PublicKeyToken=null" >
<Modularity:ModuleInfo.DependsOn>
    <sys:String>ModuleE</sys:String>
</Modularity:ModuleInfo.DependsOn>
</Modularity:ModuleInfo>
```

Specifying Dependencies in a Configuration File

The following example App.config file shows where Module D depends on Module B.

```
XML App.config
<modules>
  <module assemblyFile="Modules/ModuleD.dll" moduleType="ModuleD.ModuleD, ModuleD"
moduleName="ModuleD">
    <dependencies>
      <dependency moduleName="ModuleB"/>
    </dependencies>
</module>
```

Loading Modules on Demand

To load modules on demand, you need to specify that they should be loaded into the module catalog with the **InitializationMode** set to **OnDemand**. After you do that, you need to write the code in your application to request that the module be loaded.

Specifying On-Demand Loading in Code

You use attributes to specify that a module is on-demand, as shown in the following code example.

```csharp
C# Bootstrapper.cs
protected override void ConfigureModuleCatalog()
{
  Type moduleCType = typeof(ModuleC);
  this.ModuleCatalog.AddModule(new ModuleInfo()
  {
      ModuleName = moduleCType.Name,
      ModuleType = moduleCType.AssemblyQualifiedName,
      InitializationMode = InitializationMode.OnDemand
  });
}
```

Specifying On-Demand Loading in XAML

You can specify the **InitializationMode.OnDemand** when you define your module catalog in XAML, as shown in the following code example.

```xml
XAML ModulesCatalog.xaml
...
 <Modularity:ModuleInfoGroup InitializationMode="OnDemand">
        <Modularity:ModuleInfo Ref="ModuleE.xap" ModuleName="ModuleE"
ModuleType="ModuleE.ModuleE, ModuleE, Version=1.0.0.0, Culture=neutral,
PublicKeyToken=null" />
...
```

Specifying On-Demand Loading in a Configuration File

You can specify the **InitializationMode.OnDemand** when you define your module catalog in the App.config file, as shown in the following code example.

```xml
XML App.config
...
<module assemblyFile="Modules/ModuleC.dll" moduleType="ModuleC.ModuleC, ModuleC"
moduleName="ModuleC" startupLoaded="false"/>
...
```

Requesting On-Demand Loading of a Module

After a module is specified as on demand, the application can then ask the module to be loaded. The code that initiates the loading needs to obtain a reference to the **IModule Manager** service registered with the container by the bootstrapper, as shown in the following example.

```C#
private void OnLoadModuleCClick(object sender, RoutedEventArgs e)
{
    moduleManager.LoadModule("ModuleC");
}
```

DOWNLOADING REMOTE MODULES IN THE BACKGROUND

Downloading modules in the background after the application starts or only when the user needs them can improve application startup time.

Preparing a Module for Remote Download

In Silverlight applications, modules are packaged into .xap files. To download a module separately from the application, create a separate .xap file. You can choose to put multiple modules in a single .xap file to optimize the number of download requests versus download size of each .xap file.

> **Note:** *For each .xap file, you will need to create a new Silverlight application project. In Visual Studio 2008 and 2010, only application projects produce a separate .xap file. You won't need the App.xaml or MainPage.xaml files in these projects.*

Tracking Download Progress

The **ModuleManager** class provides an event for applications to track the download progress of modules. This class shows the bytes downloaded versus the total bytes to receive, as well as the progress expressed as a percentage. You can use this class to display visual progress indicators to the user as features are downloaded, as shown in the following examples.

```C#
this.moduleManager.ModuleDownloadProgressChanged +=
this.ModuleManager_ModuleDownloadProgressChanged;
```

```C#
void ModuleManager_ModuleDownloadProgressChanged(object sender,
    ModuleDownloadProgressChangedEventArgs e)
{
    ...
}
```

DETECTING WHEN A MODULE HAS BEEN LOADED

The **ModuleManager** service provides an event that applications can use to track when a module loads or fails to load. You can get a reference to this service through dependency injection of the **IModuleManager** interface, as shown in the following examples.

```C#
this.moduleManager.LoadModuleCompleted += this.ModuleManager_LoadModuleCompleted;
```

```C#
void ModuleManager_LoadModuleCompleted(object sender, LoadModuleCompletedEventArgs e)
{
    ...
}
```

To keep the application and modules loosely coupled, you should avoid using this event to integrate the module with the application. Instead, the module's **Initialize** method should handle integration with the application.

The **LoadModuleCompletedEventArgs** contains an **IsErrorHandled** property. If a module fails to load and the application wants to prevent the **ModuleManager** from logging the error and throwing an exception, it can set this property to **true**.

> **Note:** *After a module is loaded and initialized, the module assembly cannot be unloaded. The module instance reference will not be held by the Prism libraries; therefore, the module class instance may be garbage collected after initialization is complete.*

MODULES IN MEF

This section highlights the differences that you will encounter if you choose to use MEF as your dependency injection container.

> **Note:** *With MEF, the **MefModuleManager** is used by the **MefBootstrapper**. It extends the **ModuleManager** and implements the **IPartImportsSatisfied Notification** interface to ensure that the **ModuleCatalog** is updated when new types are imported by MEF.*

Using MEF to Register Modules Programmatically

When using MEF, you can apply the **ModuleExport** attribute to module classes to have MEF automatically discover the types. The following is an example.

```C#
[ModuleExport(typeof(ModuleB))]
public class ModuleB : IModule
{
    ...
}
```

You can also use MEF to discover and load modules by using the **AssemblyCatalog** class, which can be used to discover all the exported module classes in an assembly, and the **AggregateCatalog** class, which allows multiple catalogs to be combined into one logical catalog. By default, the Prism **MefBootstrapper** class creates an **AggregateCatalog** instance. You can then override the **ConfigureAggregateCatalog** method to register assemblies, as shown in the following code example.

```C#
protected override void ConfigureAggregateCatalog()
{
    base.ConfigureAggregateCatalog();
    //Module A is referenced in in the project and directly in code.
    this.AggregateCatalog.Catalogs.Add(
    new AssemblyCatalog(typeof(ModuleA).Assembly));

    this.AggregateCatalog.Catalogs.Add(
        new AssemblyCatalog(typeof(ModuleC).Assembly));
}
```

The Prism **MefModuleManager** implementation keeps the MEF **AggregateCatalog** and the Prism **ModuleCatalog** synchronized, thereby allowing Prism to discover modules added via the **ModuleCatalog** or the **AggregateCatalog**.

> **Note:** *MEF uses* **Lazy<T>** *extensively to prevent instantiation of exported and imported types until the* **Value** *property is used.*

Using MEF to Discover Modules in a Directory

MEF provides a **DirectoryCatalog** that you can use to inspect a directory for assemblies that contain modules (and other MEF exported types). In this case, you override the **ConfigureAggregateCatalog** method to register the directory. This approach is only available in WPF.

To use this approach, you first need to use the **ModuleExport** attribute to apply the module names and dependencies to your modules, as shown in the following code example. This allows MEF to import the modules and allows Prism to keep the **Module Catalog** updated.

```C#
protected override void ConfigureAggregateCatalog()
{
    base.ConfigureAggregateCatalog();

    DirectoryCatalog catalog = new DirectoryCatalog("DirectoryModules");
    this.AggregateCatalog.Catalogs.Add(catalog);
}
```

Using MEF to Specify Dependencies in Code

For WPF applications that use MEF, use the **ModuleExport** attribute, as shown in the following example.

```
C# (when using MEF)
[ModuleExport(typeof(ModuleA), DependsOnModuleNames = new string[] { "ModuleD" })]
public class ModuleA : IModule
{
    ...
}
```

Because MEF allows you to discover modules at run time, you may also discover new dependencies between modules at run time. Although you can use MEF with the **ModuleCatalog**, it is important to remember that the **ModuleCatalog** validates the dependency chain when it is loaded from XAML or configuration (before any modules are loaded). If a module is listed in the **ModuleCatalog** and then loaded using MEF, the **ModuleCatalog** dependencies will be used, and the **DependsOnModuleNames** attribute will be ignored. Using MEF with a **ModuleCatalog** is most common in Silverlight applications that have modules in separate .xap files.

Using MEF to Specify On-Demand Loading

If you are using MEF and the **ModuleExport** attribute to specify modules and module dependencies, you can use the **InitializationMode** property to specify that a module should be loaded on demand, as shown in the following example.

```
C#
[ModuleExport(typeof(ModuleC), InitializationMode = InitializationMode.OnDemand)]
public class ModuleC : IModule
{
}
```

Using MEF to Prepare a Module for Remote Download

Prism applications that use MEF use MEF's **DeploymentCatalog** class to download .xap files and discover the assemblies and types within those .xap files. The **MefXapModuleTypeLoader** adds each **DeploymentCatalog** to the **AggregateCatalog**.

If two different .xap files are added and contain the same shared assembly, the same types are imported again. This can cause recomposition errors when the type is meant to be a singleton and is in an assembly shared between modules. The **Microsoft.Practices.Prism.MefExtensions.dll** is an example of such an assembly.

To avoid duplicate imports, open each module project's references and mark those shared DLLs as **'Copy Local'=false**. This stops that assembly from being packaged in the module's .xap file and being imported again. It also reduces the overall size of each .xap file. You need to ensure that either the application references the shared assembly or the application downloads a .xap file that contains the shared assemblies before the module .xap files are downloaded.

More Information

For more information about assembly caching, see "How to: Use Assembly Library Caching" on MSDN: http://msdn.microsoft.com/en-us/library/dd833069(VS.95).aspx.

To learn more about modularity in Prism, see the following:

- Modularity QuickStarts for WPF on MSDN:
  http://msdn.microsoft.com/en-us/library/ff921068(PandP.40).aspx.

- Modularity QuickStarts for Silverlight on MSDN:
  http://msdn.microsoft.com/en-us/library/ff921163(PandP.40).aspx.

For information about the modularity features that can be extended in the Prism Library, see "Modules" in "Extending Prism" on MSDN:

http://msdn.microsoft.com/en-us/library/gg430866(PandP.40).aspx.

To access web resources more easily, see the online version of the bibliography on MSDN:

http://msdn.microsoft.com/en-us/library/gg405487(PandP.40).aspx.

5

Implementing the MVVM Pattern

The Model-View-ViewModel (MVVM) pattern helps you to cleanly separate the business and presentation logic of your application from its user interface (UI). Maintaining a clean separation between application logic and UI helps to address numerous development and design issues and can make your application much easier to test, maintain, and evolve. It can also greatly increase code re-use opportunities and allows developers and UI designers to collaborate more easily as they develop their respective parts of the application.

The MVVM pattern separates the UI of the application and the underlying presentation and business logic into three separate classes: the view, which encapsulates the UI and UI logic; the view model, which encapsulates presentation logic and state; and the model, which encapsulates the application's business logic and data.

Prism includes samples and reference implementations that show how to implement the MVVM pattern in a Silverlight or Windows Presentation Foundation (WPF) application. The Prism Library also provides features that can help you implement the pattern in your own applications. These features embody the most common practices for implementing the MVVM pattern and are designed to support testability and to work well with Visual Studio and Expression Blend software.

This chapter provides an overview of the MVVM pattern and describes how to implement its fundamental characteristics. Chapter 6 describes how to use the Prism Library to implement more advanced MVVM scenarios.

Class Responsibilities and Characteristics

The MVVM pattern is a close variant of the Presentation Model pattern, optimized to take advantage of some of the core capabilities of WPF and Silverlight, such as data binding, data templates, commands, and behaviors.

In the MVVM pattern, the view encapsulates the UI and any UI logic, the view model encapsulates presentation logic and state, and the model encapsulates business logic and data. The view interacts with the view model through data binding, commands, and change notification events. The view model queries, observes, and coordinates updates to the model, converting, validating, and aggregating data as necessary for display in the view.

The following illustration shows the three MVVM classes and their interactions.

The MVVM classes and their interactions

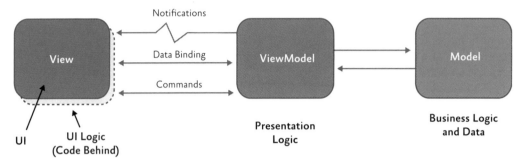

As with all separated presentation patterns, the key to using the MVVM pattern effectively lies in understanding the appropriate way to factor your application's code into the correct classes, and in understanding the ways in which these classes interact in various scenarios. The following sections describe the responsibilities and characteristics of each of the classes in the MVVM pattern.

The View Class

The view's responsibility is to define the structure and appearance of what the user sees on the screen. Ideally, the code-behind file for a view contains only a constructor that calls the **InitializeComponent** method. In some cases, the code-behind file may contain UI logic code that implements visual behavior that is difficult or inefficient to express in Extensible Application Markup Language (XAML), such as complex animations, or the code needs to directly manipulate visual elements that are part of the view. You should not put any logic code in the view that you need to unit test. Typically, logic code in the view's code-behind file will be tested by using a UI automation testing approach.

In Silverlight and WPF, data binding expressions in the view are evaluated against the view's data context. In MVVM, the view's data context is set to the view model. The view model implements properties and commands to which the view can bind and notifies the view of any changes in state through change notification events. There is typically a one-to-one relationship between a view and its view model.

Typically, views are **Control**-derived or **UserControl**-derived classes. However, in some cases, the view may be represented by a data template, which specifies the UI elements to be used to visually represent an object when it is displayed. Using data templates, a visual designer can easily define how a view model will be rendered or can modify its default visual representation without changing the underlying object itself or the behavior of the control that is used to display it.

Data templates can be thought of as views that do not have a code-behind file. They are designed to bind to a specific view model type whenever one is required to be displayed in the UI. At run time, the view, as defined by the data template, will be automatically instantiated and its data context set to the corresponding view model.

In WPF, you can associate a data template with a view model type at the application level. WPF will then automatically apply the data template to any view model objects of the specified type whenever they are displayed in the UI. This is known as implicit data templating. In Silverlight, you have to explicitly specify the data template for a view model object within the control that is to display it. In either case, the data template can be defined in-line with the control that uses it or in a resource dictionary outside the parent view and declaratively merged into the view's resource dictionary.

To summarize, the view has the following key characteristics:

- The view is a visual element, such as a window, page, user control, or data template. The view defines the controls contained in the view and their visual layout and styling.

- The view references the view model through its **DataContext** property. The controls in the view are data bound to the properties and commands exposed by the view model.

- The view may customize the data binding behavior between the view and the view model. For example, the view may use value converters to format the data to be displayed in the UI, or it may use validation rules to provide additional input data validation to the user.

- The view defines and handles UI visual behavior, such as animations or transitions that may be triggered from a state change in the view model or by the user's interaction with the UI.

- The view's code-behind file may define UI logic to implement visual behavior that is difficult to express in XAML or that requires direct references to the specific UI controls defined in the view.

THE VIEW MODEL CLASS

The view model in the MVVM pattern encapsulates the presentation logic and data for the view. It has no direct reference to the view or any knowledge about the view's specific implementation or type. The view model implements properties and commands to which the view can bind data and notifies the view of any state changes through change notification events. The properties and commands that the view model provides define the functionality to be offered by the UI, but the view determines how that functionality is to be rendered.

The view model is responsible for coordinating the view's interaction with any model classes that are required. Typically, there is a one-to many-relationship between the view model and the model classes. The view model might expose model classes directly to the view so that controls in the view can bind data directly to them. In this case, the model classes will need to be designed to support data binding and the relevant change notification events. For more information about this scenario, see the section, "Data Binding," later in this chapter.

The view model may convert or manipulate model data so that it can be easily consumed by the view. The view model may define additional properties specifically to support the view. These properties would not normally be part of (or could not be added to) the model. For example, the view model may combine the value of two fields to make it easier for the view to be presented, or it may calculate the number of characters remaining for input in fields with a maximum length. The view model may also implement data validation logic to ensure data consistency.

The view model may define logical states the view can use to provide visual changes in the UI. The view may define layout or styling changes that reflect the state of the view model. For example, the view model may define a state that indicates that data is being submitted asynchronously to a web service. The view can display an animation while it is in this state to provide visual feedback to the user.

Typically, the view model will define commands or actions that can be represented in the UI and that the user can invoke. A common example is when the view model provides a **Submit** command that allows the user submit data to a web service or to a data repository. The view might represent that command with a button so that the user can click the button to submit the data. Typically, when the command becomes unavailable, its associated UI representation becomes disabled. Commands provide a way to encapsulate user actions and to cleanly separate them from their visual representation in the UI.

To summarize, the view model has the following key characteristics:

- The view model is a non-visual class and does not derive from any WPF or Silverlight base class. It encapsulates the presentation logic required to support a use case or user task in the application. The view model is testable independently of the view and the model.

- Typically, the view model does not reference the view directly. It implements properties and commands to which the view can bind data. It uses the **INotify PropertyChanged** and **INotifyCollectionChanged** interfaces to generate change notification events that notify the view of any state changes.

- The view model coordinates the view's interaction with the model. It may convert or manipulate data so that it can be easily consumed by the view, and it might implement additional properties that may not be present on the model. It may also use the **IDataErrorInfo** or **INotifyDataErrorInfo** interfaces to implement data validation.

- The view model may define logical states that the view can represent visually to the user.

View or View Model?

In many situations, determining where certain functionality should be implemented is not obvious. The general rule of thumb is that anything concerned with the specific visual appearance of the UI on the screen and that could be restyled later (even if you are not currently planning to restyle it) should go into the view, and anything that is important to the logical behavior of the application should go into the view model. In addition, because the view model should have no explicit knowledge of the specific visual elements in the view, code to programmatically manipulate visual elements within the view should reside in the view's code-behind file or be encapsulated in a behavior. Similarly, code to retrieve or manipulate data items that are to be displayed in the view through data binding should reside in the view model.

For example, the highlight color of the selected item in a list box should be defined in the view, but the list of items to display, and the reference to the selected item itself, should be defined by the view model.

THE MODEL CLASS

The model in the MVVM pattern encapsulates business logic and data. Business logic is defined as any application logic that is concerned with the retrieval and management of application data and with making sure that any business rules that ensure data consistency and validity are imposed. To maximize re-use opportunities, models should not contain any use case–specific or user task–specific behavior or application logic.

Typically, the model represents the client-side domain model for the application. It can define data structures based on the application's data model and any supporting business and validation logic. The model may also include the code to support data access and caching, although in most cases, a separate data repository or service is employed for this. Often, the model and data access layer are generated as part of a data access or service strategy, such as the ADO.NET Entity Framework, WCF Data Services, or WCF RIA Services.

Typically, the model implements the facilities that make it easy to bind to the view. This usually means that it supports property and collection changed notification through the **INotifyPropertyChanged** and **INotifyCollectionChanged** interfaces. Models classes that represent collections of objects typically derive from the **ObservableCollection<T>** class, which provides an implementation of the **INotifyCollectionChanged** interface.

The model may also support data validation and error reporting through the **IData ErrorInfo** (or **INotifyDataErrorInfo**) interfaces. These interfaces allow WPF and Silverlight data binding to be notified when values change so that the UI can be updated. They also enable support for data validation and error reporting in the UI layer.

What if your model classes do not implement the required interfaces?
You may have to work with model objects that do not implement the **INotify PropertyChanged**, **INotifyCollectionChanged**, **IDataErrorInfo**, *or* **INotify DataErrorInfo** *interfaces. In those cases, the view model may need to wrap the model objects and expose the required properties to the view. The values for these properties will be provided directly by the model objects. The view model will implement the required interfaces for the properties it exposes so that the view can easily bind data to them.*

The model has the following key characteristics:
- The model classes are non-visual classes that encapsulate the application's data and business logic. They are responsible for managing the application's data and for ensuring its consistency and validity by encapsulating the required business rules and data validation logic.
- The model classes do not directly reference the view or view model classes and have no dependency on how they are implemented.

- The model classes typically provide property and collection change notification events through the **INotifyPropertyChanged** and **INotifyCollectionChanged** interfaces. This allows them to be easily data bound in the view. Model classes that represent collections of objects typically derive from the **ObservableCollection<T>** class.

- The model classes typically provide data validation and error reporting through either the **IDataErrorInfo** or **INotifyDataErrorInfo** interfaces.

- The model classes are typically used in conjunction with a service or repository that encapsulates data access and caching.

Class Interactions

The MVVM pattern provides a clean separation between an application's user interface, its presentation logic, and its business logic and data by separating each into separate classes. Therefore, when you implement MVVM, it is important to factor in your application's code to the correct classes, as described in the previous section.

Well-designed view, view model, and model classes will not only encapsulate the correct type of code and behavior; they will also be designed so that they can easily interact with each other via data binding, commands, and data validation interfaces.

The interactions between the view and its view model are perhaps the most important to consider, but the interactions between the model classes and the view model are also important. The following sections describe the various patterns for these interactions and describe how to design for them when you implement the MVVM pattern in your applications.

Data Binding

Data binding plays a very important role in the MVVM pattern. WPF and Silverlight both provide powerful data binding capabilities. Your view model and (ideally) your model classes should be designed to support data binding so that they can take advantage of these capabilities. Typically, this means that they must implement the correct interfaces.

Silverlight and WPF data binding supports multiple data binding modes. With one-way data binding, UI controls can be bound to a view model so that they reflect the value of the underlying data when the display is rendered. Two-way data binding will also automatically update the underlying data when the user modifies it in the UI.

To ensure that the UI is kept up to date when the data changes in the view model, it should implement the appropriate change notification interface. If it defines properties that can be data bound, it should implement the **INotifyPropertyChanged** interface. If the view model represents a collection, it should implement the **INotifyCollection-Changed** interface or derive from the **ObservableCollection<T>** class that provides an implementation of this interface. Both of these interfaces define an event that is raised whenever the underlying data is changed. Any data-bound controls will be updated automatically when these events are raised.

In many cases, a view model will define properties that return objects (and which, in turn, may define properties that return additional objects). WPF and Silverlight data binding supports using the **Path** property to bind to nested properties. Therefore, it is very common for a view's view model to return references to other view model or model classes. All view model and model classes accessible to the view should implement the **INotifyPropertyChanged** or **INotifyCollectionChanged** interfaces, as appropriate.

The following sections describe how to implement the required interfaces to support data binding within the MVVM pattern.

Implementing INotifyPropertyChanged

Implementing the **INotifyPropertyChanged** interface in your view model or model classes allows them to provide change notifications to any data-bound controls in the view when the underlying property value changes. Implementing this interface is straightforward, as shown in the following code example (see the **Questionnaire** class in the Basic MVVM QuickStart).

```csharp
public class Questionnaire : INotifyPropertyChanged
{
    private string favoriteColor;
    public event PropertyChangedEventHandler PropertyChanged;
    ...
    public string FavoriteColor
    {
        get { return this.favoriteColor; }
        set
        {
            if (value != this.favoriteColor)
            {
                this.favoriteColor = value;
                if (this.PropertyChanged != null)
                {
                    this.PropertyChanged(this,
                        new PropertyChangedEventArgs("FavoriteColor"));
                }
            }
        }
    }
}
```

Implementing the **INotifyPropertyChanged** interface on many view model classes can be repetitive and error-prone because of the need to specify the property name in the event argument. However, the Prism Library provides a convenient base class from which you can derive your view model classes. This base class implements the **INotify PropertyChanged** interface in a type-safe manner, as shown in the following example.

```
C#
public class NotificationObject : INotifyPropertyChanged
{
    public event PropertyChangedEventHandler PropertyChanged;
    ...
    protected void RaisePropertyChanged<T>(
                        Expression<Func<T>> propertyExpression)
    {...}

    protected virtual void RaisePropertyChanged(string propertyName)
    {...}
}
```

An inherited view model class can raise the property change event by either invoking **RaisePropertyChanged** with the property name specified or using a lambda expression that refers to the property, as shown in the following example.

```
C#
public string CurrentState
{
    get { return this.currentState; }
    set
    {
        if (this.currentState != value)
        {
            this.currentState = value;
            this.RaisePropertyChanged(() => this.CurrentState);
        }
    }
}
```

Note: *Using a lambda expression in this way incurs a small performance cost because the lambda expression has to be evaluated for each call. The benefit is that this approach provides compile-time type safety and refactoring support if you rename a property. Although the performance cost is small and would not typically impact your application, the costs can accrue if you have many change notifications. In this case, you should consider using the non-lambda method overload.*

Often, your model or view model will include properties whose values are calculated from other properties in the model or view model. When handling changes to properties, be sure to also raise notification events for any calculated properties.

Implementing INotifyCollectionChanged
Your view model or model class may represent a collection of items, or it may define one or more properties that return a collection of items. In either case, it is likely that you will want to display the collection in an **ItemsControl**, such as a **ListBox**, or in a **DataGrid**

control in the view. These controls can be data bound to a view model that represents a collection or to a property that returns a collection via the **ItemSource** property, as shown in the following example.

XAML
```
<DataGrid ItemsSource="{Binding Path=LineItems}" />
```

To properly support change notification requests, the view model or model class, if it represents a collection, should implement the **INotifyCollectionChanged** interface (in addition to the **INotifyPropertyChanged** interface). If the view model or model class defines a property that returns a reference to a collection, the collection class returned should implement the **INotifyCollectionChanged** interface.

However, implementing the **INotifyCollectionChanged** interface can be challenging because it must provide notifications when items are added, removed, or changed within the collection. Instead of directly implementing the interface, it is often easier to use or derive from a collection class that already implements it. The **ObservableCollection<T>** class provides an implementation of this interface and is commonly used as either a base class or to implement properties that represent a collection of items.

If you need to provide a collection to the view for data binding, and you do not need to track the user's selection or support filtering, sorting, or grouping of the items in the collection, you can simply define a property in your view model that returns a reference to the **ObservableCollection<T>** instance. The following example illustrates this approach.

C#
```csharp
public class OrderViewModel : INotifyPropertyChanged
{
    public OrderViewModel(IOrderService orderService)
    {
        this.LineItems = new ObservableCollection<OrderLineItem>(
                         orderService.GetLineItemList());
    }

    public ObservableCollection<OrderLineItem> LineItems { get; private set; }
}
```

If you obtain a reference to a collection class (for example, from another component or service that does not implement **INotifyCollectionChanged**), you can often wrap that collection in an **ObservableCollection<T>** instance by using one of the constructors that take an **IEnumerable<T>** or **List<T>** parameter.

Implementing ICollectionView

The preceding code example shows how to implement a simple view model property that returns a collection of items that can be displayed via data-bound controls in the view. Because the **ObservableCollection<T>** class implements the **INotifyCollectionChanged** interface, the controls in the view will be updated automatically to reflect the current list of items in the collection as items are added or removed.

However, you may need to more finely control how the collection of items is displayed in the view, or track the user's interaction with the displayed collection of items, from within the view model itself. For example, you might need to allow the collection of items to be filtered or sorted according to presentation logic implemented in the view model, or you might need to keep track of the currently selected item in the view so that commands implemented in the view model can act on the currently selected item.

WPF and Silverlight support these scenarios by providing various classes that implement the **ICollectionView** interface. This interface provides properties and methods to allow a collection to be filtered, sorted, or grouped, and to allow the currently selected item to be tracked or changed. Both Silverlight and WPF provide implementations of this interface: Silverlight provides the **PagedCollectionView** class, and WPF provides the **ListCollectionView** class.

Collection view classes work by wrapping an underlying collection of items so that they can provide automatic selection tracking and sorting, filtering, and paging for them. You can use the **CollectionViewSource** class to create an instance of these classes programmatically or declaratively in XAML.

> **Note:** *In WPF, a default collection view will actually be created automatically whenever a control is bound to a collection. In Silverlight, a collection view will be created automatically only if the bound collection supports the* **ICollectionViewFactory** *interface.*

Collection view classes can be used by the view model to keep track of important state information for the underlying collection, while maintaining a clean separation of concerns between the UI in the view and the underlying data in the model. In effect, **CollectionViews** are view models that are designed specifically to support collections.

Therefore, if you need to implement filtering, sorting, grouping, or selection tracking of items in the collection from within your view model, your view model should create an instance of a collection view class for each collection to be exposed to the view. You can then subscribe to selection changed events, such as the **CurrentChanged** event, or control filtering, sorting, or grouping by using the methods provided by the collection view class from within your view model.

The view model should implement a read-only property that returns an **ICollection View** reference so that controls in the view can bind data to the collection view object and interact with it. All WPF and Silverlight controls that derive from the **ItemsControl** base class can automatically interact with **ICollectionView** classes.

The following code example shows the use of the **PagedCollectionView** in Silverlight to keep track of the currently selected customer.

```
C#
public class MyViewModel : INotifyPropertyChanged
{
    public ICollectionView Customers { get; private set; }

    public MyViewModel(ObservableCollection<Customer> customers)
    {
```

```
        // Initialize the CollectionView for the underlying model
        // and track the current selection.
        Customers = new PagedCollectionView(customers);
        Customers.CurrentChanged +=
                            new EventHandler(SelectedItemChanged);
    }

    private void SelectedItemChanged(object sender, EventArgs e)
    {
        Customer current = Customers.CurrentItem as Customer;
        ...
    }
}
```

In the view, you can then bind an **ItemsControl**, such as a **ListBox**, to the **Customers** property on the view model by using its **ItemsSource** property, as shown in the following example.

XAML
```
<ListBox ItemsSource="{Binding Path=Customers}">
    <ListBox.ItemTemplate>
        <DataTemplate>
            <StackPanel>
                <TextBlock Text="{Binding Path=Name}"/>
            </StackPanel>
        </DataTemplate>
    </ListBox.ItemTemplate>
</ListBox>
```

When the user selects a customer in the UI, the view model will be informed so that it can apply the commands that relate to the currently selected customer. The view model can also programmatically change the current selection in the UI by calling methods on the collection view object, as shown in the following code example.

C#
```
Customers.MoveCurrentToNext();
```

When the selection changes in the collection view, the UI is automatically updated to visually represent the selected state of the item. The implementation is similar for WPF, although the **PagedCollectionView** in the preceding example will typically be replaced with a **ListCollectionView** or **BindingListCollectionView** class, as shown in the following example.

C#
```
Customers = new ListCollectionView(_model);
Customers.CurrentChanged += new EventHandler(SelectedItemChanged);
```

COMMANDS

In addition to providing access to the data to be displayed or edited in the view, the view model will typically define one or more actions or operations that can be performed by the user. In WPF and Silverlight, actions or operations that the user can perform through the UI are typically defined as commands. Commands provide a convenient way to represent actions or operations that can be easily bound to controls in the UI. They encapsulate the actual code that implements the action or operation and help to keep it decoupled from its actual visual representation in the view.

Commands can be visually represented, and users can invoke them in many different ways as they interact with the view. In most cases, commands are invoked as a result of a mouse click, but they can also be invoked as a result of shortcut key presses, touch gestures, or any other input events. Controls in the view are data bound to the view model's commands so that the user can invoke them by whatever input event or gesture the control defines. Interaction between the UI controls in the view and the command can be two-way. In a two-way interaction, the command can be invoked as the user interacts with the UI, and the UI can be automatically enabled or disabled as the underlying command becomes enabled or disabled.

The view model can implement a command as either a command method or as a command object (an object that implements the **ICommand** interface). In either case, the view's interaction with the command can be defined declaratively without requiring complex event handling code in the view's code-behind file. For example, certain controls in WPF and Silverlight inherently support commands and provide a **Command** property that can be data bound to an **ICommand** object provided by the view model. In other cases, a command behavior can be used to associate a control with a command method or command object provided by the view model.

> **Note:** *A behavior is a powerful and flexible extensibility mechanism that can be used to encapsulate interaction logic and activity that can then be declaratively associated with controls in the view. Command behaviors can be used to associate command objects or methods with controls that were not specifically designed to interact with commands.*

The following sections describe how to implement commands in your view—as command methods or as command objects—and how to associate them with controls in the view.

Implementing Command Objects

A command object is an object that implements the **ICommand** interface. This interface defines an **Execute** method, which encapsulates the operation itself, and a **CanExecute** method, which indicates whether the command can be invoked at a particular time. Both of these methods take a single argument as the parameter for the command. The encapsulation of the implementation logic for an operation in a command object means that it can be more easily unit tested and maintained.

Implementing the **ICommand** interface is straightforward. However, there are a number of implementations of this interface that you can readily use in your application. For example, you can use the **ActionCommand** class from the Expression Blend SDK or the **DelegateCommand** class provided by Prism.

The Prism **DelegateCommand** class encapsulates two delegates that each reference a method implemented within your view model class. It inherits from the **DelegateCommand Base** class, which implements the **ICommand** interface's **Execute** and **CanExecute** methods by invoking these delegates. You specify the delegates to your view model methods in the **DelegateCommand** class constructor, which is defined as follows.

```csharp
// C# DelegateCommand.cs
public class DelegateCommand<T> : DelegateCommandBase
{
public DelegateCommand(Action<T> executeMethod,Func<T,bool> canExecuteMethod):
base((o) => executeMethod((T)o), (o) => canExecuteMethod((T)o))
    {
        ...
    }
}
```

For example, the following code example shows how a **DelegateCommand** instance, which represents a **Submit** command, is constructed by specifying delegates to the **OnSubmit** and **CanSubmit** view model methods. The command is then exposed to the view via a read-only property that returns a reference to an **ICommand**.

```csharp
// C#
public class QuestionnaireViewModel
{
    public QuestionnaireViewModel()
    {
      this.SubmitCommand = new DelegateCommand<object>(
                        this.OnSubmit, this.CanSubmit);
    }

    public ICommand SubmitCommand { get; private set; }

    private void OnSubmit(object arg)   {...}
    private bool CanSubmit(object arg)  { return true; }
}
```

When the **Execute** method is called on the **DelegateCommand** object, it simply uses the delegate that you specified in the constructor to forward the call to the method in your view model class. Similarly, when the **CanExecute** method is called, the corresponding method in your view model class is called. The delegate to the **CanExecute** method in the constructor is optional. If a delegate is not specified, **DelegateCommand** will always return **true** for **CanExecute**.

The **DelegateCommand** class is a generic type. The type argument specifies the type of the command parameter passed to the **Execute** and **CanExecute** methods. In the preceding example, the command parameter is of type **object**. Prism also provides a non-generic version of the **DelegateCommand** class for use when a command parameter is not required.

The view model can indicate a change in the command's **CanExecute** status by calling the **RaiseCanExecuteChanged** method on the **DelegateCommand** object. This causes the **CanExecuteChanged** event to be raised. Any controls in the UI that are bound to the command will update their enabled status to reflect the availability of the bound command.

Other implementations of the **ICommand** interface are available. The **ActionCommand** class provided by the Expression Blend SDK is similar to Prism's **DelegateCommand** class described earlier, but it supports only a single **Execute** method delegate. Prism also provides the **CompositeCommand** class, which allows **DelegateCommands** to be grouped together for execution. For more information about using the **Composite Command** class, see "Composite Commands" in Chapter 6, "Advanced MVVM Scenarios."

Invoking Command Objects from the View

There are a number of ways in which a control in the view can be associated with a command object proffered by the view model. Certain WPF and Silverlight 4 controls, notably **ButtonBase** derived controls, such as **Button** or **RadioButton**, and **Hyperlink**, or **MenuItem** derived controls, can be easily data bound to a command object through the **Command** property, as shown in the following example. WPF also supports binding a view model **ICommand** to a **KeyGesture**.

XAML
```
<Button Command="{Binding Path=SubmitCommand}" CommandParameter="SubmitOrder"/>
```

You can also optionally define a command parameter by using the **CommandParameter** property. You specify the type of the expected argument in the **Execute** and **CanExecute** target methods. The control will automatically invoke the target command when the user interacts with that control, and the command parameter, if provided, will be passed as the argument to the command's **Execute** method. In the preceding example, the button will automatically invoke the **SubmitCommand** when it is clicked. Additionally, if a **CanExecute** handler is specified, the button will be automatically disabled if **CanExecute** returns **false**, and it will be enabled if it returns **true**.

An alternative approach is to use Expression Blend interaction triggers and **Invoke CommandAction** behavior, as shown in the following example.

XAML
```
<Button Content="Submit" IsEnabled="{Binding CanSubmit}">
    <i:Interaction.Triggers>
        <i:EventTrigger EventName="Click">
            <i:InvokeCommandAction Command="{Binding SubmitCommand}"/>
        </i:EventTrigger>
    </i:Interaction.Triggers>
</Button>
```

This approach can be used for any control to which you can attach an interaction trigger. It is especially useful if you want to attach a command to a control that does not derive from **ButtonBase**, or when you want to invoke the command on an event other than the click event. Again, if you need to supply parameters for your command, you can use the **CommandParameter** property.

Unlike controls that can be bound directly to a command, **InvokeCommandAction** does not automatically enable or disable the control based on the command's **CanExecute** value. To implement this behavior, you have to bind the **IsEnabled** property of the control directly to a suitable property on the view model, as shown earlier.

> **Command-Enabled Controls vs. Behaviors**
>
> *WPF and Silverlight 4 controls that support commands allow you to declaratively hook up a control to a command. These controls will invoke the specified command when the user interacts with the control in a specific way. For example, for a **Button** control, the command will be invoked when the user clicks the button. This event associated with the command is fixed and cannot be changed.*
>
> *Behaviors also allow you to connect a control to a command in a declarative fashion. However, behaviors can be associated with a range of events raised by the control, and they can be used to conditionally invoke an associated command object or a command method on the view model. In other words, behaviors can address many of the same scenarios as command-enabled controls, and they may provide a greater degree of flexibility and control.*
>
> *You will need to choose when to use command-enabled controls and when to use behaviors, as well as which kind of behavior to use. If you prefer to use a single mechanism to associate controls in the view with functionality in the view model or for consistency, you should consider using behaviors, even for controls that inherently support commands.*
>
> *If you only need to use command-enabled controls to invoke commands on the view model, and if you are happy with the default events to invoke the command, behaviors may not be required. Similarly, if your developers or UI designers will not be using Expression Blend, you may prefer command-enabled controls (or custom attached behaviors) because of the additional syntax required for Expression Blend behaviors.*

Invoking Command Methods from the View

An alternative approach to implementing commands as **ICommand** objects is to implement them simply as methods in the view model and then to use behaviors to invoke those methods directly from the view.

This can be achieved in a similar way to the invocation of commands from behaviors, as shown in the previous section. However, instead of using **InvokeCommandAction**, you use the **CallMethodAction**. The following code example calls the (parameter-less) **Submit** method on the underlying view model.

```XAML
<Button Content="Submit" IsEnabled="{Binding CanSubmit}">
    <i:Interaction.Triggers>
        <i:EventTrigger EventName="Click">
            <i:CallMethodAction TargetObject="{Binding}" Method="Submit"/>
        </i:EventTrigger>
    </i:Interaction.Triggers>
</Button>
```

The **TargetObject** is bound to the underlying data context (which is the view model) by the **{Binding}** expression. The **Method** parameter specifies the method to invoke.

Note: CallMethodAction *does not support parameters. If you need to pass parameters to the target method, you have to provide the values as properties on the view model, switch to using a command with an* **InvokeCommandAction**, *or write your own version of the* **CallMethodAction** *that will pass parameters.*

DATA VALIDATION AND ERROR REPORTING

Your view model or model will often be required to perform data validation and to signal any data validation errors to the view so that the user can act to correct them.

Silverlight and WPF provide support for managing data validation errors that occur when individual properties that are bound to controls in the view are changed. For single properties that are data-bound to a control, the view model or model can signal a data validation error within the property setter by rejecting an incoming bad value and throwing an exception. If the **ValidatesOnExceptions** property on the data binding is **true**, the data binding engine in WPF and Silverlight will handle the exception and display a visual cue to the user that there is a data validation error.

However, where possible, you should avoid throwing exceptions with properties in this way. An alternative approach is to implement the **IDataErrorInfo** or **INotifyData ErrorInfo** interfaces on your view model or model classes. These interfaces allow your view model or model to perform data validation for one or more property values and to return an error message to the view so that the user can be notified of the error.

Implementing IDataErrorInfo

The **IDataErrorInfo** interface provides basic support for property data validation and error reporting. It defines two read-only properties: an indexer property, with the property name as the indexer argument, and an **Error** property. Both properties return a string value.

The indexer property allows the view model or model class to provide an error message specific to the named property. An empty string or null return value indicates to the view that the changed property value is valid. The **Error** property allows the view model or model class to provide an error message for the entire object. Note, however, that this property is not currently called by the Silverlight or WPF data binding engine.

The **IDataErrorInfo** indexer property is accessed when a data-bound property is first displayed, and whenever it is subsequently changed. Because the indexer property is called for all properties that change, you should be careful to ensure that data validation is as fast and as efficient as possible.

When binding controls in the view to properties you want to validate through the **IDataErrorInfo** interface, set the **ValidatesOnDataErrors** property on the data binding to **true**. This will ensure that the data binding engine will request error information for the data-bound property. See the following example.

```XAML
<TextBox
Text="{Binding Path=CurrentEmployee.Name, Mode=TwoWay, ValidatesOnDataErrors=True,
NotifyOnValidationError=True}"
/>
```

Implementing INotifyDataErrorInfo

The **INotifyDataErrorInfo** interface is more flexible than the **IDataErrorInfo** interface. It supports multiple errors for a property, asynchronous data validation, and the ability to notify the view if the error state changes for an object. However, **INotifyDataErrorInfo** is currently supported in Silverlight 4 only, and is not available in WPF 4.

The **INotifyDataErrorInfo** interface defines a **HasErrors** property, which allows the view model to indicate whether an error (or multiple errors) for any properties exist, and a **GetErrors** method, which allows the view model to return a list of error messages for a particular property.

The **INotifyDataErrorInfo** interface also defines an **ErrorsChanged** event. This supports asynchronous validation scenarios in Silverlight by allowing the view or view model to use an **ErrorsChanged** event to signal a change in error state for a particular property. Property values can be changed in a number of ways, and not just by using data binding—for example, as a result of a web service call or background calculation. The **ErrorsChanged** event allows the view model to inform the view of an error as soon as a data validation error has been identified.

To support **INotifyDataErrorInfo**, you will need to maintain a list of errors for each property. The Model-View-ViewModel Reference Implementation (MVVM RI) demonstrates one way to do this by using an **ErrorsContainer** collection class that tracks all the validation errors in the object. It also raises notification events if the error list changes. The following code example shows a **DomainObject** (a root model object) and an example implementation of **INotifyDataErrorInfo** using the **ErrorsContainer** class.

```C#
public abstract class DomainObject : INotifyPropertyChanged,
                                     INotifyDataErrorInfo
{

    private ErrorsContainer<ValidationResult> errorsContainer =
                new ErrorsContainer<ValidationResult>(
                    pn => this.RaiseErrorsChanged( pn ) );

    public event EventHandler<DataErrorsChangedEventArgs> ErrorsChanged;

    public bool HasErrors
    {
        get { return this.ErrorsContainer.HasErrors; }
    }
```

```
    public IEnumerable GetErrors(string propertyName)
    {
        return this.errorsContainer.GetErrors(propertyName);
    }

    protected void RaiseErrorsChanged(string propertyName)
    {
        var handler = this.ErrorsChanged;
        if (handler != null)
        {
            handler(this, new DataErrorsChangedEventArgs(propertyName));
        }
    }
    ...
}
```

In Silverlight, any controls that are data bound to properties on the view model will automatically subscribe to the **INotifyDataErrorInfo** event and display error information on the control if the property contains an error.

Construction and Configuration

The MVVM pattern helps you to cleanly separate your UI from your presentation and business logic and data, so implementing the right code in the right class is an important first step in using the MVVM pattern effectively. Managing the interactions between the view and view model classes through data binding and commands are also important aspects to consider. The next step is to consider how the view, view model, and model classes are instantiated and associated with each other at run time.

> **Note:** *Choosing an appropriate strategy to manage this step is especially important if you are using a dependency injection container in your application. Both the Managed Extensibility Framework (MEF) and the Unity Application Block (Unity) allow you to specify dependencies between the view, view model, and model classes and to have them fulfilled by the container. More advanced MVVM scenarios are discussed in the next chapter.*

Typically, there is a one-to-one relationship between a view and its view model. The view and view model are loosely coupled via the view's data context property. This allows visual elements and behaviors in the view to be data bound to properties, commands, and methods on the view model. You will need to decide how to manage the instantiation of the view and view model classes and how to associate them via the **DataContext** property at run time.

You must take care when constructing and connecting the view and view model to ensure that loose coupling is maintained. As noted in the previous section, ideally, the view model should not depend on any specific implementation of a view. Similarly, the view should not depend on any specific implementation of a view model.

Note: *The view will **implicitly** depend on specific properties, commands, and methods on the view model because of the data bindings it defines. If the view model does not implement the required property, command, or method, a run-time exception will be generated by the data binding engine, which will be displayed in the Visual Studio output window during debugging.*

There are multiple ways that the view and the view model can be constructed and associated at run time. The most appropriate approach for your application will depend largely on whether you create the view or the view model first, and whether you do this programmatically or declaratively. The following sections describe common ways in which the view and view model classes can be created and associated with each other at run time.

CREATING THE VIEW MODEL USING XAML

Perhaps the simplest approach is for the view to declaratively instantiate its corresponding view model in XAML. When the view is constructed, the corresponding view model object will also be constructed. You can also specify in XAML that the view model be set as the view's data context.

The XAML-based approach is demonstrated in the QuestionnaireView.xaml file in the Basic MVVM QuickStart. In that example, the **QuestionnaireViewModel** instance is defined in the **QuestionnaireView**'s XAML, as shown in the following example.

```XAML
<UserControl.DataContext>
    <my:QuestionnaireViewModel/>
</UserControl.DataContext>
```

When the **QuestionnaireView** is created, an instance of the **QuestionnaireView Model** is automatically constructed and set as the view's data context. This approach requires your view model to have a default (parameter-less) constructor.

The declarative construction and assignment of the view model by the view has the advantage of being simple and working well in design-time tools such as Expression Blend or Visual Studio. The disadvantage of this approach is that the view has knowledge of the corresponding view model type.

CREATING THE VIEW MODEL PROGRAMMATICALLY

Another approach is for the view to instantiate its corresponding view model instance programmatically in its constructor. It can then set it as its data context, as shown in the following code example.

```C#
public QuestionnaireView()
{
    InitializeComponent();
    this.DataContext = new QuestionnaireViewModel();
}
```

The programmatic construction and assignment of the view model within the view's code-behind file has the advantage of being simple and working well in design-time tools such as Expression Blend or Visual Studio. The disadvantages of this approach are that the view needs to have knowledge of the corresponding view model type and that it requires code in the view's code-behind file. Using a dependency injection container, such as Unity or MEF, can help to maintain loose coupling between the view and view model. For more information, see Chapter 3, "Managing Dependencies Between Components."

CREATING A VIEW DEFINED AS A DATA TEMPLATE

A view can be defined as a data template and associated with a view model type. Data templates can be defined as resources, or they can be defined inline within the control that will display the view model. The content of the control is the view model instance, and the data template is used to visually represent that instance. WPF and Silverlight will automatically instantiate the data template and set its data context to the view model instance at run time. This technique is an example of a situation in which the view model is instantiated first, followed by the creation of the view.

Data templates are flexible and lightweight. The UI designer can use them to easily define the visual representation of a view model without requiring any complex code. Data templates are restricted to views that do not require any UI logic (code-behind). Microsoft Expression Blend can be used to design and edit data templates.

The following example shows an **ItemsControl** that is bound to a list of customers. Each customer object in the underlying collection is a view model instance. The view for the customer is defined by an inline data template. In the example, the view for each customer view model consists of a **StackPanel** with a label and a **TextBox** control bound to the **Name** property on the view model.

```XAML
<ItemsControl ItemsSource="{Binding Customers}">
    <ItemsControl.ItemTemplate>
        <DataTemplate>
            <StackPanel Orientation="Horizontal">
                <TextBlock VerticalAlignment="Center" Text="Customer Name: " />
                <TextBox Text="{Binding Name}" />
            </StackPanel>
        </DataTemplate>
    </ItemsControl.ItemTemplate>
</ItemsControl>
```

You can also define a data template as a resource. The following example shows the data template defined as a resource and applied to a content control via the **Static Resource** markup extension.

```XAML
<UserControl ...>
    <UserControl.Resources>
        <DataTemplate x:Key="CustomerViewTemplate">
```

```
                <local:CustomerContactView />
        </DataTemplate>
    </UserControl.Resources>

    <Grid>
        <ContentControl Content="{Binding Customer}"
                ContentTemplate="{StaticResource CustomerViewTemplate}" />
    </Grid>
</Window>
```

In this example, the data template wraps a concrete view type. This allows the view to define code-behind behavior. In this way, the data template mechanism can be used to externally provide the association between the view and the view model. Although the preceding example shows the template in the **UserControl** resources, it can also be placed in application's resources for reuse. You can find an example of using data templates to instantiate views and associate them with their view models in the MVVM QuickStart file QuestionnaireView.xaml.

Key Decisions

When you decide to use the MVVM pattern to construct your application, you will have to make certain design choices that will be difficult to change later on. Generally, these decisions are application-wide and their consistent use throughout the application will improve developer and designer productivity. The following summarizes the most important decisions that you will need to make when implementing the MVVM pattern:

- **Decide on the approach to view and view model construction that you will use**. You need to decide if your application will construct the views or the view models first and whether it will use a dependency injection container, such as Unity or MEF. You will usually want this to be consistent application-wide. For more information, see the section, "Construction and Configuration," in this chapter and the section "Advanced Construction and Configuration," in Chapter 6, "Advanced MVVM Scenarios."

- **Decide if you will expose commands from your view models as command methods or command objects**. Command methods are simple to expose and can be invoked through behaviors in the view. Command objects can neatly encapsulate the command and enabled/disabled logic and can be invoked through behaviors or by using the **Command** property on **ButtonBase**-derived controls. To make it easier on your developers and designers, it is a good idea to make this an application-wide choice. For more information, see the section, "Commands," in this chapter.

- **Decide how your view models and models will report errors to the view**. Your models can either support **IDataErrorInfo** or, if using Silverlight, **INotifyData ErrorInfo**. Not all models may need to report error information, but for those that do, it is preferable to have a consistent approach for your developers. For more information, see the section, "Data Validation and Error Reporting," in this chapter.

- **Decide whether Expression Blend design-time data support is important to your team**. If you will use Expression Blend to design and maintain your UI and want to see design-time data, make sure that your views and view models offer constructors that do not have parameters and that your views provide a design-time data context. Alternatively, consider using the design-time features provided by Expression Blend by using design-time attributes such as **d:DataContext** and **d:DesignSource**. For more information, see "Guidelines for Creating Designer Friendly Views" in Chapter 7, "Composing the User Interface."

More Information

For more information about data binding in WPF, see "Data Binding" on MSDN:
> http://msdn.microsoft.com/en-us/library/ms750612.aspx.

For more information about data binding in Silverlight, see "Data Binding" on MSDN:
> http://msdn.microsoft.com/en-us/library/cc278072(VS.95).aspx.

For more information about binding to collections in WPF, see "Binding to Collections" in "Data Binding Overview" on MSDN:
> http://msdn.microsoft.com/en-us/library/ms752347.aspx.

For more information about binding to collections in Silverlight, see "Binding to Collections" in "Data Binding" on MSDN:
> http://msdn.microsoft.com/en-us/library/cc278072(VS.95).aspx.

For more information about the Presentation Model pattern, see "Presentation Model" on Martin Fowler's website:
> http://www.martinfowler.com/eaaDev/PresentationModel.html.

For more information about data templates, see "Data Templating Overview" on MSDN:
> http://msdn.microsoft.com/en-us/library/ms742521.aspx.

For more information about MEF, see "Managed Extensibility Framework Overview" on MSDN:
> http://msdn.microsoft.com/en-us/library/dd460648.aspx.

For more information about Unity, see "Unity Application Block" on MSDN:
> http://www.msdn.com/unity.

For more information about **DelegateCommand** and **CompositeCommand**, see Chapter 9, "Communicating Between Loosely Coupled Components."

To access web resources more easily, see the online version of the bibliography on MSDN:
> http://msdn.microsoft.com/en-us/library/gg405487(PandP.40).aspx.

6 Advanced MVVM Scenarios

The previous chapter described how to implement the basic elements of the Model-View-ViewModel (MVVM) pattern by separating your application's user interface (UI), presentation logic, and business logic into three separate classes (the view, view model, and model), implementing the interactions between those classes (through data binding, commands, and data validation interfaces), and by implementing a strategy to handle construction, connection, and configuration of the MVVM classes.

Implementing the MVVM pattern using these basic elements will probably support many of the scenarios in your application. However, you may encounter more sophisticated scenarios that require the basic MVVM pattern to be extended or that require more advanced techniques to be applied. This is more likely to be true if your application is large or complex, but you may also encounter these scenarios in smaller applications. The Prism Library provides components that implement many of these techniques, allowing you to more easily use them in your own applications.

This chapter describes some sophisticated scenarios and how the MVVM pattern can support them. The next section explains how commands can be chained together or associated with child views and how they can be extended to support custom requirements. The following sections then describe how to handle asynchronous data requests and subsequent UI interactions and how to handle interaction requests between the view and the view model.

The section, "Advanced Construction and Configuration," contains guidance about handling construction, connection, and configuration when using a dependency injection container, such as the Unity Application Block (Unity), or when using the Managed Extensibility Framework (MEF). The final section describes how you can test MVVM applications by providing guidance on unit testing your application's view model and model classes, and on testing behaviors.

Commands

Commands provide a way to separate the command's implementation logic from its UI representation. Data binding or behaviors provide a way to declaratively associate elements in the view with commands proffered by the view model. The "Commands" section in Chapter 5, "Implementing the MVVM Pattern," described how commands can be implemented as command objects or command methods in the view model, and how they can be invoked from controls in the view by using either behaviors or the built-in **Command** property provided by certain controls.

> **WPF Routed Commands**: *Commands implemented as command objects or command methods in the MVVM pattern differ somewhat from WPF's built-in implementation of commands named routed commands (Silverlight does not have any routed command implementations). WPF routed commands deliver command messages by routing them through elements in the UI tree (specifically, the logical tree). Therefore, command messages are routed up or down the UI tree from the focused element, or they are routed to an explicitly specified target element. By default, they are not routed to components outside of the UI tree, such as the view model associated with the view. However, WPF-routed commands can use a command handler defined in the view's code-behind file to forward the command call to the view model class.*

Composite Commands

In many cases, a command defined by a view model will be bound to controls in the associated view so that the user can directly invoke the command from within the view. However, in some cases, you may want to be able to invoke commands on one or more view models from a control in a parent view in the application's UI.

For example, if your application allows the user to edit multiple items at the same time, you may want to allow the user to save all the items by using a single command represented by a button in the application's toolbar or ribbon. In this case, the **Save All** command will invoke each of the **Save** commands implemented by the view model instance for each item, as shown in the following illustration.

Implementing the SaveAll composite command

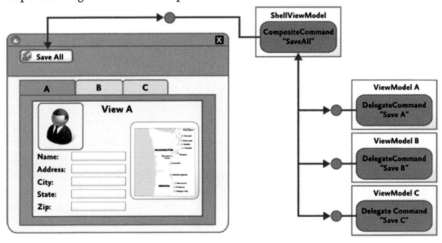

Prism supports this scenario through the **CompositeCommand** class.

The **CompositeCommand** class is a command that is composed from multiple child commands. When the composite command is invoked, each of its child commands is invoked in turn. It is useful if you need to represent a group of commands as a single command in the UI or if you want to invoke multiple commands to implement a logical command.

For example, the **CompositeCommand** class is used in the Stock Trader Reference Implementation (Stock Trader RI) to implement the **SubmitAllOrders** command represented by the **Submit All** button in the buy/sell view. When the user clicks the **Submit All** button, each **SubmitCommand** defined by the individual buy/sell transactions is executed.

The **CompositeCommand** class maintains a list of child commands (**Delegate Command** instances). The **Execute** method of the **CompositeCommand** class simply calls the **Execute** method on each of the child commands in turn. Similarly, the **CanExecute** method calls the **CanExecute** method of each child command. However, if any of the child commands cannot be executed, the **CanExecute** method will return **false**. In other words, by default, a **CompositeCommand** can only be executed when all the child commands can be executed.

Registering and Unregistering Child Commands

Child commands are registered or unregistered by the **RegisterCommand** and **Unregister Command** methods. In the Stock Trader RI, for example, the **Submit** and **Cancel** commands for each buy/sell order are registered with the **SubmitAllOrders** and **Cancel AllOrders** composite commands, as shown in the following code example (see the **OrdersController** class).

```
C# OrdersController.cs
commandProxy.SubmitAllOrdersCommand.RegisterCommand(
                    orderCompositeViewModel.SubmitCommand );
commandProxy.CancelAllOrdersCommand.RegisterCommand(
                    orderCompositeViewModel.CancelCommand );
```

Note: *The* **commandProxy** *object in the preceding example provides instance access to the* **Submit** *and* **Cancel** *composite commands, which are defined statically. For more information, see the class file StockTraderRICommands.cs.*

Executing Commands in Active Child Views

Often, your application will need to display a collection of child views in the application's UI. Each child view will have a corresponding view model that, in turn, might implement one or more commands. You can use composite commands to represent the commands implemented by child views in the application's UI and help to coordinate how they are invoked from within the parent view. To support these scenarios, the Prism **Composite Command** and **DelegateCommand** classes have been designed to work with Prism regions.

Prism regions, described in section, "Regions," in Chapter 7, "Composing the User Interface," provide a way for child views to be associated with logical placeholders in the application's UI. They are often used to decouple the layout of child views from their logical placeholders and placeholder positions in the UI. Regions are based on named placeholders that are attached to specific layout controls. The following illustration shows an example in which each child view has been added to the region named **EditRegion**, and the UI designer has chosen to use a **Tab** control to lay out the views in that region.

Defining the EditRegion using a Tab control

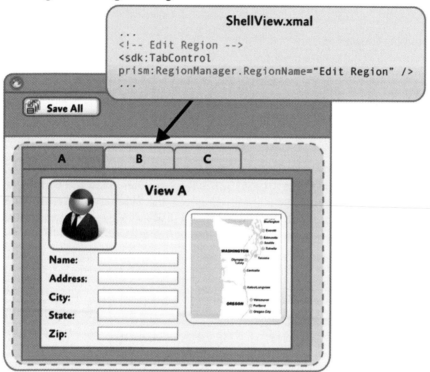

Typically, composite commands at the parent view level will be used to coordinate how commands at the child view level are invoked. In some cases, you will want the commands for all shown views to be executed at one time, as in the **Save All** command example described earlier. In other cases, you will want the command to be executed only on the active view. In this case, the composite command will execute the child commands only on views that are deemed to be active; it will not execute the child commands on views that are not active. For example, you may want to implement a **Zoom** command on the application's toolbar or ribbon that causes only the currently active item to be zoomed, as shown in the following diagram.

Defining the EditRegion using a Tab control

To support this scenario, Prism provides the **IActiveAware** interface. The **IActive Aware** interface defines an **IsActive** property that returns **true** when the implementer is active, and an **IsActiveChanged** event that is raised whenever the active state is changed.

You can implement the **IActiveAware** interface on child views or view models. It is primarily used to track the active state of a child view in a region. Whether or not a view is active is determined by the region adapter that coordinates the views in the specific region control. For example, the **Tab** control shown earlier uses a region adapter that sets the view in the currently selected tab to **active**.

The **DelegateCommand** class also implements the **IActiveAware** interface. The **CompositeCommand** can be configured to evaluate the active status of child **Delegate Commands** (in addition to the **CanExecute** status) by specifying **true** for the **monitor CommandActivity** parameter in the constructor. When this parameter is set to **true**, the **CompositeCommand** class will consider each child **DelegateCommand**'s active status when determining the return value for the **CanExecute** method and when executing child commands within the **Execute** method.

When the **monitorCommandActivity** parameter is **true**, the **CompositeCommand** class exhibits the following behavior:

- **CanExecute**. Returns **true** only when all active commands can be executed. Child commands that are inactive will not be considered at all.

- **Execute**. Executes all active commands. Child commands that are inactive will not be considered at all.

You can use this functionality to implement the example described earlier. By implementing the **IActiveAware** interface on your child view models, you will be notified when your child view becomes active or inactive in the region. When the child view's active status changes, you can update the active status of the child commands. Then, when the user invokes the **Zoom** composite command, the **Zoom** command on the active child view will be invoked.

COMMANDS WITHIN COLLECTIONS

When you display a collection of items in a view, you may need the UI for each item in the collection to be associated with a command at the parent view level (instead of at the item level).

For example, in the application shown in the following illustration, the view displays a collection of items in a **ListBox** control, and the data template used to display each item defines a **Delete** button that allows the user to delete individual items from the collection.

Binding commands within collections

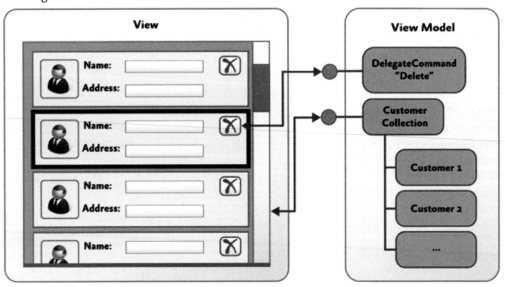

Because the view model implements the **Delete** command, the challenge is to associate the **Delete** button in the UI for each item to the **Delete** command implemented by the view model. The difficulty arises because the data context for each of the items in the **ListBox** references the item in the collection instead of the parent view model that implements the **Delete** command.

One approach to this problem is to use the **ElementName** binding property to bind the button in the data template to the command in the parent view. This ensures that the binding is relative to the parent control and not relative to the data template. The following Extensible Application Markup Language (XAML) example illustrates this technique.

XAML
```xaml
<Grid x:Name="root">
    <ListBox ItemsSource="{Binding Path=Items}">
        <ListBox.ItemTemplate>
            <DataTemplate>
  <Button Content="{Binding Path=Name}"
        Command="{Binding ElementName=root, Path=DataContext.DeleteCommand}" />
            </DataTemplate>
        </ListBox.ItemTemplate>
    </ListBox>
</Grid>
```

The content of the button control in the data template is bound to the **Name** property on the item in the collection. However, the command for the button is bound via the root element's data context to the **Delete** command. This allows the button to be bound to the command at the parent view level instead of at the item level. You can use the **CommandParameter** property to specify the item to which the command is to be applied, or you can implement the command to operate on the currently selected item (by using a **CollectionView**).

COMMAND BEHAVIORS

In Silverlight 3 and earlier versions, Silverlight did not offer controls that directly supported commands. The **ICommand** interface was available, but no controls implemented the **Command** property to allow them to be directly hooked up to an **ICommand** implementation. To overcome this limitation, and to support MVVM commanding patterns in Silverlight 3, the Prism Library (version 2.0) provided a mechanism to allow any Silverlight control to be bound to a command object by using an attached behavior. This mechanism also worked in WPF, which allowed view model implementations to be reused in both Silverlight and WPF applications.

The following example shows how the Prism command behaviors are used to bind a command object defined on a view model to a button's click event.

XAML OrdersView.xaml
```xaml
<Button Content="Submit All"
   prism:Click.Command="{Binding Path=SubmitAllCommand}"
   prism:Click.CommandParameter="{Binding Path=TickerSymbol}" />
```

Silverlight 4 added support for the **Command** property to all **Hyperlink**-derived and **ButtonBase**-derived controls, allowing them to be bound directly to command objects in the same way that they are in WPF. The use of the **Command** property for these controls is described in the section, "Commands," in Chapter 5, "Implementing the MVVM Pattern." However, Prism command behaviors remain in the Prism Library for backward compatibility reasons and to support the development of custom behaviors, as described later in this chapter.

The behavior approach is a generally applicable technique for implementing and encapsulating interactive behavior in a way that can be easily applied to controls in the view. The use of behaviors to support commands as shown earlier is just one of the many scenarios that behaviors can support. Microsoft Expression Blend now provides a variety of behaviors, including the **InvokeCommandAction** and the **CallMethodAction** described in the section, "Invoking Command Methods from the View," in Chapter 5, "Implementing the MVVM Pattern," and a software development kit (SDK) to allow the development of custom behaviors. Expression Blend provides drag-and-drop creation and property editing support for behaviors, which greatly simplifies the task of adding behaviors.

Although the introduction of support for command-enabled controls in Silverlight 4, and the introduction of the Expression Blend Behaviors SDK, obviates much of the need for Prism command behaviors, you may find their compact syntax and implementation and their extensibility to be useful.

Extending Prism Command Behaviors

Prism command behaviors are based on an attached behavior pattern. This pattern connects events raised by controls to the command objects provided by the view model. The Prism command behavior is comprised of two parts: an attached property and a behavior object. The attached property establishes a relationship between the target control and the behavior object. The behavior object monitors the target control and takes action based on events or state changes in the control or the view model.

The Prism command behavior executes commands based on the **Click** event of a **ButtonBase**-derived control by providing the **ButtonBaseClickCommandBehavior** class and a property to attach it to the click event of a target control. The following illustration shows the relationship between **ButtonBase**, **ButtonBaseClickCommandBehavior**, and the **ICommand** object provided by the view model.

Forwarding a ButtonClick event to an ICommand

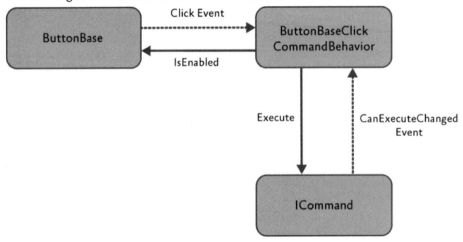

Your application may need to invoke commands from controls or events other than the **Click** event from **ButtonBase**, or you may need to customize the way in which the behavior interacts with the target control or the view model to which it is bound. In these cases, you will need to define your own attached property and/or behavior implementation.

The Prism Library provides the **CommandBehaviorBase\<T>** class to make it easier to create behaviors that interact with **ICommand** objects. This class invokes the command, and then monitors changes in the command's **CanExecuteChanged** event. It can be used to extend command support in both Silverlight and WPF.

To create a custom behavior, create a class that inherits from **CommandBehaviorBase\<T>** and targets the control you want to monitor. The type parameter for this class specifies the type of the control to which the behavior can be attached. In the constructor of your class, you can subscribe to the events that you want to monitor from the control. The following code example shows the implementation of the **ButtonBaseClickCommand Behavior** class.

```C#
public class ButtonBaseClickCommandBehavior : CommandBehaviorBase<ButtonBase>
{
    public ButtonBaseClickCommandBehavior(ButtonBase clickableObject)
        : base(clickableObject)
    {
        clickableObject.Click += OnClick;
    }

    private void OnClick(object sender, System.Windows.RoutedEventArgs e)
    {
        ExecuteCommand();
    }
}
```

Using the **CommandBehaviorBase\<T>** class, you can define custom behavior classes of your own. This allows you to customize how the behavior interacts with the target control or the command provided by the view model. For example, you could define a behavior that invokes the bound command based on a different control event or that changes the visual state of the control based on the **CanExecute** status of the bound command.

To support the declarative attachment of the command behavior to the target control, an attached property is used. The attached property allows the behavior to be attached to the control in XAML and manages the construction and association of the behavior implementation with the target control. The attached property is defined within a static class. Prism command behaviors are based on the convention that the name of the static class refers to the event that is used to invoke the command. The name of the attached property refers to the type of the object being data bound. Therefore, the Prism command behaviors described earlier use a static class named **Click**, which defines an attached property named **Command**. This allows the use of the **Click.Command** syntax shown earlier.

The command behavior object itself is also associated with the target control via an attached property. However, this attached property is private to the static class and is not visible to the developer, as shown below.

```C#
public static readonly DependencyProperty CommandProperty =
                        DependencyProperty.RegisterAttached(
                            "Command",
                            typeof(ICommand),
                            typeof(Click),
                            new PropertyMetadata(OnSetCommandCallback));

private static readonly DependencyProperty ClickCommandBehaviorProperty =
                        DependencyProperty.RegisterAttached(
                            "ClickCommandBehavior",
                            typeof(ButtonBaseClickCommandBehavior),
                            typeof(Click),
                            null);
```

The implementation of the **Command** attached property creates an instance of the **ButtonBaseClickCommandBehavior** class by using the **OnSetCommandCallback** callback method, as shown in the following code example.

```C#
private static void OnSetCommandCallback(DependencyObject dependencyObject,
DependencyPropertyChangedEventArgs e)
{
    ButtonBase buttonBase = dependencyObject as ButtonBase;
    if (buttonBase != null)
    {
        ButtonBaseClickCommandBehavior behavior = GetOrCreateBehavior(buttonBase);
        behavior.Command = e.NewValue as ICommand;
    }
}

private static void OnSetCommandParameterCallback(DependencyObject dependencyObject,
DependencyPropertyChangedEventArgs e)
{
    ButtonBase buttonBase = dependencyObject as ButtonBase;
    if (buttonBase != null)
    {
        ButtonBaseClickCommandBehavior behavior = GetOrCreateBehavior(buttonBase);
        behavior.CommandParameter = e.NewValue;
    }
}
```

```
private static ButtonBaseClickCommandBehavior GetOrCreateBehavior(
                                                ButtonBase buttonBase)
{
    ButtonBaseClickCommandBehavior behavior =
        buttonBase.GetValue(ClickCommandBehaviorProperty) as
            ButtonBaseClickCommandBehavior;
    if ( behavior == null )
    {
        behavior = new ButtonBaseClickCommandBehavior(buttonBase);
        buttonBase.SetValue(ClickCommandBehaviorProperty, behavior);
    }

    return behavior;
}
```

Handling Asynchronous Interactions

Your view model will often need to interact with the services and components in your application that communicate asynchronously instead of synchronously. This is especially true if you are building a Silverlight application or interacting with web services or other resources over the network, or if your application uses background tasks to perform calculations or I/O. Performing these operations asynchronously ensures that your application remains responsive, which is essential for delivering a good user experience.

When the user initiates an asynchronous request or background task, it is difficult to predict when the response will arrive (or even if it will arrive) and which thread it will return on. Because the UI can be updated only in the UI thread, you will often need to update the UI by dispatching a request on the UI thread.

RETRIEVING DATA AND INTERACTING WITH WEB SERVICES

When interacting with web services or other remote access technologies, you will often encounter the IAsyncResult pattern. In this pattern, instead of invoking a method such as **GetQuestionnaire**, you use a pair of methods: **BeginGetQuestionnaire** and **EndGet Questionnaire**. To initiate the asynchronous call, you call **BeginGetQuestionnaire**. To get the results or determine if there an exception occurred when the target method was invoked, you call **EndGetQuestionnaire** when the call is complete.

To determine when to call **EndGetQuestionnaire**, you can either poll for completion or (preferably) specify a callback during the call to **BeginGetQuestionnaire**. With the callback approach, your callback method will be called when the target method completes its execution, allowing you to call **EndGetQuestionnaire** from there, as shown in the following example.

C#
```
IAsyncResult asyncResult =
this.service.BeginGetQuestionnaire(GetQuestionnaireCompleted,
                        null // object state, not used in this example);
```

```
private void GetQuestionnaireCompleted(IAsyncResult result)
{
   try
   {
     questionnaire = this.service.EndGetQuestionnaire(ar);
   }
   catch (Exception ex)
   {
     // Do something to report the error.
   }
}
```

It is important to note that in calls to the **End** method (in this case, **EndGet Questionnaire**), any exceptions that occurred during the execution of the request will be raised. Your application must handle these exceptions, and it may need to report them in a thread-safe way via the UI. If your application does not handle the exceptions, the thread will end and you will not be able to process the results.

Because the response usually is not on the UI thread, if you plan to modify anything that will affect UI state, you will need to dispatch the response to the UI thread by using either the thread **Dispatcher** or the **SynchronizationContext** objects. In WPF and Silverlight, you will typically use the dispatcher.

In the following code example, the **Questionnaire** object is retrieved asynchronously, and then it is set as the data context for the **QuestionnaireView**. In Silverlight, you can use the **CheckAccess** method of the dispatcher to see whether you are on the UI thread. If you are not, you will need to use the **BeginInvoke** method to have the request carried out on the UI thread.

```C#
var dispatcher = System.Windows.Deployment.Current.Dispatcher;
if (dispatcher.CheckAccess())
{
    QuestionnaireView.DataContext = questionnaire;
}
else
{
    dispatcher.BeginInvoke(
          () => { Questionnaire.DataContext = questionnaire; });
}
```

The Model-View-ViewModel Reference Implementation (MVVM RI) shows an example of how to consume an **IAsyncResult**-based service interface similar to the preceding examples. It also wraps the service to provide a simpler callback mechanism for the consumer and handles the dispatch of the callback to the caller's thread. For example, the following code example shows retrieval of the questionnaire.

```C#
this.questionnaireRepository.GetQuestionnaireAsync(
    (result) =>
    {
        this.Questionnaire = result.Result;
    });
```

The **result** object that is returned wraps the retrieved result, in addition to errors that may have occurred. The following code example shows how the errors could be evaluated.

```C#
this.questionnaireRepository.GetQuestionnaireAsync(
    (result) =>
    {
        if (result.Error == null) {
          this.Questionnaire = result.Result;
          ...
        }
        else
        {
          // Handle error.
        }
    })
```

User Interaction Patterns

Frequently, an application needs to notify the user that an event has occurred or ask for confirmation before proceeding with an operation. These interactions are often brief interactions designed to simply inform the user of a change in the application or to obtain a simple response. Some of these interactions may appear modal to the user, such as when the UI displays a dialog box or a message box, or they may appear non-modal, such as when the UI displays a toast notification or a pop-up window.

There are multiple ways to interact with the user in these cases, but implementing them in an MVVM-based application in a way that preserves a clean separation of concerns can be challenging. For example, in a non-MVVM application, you could use the **MessageBox** class in the UI's code-behind file to prompt the user for a response. In an MVVM application, this would not be appropriate because it would break the separation of concerns between the view and the view model.

In the MVVM pattern, the view model is responsible for initiating an interaction with the user and for consuming and processing any response, while the view is responsible for actually managing the interaction with the user by employing whatever user experience is appropriate. Preserving the separation of concerns between the presentation logic implemented in the view model, and the user experience implemented by the view, helps to improve testability and flexibility.

There are two common approaches to implementing these kinds of user interactions in the MVVM pattern. One approach is to implement a service that can be used by the view model to initiate interaction with the user, thereby preserving its independence from the view's implementation. Another approach uses events raised by the view model to express the intent to interact with the user, along with components in the view that are bound to these events and that manage the visual aspects of the interaction. Each of these approaches is described in the following sections.

USING AN INTERACTION SERVICE

In this approach, the view model relies on an interaction service component to initiate interaction with the user by using a message box. This approach supports a clean separation of concerns and testability by encapsulating the visual implementation of the interaction in a separate service component. Typically, the view model has a dependency on an interaction service interface, and it uses dependency injection or a service locator to acquire a reference to the interaction service's implementation.

After the view model has a reference to the interaction service, it can programmatically request interaction with the user whenever necessary. The interaction service implements the visual aspects of the interaction, as shown in the following illustration. Using an interface reference in the view model allows different implementations to be used, according to the implementation requirements of the user interface. For example, implementations of the interaction service for WPF and Silverlight could be provided, thus allowing for greater reuse of the application's presentation logic.

Using an interaction service to interact with the user

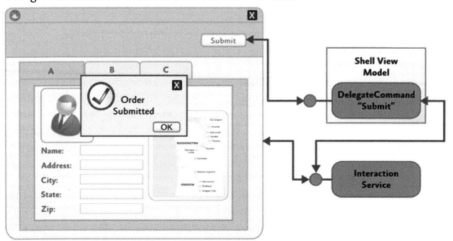

You can use a blocking method call to implement modal interactions in a synchronous way, as shown in the following code example. Examples of this type of interaction are those in which a user is presented with a **MessageBox** or modal pop-up window to obtain a specific response before execution can continue.

```C#
var result =
    interactionService.ShowMessageBox(
        "Are you sure you want to cancel this operation?",
        "Confirm",
        MessageBoxButton.OK );
if (result == MessageBoxResult.Yes)
{
    CancelRequest();
}
```

However, one of the disadvantages of this approach is that it forces a synchronous programming model that is not shared by other interaction mechanisms in Silverlight, resulting in numerous problems when you implement the interaction service. An alternative asynchronous implementation allows the view model to provide a callback to execute on completion of the interaction. The following code illustrates this approach.

```C#
interactionService.ShowMessageBox(
    "Are you sure you want to cancel this operation?",
    "Confirm",
    MessageBoxButton.OK,
    result =>
    {
        if (result == MessageBoxResult.Yes)
        {
            CancelRequest();
        }
    });
```

The asynchronous approach provides greater flexibility when implementing the interaction service by allowing modal and non-modal interactions to be implemented. For example, in WPF, the **MessageBox** class can be used to implement a truly modal interaction with the user; whereas, in Silverlight, a pop-up window can be used to implement a pseudo-modal interaction with the user.

USING INTERACTION REQUEST OBJECTS

Another approach to implementing simple user interactions in the MVVM pattern is to allow the view model to make interaction requests directly to the view itself by using an interaction request object coupled with a behavior in the view. The interaction request object encapsulates the details of the interaction request and its response, and uses events to communicate with the view. The view subscribes to these events to initiate the user experience portion of the interaction. The view will typically encapsulate the user experience of the interaction in a behavior that is data-bound to the interaction request object provided by the view model, as shown in the following illustration.

Using an interaction request object to interact with the user

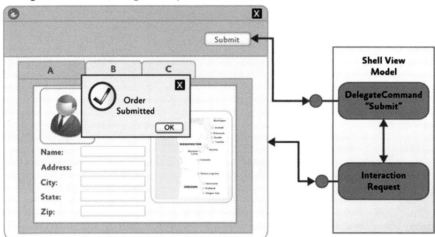

This approach provides a simple, yet flexible, mechanism that preserves a clean separation between the view model and the view—it allows the view model to encapsulate the application's presentation logic, including any required user interactions, while allowing the view to fully encapsulate the visual aspects of the interaction. The view model's implementation, including its expected interactions with the user through the view, can be easily tested, and the UI designer has a lot of flexibility in choosing how to implement the interaction within the view by using behaviors that encapsulate the different user experiences for the interaction.

This approach is consistent with the MVVM pattern, enabling the view to reflect state changes it observes on the view model and using two-way data binding for communication between the two. The encapsulation of the non-visual elements of the interaction in an interaction request object, and the use of a corresponding behavior to manage the visual elements of the interaction, are very similar to the way in which command objects and command behaviors are used.

This approach is the one that Prism uses. The Prism Library directly supports this pattern through the **IInteractionRequest** interface and the **InteractionRequest<T>** class. The **IInteractionRequest** interface defines an event to initiate the interaction. Behaviors in the view bind to this interface and subscribe to the event that it exposes. The **InteractionRequest<T>** class implements the **IInteractionRequest** interface and defines two **Raise** methods to allow the view model to initiate an interaction and to specify the context for the request, and optionally, a callback delegate.

Initiating Interaction Requests from the View Model

The **InteractionRequest<T>** class coordinates the view model's interaction with the view during an interaction request. The **Raise** method allows the view model to initiate the interaction and to specify a context object (of type **T**) and a callback method that is called after the interaction ends. The context object allows the view model to pass data and state to the view for it to be used during the interaction with the user. If a callback method was specified, the context object will be passed back to the view model. This allows any changes that the user made during the interaction to be passed back to the view model. The following code shows how an interaction request is initiated.

```C#
public interface IInteractionRequest
{
    event EventHandler<InteractionRequestedEventArgs> Raised;
}

public class InteractionRequest<T> : IInteractionRequest
{
    public event EventHandler<InteractionRequestedEventArgs> Raised;

    public void Raise(T context, Action<T> callback)
    {
        var handler = this.Raised;
        if (handler != null)
        {
            handler(
                this,
                new InteractionRequestedEventArgs(
                    context,
                    () => callback(context)));
        }
    }
}
```

Prism provides predefined context classes that support common interaction request scenarios. The **Notification** class is the base class for all context objects. You would use this class when you use an interaction request to notify the user of an important event in the application. It provides two properties—**Title** and **Content**—which will be displayed to the user. Typically, notifications are one-way; therefore, it is not expected that the user will change these values during the interaction.

The **Confirmation** class derives from the **Notification** class and adds a third property—**Confirmed**—which is used to signify that the user has confirmed or denied the operation. The **Confirmation** class is used to implement **MessageBox** style interactions where the user wants to obtain a yes/no response from the user. You can define a custom context class that derives from the **Notification** class to encapsulate whatever data and state you need to support the interaction.

To use the **InteractionRequest<T>** class, the view model class creates an instance of the **InteractionRequest<T>** class and defines a read-only property to allow the view to bind to it. When the view model initiates the request, it calls the **Raise** method, passing in the context object and, optionally, the callback delegate. The following code example shows this process.

```csharp
C#
public IInteractionRequest ConfirmCancelInteractionRequest
{
    get
    {
        return this.confirmCancelInteractionRequest;
    }
}

this.confirmCancelInteractionRequest.Raise(
    new Confirmation("Are you sure you wish to cancel?"),
    confirmation =>
    {
        if (confirmation.Confirmed)
        {
            this.NavigateToQuestionnaireList();
        }
    });
}
```

The MVVM Reference Implementation (MVVM RI) illustrates how the **IInteraction Request** interface and the **InteractionRequest<T>** class are used to implement user interactions between the view and view model in a survey application (see QuestionnaireView Model.cs).

Using Behaviors to Implement the Interaction User Experience

Because the interaction request object represents a logical interaction, the exact user experience for the interaction is defined in the view. Behaviors are often used to encapsulate the user experience for an interaction. This allows the UI designer to choose an appropriate behavior and to bind it to the interaction request object on the view model.

The view must be set up to detect an interaction request event and then present the appropriate visual display for the request. The Expression Blend Behaviors Framework supports the concept of triggers and actions. Triggers are used to initiate actions whenever a specific event is raised.

You can use the standard **EventTrigger** provided by Expression Blend to monitor an interaction request event by binding it to the interaction request objects exposed by the view model. However, the Prism Library defines a custom **EventTrigger**, named **Interaction RequestTrigger**, which automatically connects to the appropriate **Raised** event of the **IInteractionRequest** interface. This reduces the amount of XAML that you need to write and also reduces the chance that you will inadvertently enter an incorrect event name.

After the event is raised, the **InteractionRequestTrigger** will invoke the specified action. For Silverlight, the Prism Library provides the **PopupChildWindowAction** class, which displays a pop-up window to the user. When the child window is displayed, its data context is set to the context parameter of the interaction request. Using the **Content Template** property of the **PopupChildWindowAction** class, you can specify a data template to define the UI layout to be used for the **Content** property of the context object. The title of the pop-up window is bound to the **Title** property of the context object.

> **Note:** *By default, the specific type of pop-up window displayed by the* **PopupChild WindowAction** *class depends on the type of the context object. For a* **Notification** *context object, a* **NotificationChildWindow** *is displayed, while for a* **Confirmation** *context object, a* **ConfirmationChildWindow** *is displayed. The* **NotificationChild Window** *displays a simple popup window to display the notification, while the* **ConfirmationChildWindow** *also contains* **OK** *and* **Cancel** *buttons to capture the user's response. You can override this behavior by specifying a pop-up window using the* **ChildWindow** *property of the* **PopupChildWindowAction** *class.*

The following example shows how the **InteractionRequestTrigger** and the **Popup ChildWindowAction** are used to display a confirmation pop-up window to the user within the MVVM RI.

```XAML
<i:Interaction.Triggers>
    <prism:InteractionRequestTrigger
            SourceObject="{Binding ConfirmCancelInteractionRequest}">

        <prism:PopupChildWindowAction
                ContentTemplate="{StaticResource ConfirmWindowTemplate}"/>

    </prism:InteractionRequestTrigger>
</i:Interaction.Triggers>

<UserControl.Resources>
    <DataTemplate x:Key="ConfirmWindowTemplate">
        <Grid MinWidth="250" MinHeight="100">
            <TextBlock TextWrapping="Wrap" Grid.Row="0" Text="{Binding}"/>
        </Grid>
    </DataTemplate>
</UserControl.Resources>
```

> **Note:** *The data template specified by the* **ContentTemplate** *property defines the UI layout for the* **Content** *property of the context object. In the preceding code, the* **Content** *property is a string; therefore, the* **TextBlock** *is simply bound to the* **Content** *property itself.*

As the user interacts with the pop-up window, the context object is updated according to the bindings defined in the pop-up window or in the data template used to display the **Content** property of the context object. After the user closes the pop-up window, the context object is passed back to the view model, along with any updated values, via the callback method. In the confirmation example used in the MVVM RI, the default confirmation view is responsible for setting the **Confirmed** property on the supplied **Confirmation** object to **true** when the **OK** button is clicked.

You can define different triggers and actions to support other interaction mechanisms. You can implement the Prism **InteractionRequestTrigger** and **PopupChild WindowAction** classes, and use them as the basis for developing your own triggers and actions.

Advanced Construction and Configuration

To successfully implement the MVVM pattern, you need to fully understand the responsibilities of the view, model, and view model classes so that you can implement your application's code in the correct classes. Implementing the correct patterns to allow these classes to interact (through data binding, commands, interaction requests, and so on) is also an important requirement. Additionally, you should consider how the view, view model, and model classes are instantiated and associated with each other at run time.

Choosing an appropriate strategy to manage this step is especially important if you are using a dependency injection container in your application. The Managed Extensibility Framework (MEF) and the Unity Application Block (Unity) both give you the ability to specify dependencies between the view, view model, and model classes and have them fulfilled by the container at run time.

Typically, you define the view model as a dependency of the view, so that when the view is constructed (by using the container) it automatically instantiates the required view model. In turn, any components or services that the view model depends on will also be instantiated by the container. After the view model is successfully instantiated, the view sets it as its data context.

USING MEF TO CREATE THE VIEW AND VIEW MODEL

With MEF, you can use the **import** attribute to specify the view's dependency on a view model, and you can use an **export** attribute to specify the concrete view model type to be instantiated. You can use either a property or a constructor argument to import the view model into the view.

For example, the **QuestionnaireView** in the MVVM RI view declares a write-only property for the view model, together with an **import** attribute. When the view is instantiated, MEF creates an instance of the appropriate exported view model and sets the property value. The property setter assigns the view model as the view's data context, as shown in the following example.

```
C#
[Import]
public QuestionnaireViewModel ViewModel
{
    set { this.DataContext = value; }
}
```

The view model is defined and exported, as shown in the next example.

```C#
[Export]
public class QuestionnaireViewModel : NotificationObject
{

    ...

}
```

An alternative approach is to define an importing constructor on the view, as shown in the following example.

```C#
public QuestionnaireView()
{

    InitializeComponent();

}


[ImportingConstructor]
public QuestionnaireView(QuestionnaireViewModel viewModel) : this()
{

    this.DataContext = viewModel;

}
```

MEF will then instantiate the view model and pass it as an argument to the view's constructor.

> **Note:** *You can use property injection or constructor injection in both MEF and Unity; however, you may find property injection to be simpler because you do not have to maintain two constructors. Design-time tools, such as Visual Studio and Expression Blend, require that controls have a default parameter-less constructor or they cannot be displayed in the designer. Any additional constructors that you define should ensure that the default constructor is called so that view can be properly initialized by using the* **InitializeComponent** *method.*

Using Unity to Create the View and View Model

Using Unity as your dependency injection container is similar to using MEF, and both property-based and constructor-based injection are supported. The principal difference is that, in most cases, the types are not implicitly discovered at run time. Instead, they have to be registered with the container.

Typically, you define an interface in the view model so the view model's concrete type can be decoupled from the view. For example, the view can use a constructor argument to define its dependency on the view model, as shown in the following example.

```C#
public QuestionnaireView()
{
    InitializeComponent();
}

public QuestionnaireView(QuestionnaireViewModel viewModel) : this()
{
    this.DataContext = viewModel;
}
```

Note: *The default parameter-less constructor is necessary to allow the view to work in design-time tools, such as Visual Studio and Expression Blend.*

Alternatively, you can define a write-only view model property on the view, as shown in the next example. Unity will instantiate the required view model, and then call the property setter after the view is instantiated.

```C#
public QuestionnaireView()
{
    InitializeComponent();
}

[Dependency]
public QuestionnaireViewModel ViewModel
{
    set { this.DataContext = value; }
}
```

The view model type is registered with the Unity container, as shown in the following example.

```C#
IUnityContainer container;
container.RegisterType<QuestionnaireViewModel>();
```

The view can then be instantiated through the container, as shown in the next example.

```C#
IUnityContainer container;
var view = container.Resolve<QuestionnaireView>();
```

USING AN EXTERNAL CLASS TO CREATE THE VIEW AND VIEW MODEL

You may find it useful to define a controller or service class to coordinate the instantiation of the view and view model classes. This approach can be used with a dependency injection container, such as MEF or Unity, or when the view explicitly creates its required view model.

This approach is particularly useful when you implement navigation in your application. In this case, the controller is associated with a placeholder control or region in the UI, and it coordinates the construction and placement of views in that placeholder or region.

For example, the MVVM RI uses a service class to build views using a container and show them in the main page. In this example, views are specified by view names. Navigation is initiated by a call to the **ShowView** method on the UI service, as shown in the next example.

```C#
private void NavigateToQuestionnaireList()
{
    // Ask the UI service to go to the "questionnaire list" view.
    this.uiService.ShowView(ViewNames.QuestionnaireTemplatesList);
}
```

The UI service is associated with a placeholder control in the UI of the application. it encapsulates the creation of the required view, and then coordinates its appearance in the UI. The **ShowView** of the **UIService** uses the container to create an instance of the view (so that its view model and other dependencies can be fulfilled) and then displays it in the proper location, as shown in the next example.

```C#
public void ShowView(string viewName)
{
    var view = this.ViewFactory.GetView(viewName);
    this.MainWindow.CurrentView = view;
}
```

Note: *Prism provides extensive support for navigation within regions. Region navigation uses a mechanism very similar to the preceding approach, except that the region manager is responsible for coordinating the instantiation and placement of the view in the specific region. For more information, see the section, "View-Based Navigation" in Chapter 8, "Navigation."*

Testing MVVM Applications

Testing models and view models from MVVM applications is the same as testing any other classes, and the same tools and techniques—such as unit testing and mocking frameworks—can be used. However, there are some testing patterns that are typically seen in model and view model classes, and these patterns can benefit from standard testing techniques and test helper classes.

TESTING INOTIFYPROPERTYCHANGED IMPLEMENTATIONS

Implementing the **INotifyPropertyChanged** interface allows views to react to changes originated in models and view models. These changes are not limited to domain data shown in controls; they are also used to control the view, such as view model states that cause animations to be started or controls to be disabled.

Testing Simple Cases

Properties that can be updated directly by the test code can be tested by attaching an event handler to the **PropertyChanged** event and checking whether the event is raised after setting a new value for the property. Helper classes, such as the **ChangeTracker** class used in the MVVM sample projects, can be used to attach a handler and collect the results; this avoids repetitive tasks when writing tests. The following code example shows a test that uses this type of helper class.

```csharp
C#
var changeTracker = new PropertyChangeTracker(viewModel);

viewModel.CurrentState = "newState";

CollectionAssert.Contains(changeTracker.ChangedProperties, "CurrentState");
```

If a property is the result of a code-generation process that guarantees the implementation of the **INotifyPropertyChanged** interface, such as those that occur in code generated by a model designer, that property will not typically need to be tested.

Testing Computed and Non-Settable Properties

When properties cannot be set by test code, such as properties with non-public setters or read-only, calculated properties, the test code needs to stimulate the object under test to cause the change in the properties and their corresponding notifications. However, the structure of the test is the same as that of the simpler cases, as shown in the following code example. In the example, a change in a model object causes a property in a view model to change.

```C#
var changeTracker = new PropertyChangeTracker(viewModel);

var question = viewModel.Questions.First() as OpenQuestionViewModel;
question.Question.Response = "some text";

CollectionAssert.Contains(changeTracker.ChangedProperties, "UnansweredQuestions");
```

Testing Whole Object Notifications

When you implement the **INotifyPropertyChanged** interface, an object will be able to raise the **PropertyChanged** event with a null or empty string as its changed property name to indicate that all properties in the object may have changed. These cases can be tested just like the cases that notify individual property names.

TESTING INOTIFYDATAERRORINFO IMPLEMENTATIONS

There are several mechanisms available to enable bindings to perform input validation, such as throwing exceptions when properties are set, implementing the **IDataErrorInfo** interface, and (in Silverlight) implementing the **INotifyDataErrorInfo** interface. Implementing the **INotifyDataErrorInfo** interface allows for greater sophistication because it can indicate multiple errors per property and perform asynchronous and cross-property validation. Because of these capabilities, it also requires the most testing.

There are two aspects to testing **INotifyDataErrorInfo** implementations: testing that the validation rules are correctly implemented and testing that the requirements for implementations of the interface, such as raising the **ErrorsChanged** event when the result for the **GetErrors** method would be different, are met.

Testing Validation Rules

Validation logic is usually simple to test, because it is typically a self-contained process in which the output depends on the input. For each property that has validation rules associated with it, there should be tests on the results of invoking the **GetErrors** method with the validated property name for valid values, invalid values, boundary values, and so on. If the validation logic is shared, such as when the data annotation's validation attribution is used to express validation rules declaratively, the more exhaustive tests can be concentrated on the shared validation logic. On the other hand, custom validation rules must be thoroughly tested. The following example shows how valid and invalid values can be tested.

```csharp
C#
// Invalid case
var notifyErrorInfo = (INotifyDataErrorInfo)question;

question.Response = -15;

Assert.IsTrue(notifyErrorInfo.GetErrors("Response").Cast<ValidationResult>().Any());

// Valid case
var notifyErrorInfo = (INotifyDataErrorInfo)question;

question.Response = 15;
Assert.IsFalse(notifyErrorInfo.GetErrors("Response").Cast<ValidationResult>().Any());
```

Cross-property validation rules follow the same pattern, typically requiring more tests to accommodate the combination of values for the different properties.

Testing the Requirements for INotifyDataErrorInfo Implementations

Besides producing the right values for the **GetErrors** method, implementations of the **INotifyDataErrorInfo** interface must ensure that the **ErrorsChanged** event is raised appropriately whenever the result for **GetErrors** changes. Additionally, the **HasErrors** property must reflect the overall error state of the object implementing the interface.

There is no mandatory approach for implementing the **INotifyDataErrorInfo** interface. However, implementations that rely on objects that accumulate validation errors and perform the necessary notifications are typically preferred because they are simpler to test. This is because it is not necessary to verify that the requirements for all the members of the **INotifyDataErrorInfo** interface are met for each validation rule on each validated property (provided that the error management object is properly tested).

Testing the interface requirements should include at least the following verifications:

- The **HasErrors** property reflects the overall error state of the object. Setting a valid value for a previously invalid property does not result in a change for this property if other properties still have invalid values.

- The **ErrorsChanged** event is raised when the error state for a property changes, as reflected by a change in the result for the **GetErrors** method. The error state change could be going from a valid state (that is, no errors) to an invalid state and vice versa, or it can go from an invalid state to a different invalid state. The updated result for **GetErrors** is available for handlers of the **ErrorsChanged** event.

When you create test implementations for the **INotifyPropertyChanged** interface, using helper classes, such as the **NotifyDataErrorInfoTestHelper** class in the MVVM sample projects, can make writing tests for implementations of the **INotifyDataError Info** interface easier because the helper classes handle repetitive housekeeping operations and standard checks. Helper classes are particularly useful if the interface implementation does not rely on some kind of reusable errors manager. The following code example shows this type of helper class.

```C#
var helper =
    new NotifyDataErrorInfoTestHelper<NumericQuestion, int?>(
        question,
        q => q.Response);

helper.ValidatePropertyChange(
    6,
    NotifyDataErrorInfoBehavior.Nothing);
helper.ValidatePropertyChange(
    20,
    NotifyDataErrorInfoBehavior.FiresErrorsChanged
    | NotifyDataErrorInfoBehavior.HasErrors
    | NotifyDataErrorInfoBehavior.HasErrorsForProperty);
helper.ValidatePropertyChange(
    null,
    NotifyDataErrorInfoBehavior.FiresErrorsChanged
    | NotifyDataErrorInfoBehavior.HasErrors
    | NotifyDataErrorInfoBehavior.HasErrorsForProperty);
helper.ValidatePropertyChange(
    2,
    NotifyDataErrorInfoBehavior.FiresErrorsChanged);
```

TESTING ASYNCHRONOUS SERVICE CALLS

In the MVVM pattern, view models usually invoke operations on services, often asynchronously. Tests for code that invokes these operations typically use mocks or stubs as replacements for the actual services.

The standard patterns used to implement asynchronous operations provide different guarantees regarding the thread in which notifications about the status of an operation occur. Although the Event-based Asynchronous design pattern guarantees that handlers for the events are invoked on a thread that is appropriate for the application, the IAsyncResult design pattern does not provide any such guarantees. This forces the view model code that originates the call to ensure that any changes that would affect the view are posted to the UI thread.

Dealing with threading concerns requires more complicated, and typically harder to test, code. It also usually requires the tests themselves to be asynchronous. When notifications are guaranteed to occur in the UI thread, either because the standard event-based asynchronous pattern is used or because view models rely on a service access layer to marshal notifications to the appropriate thread, tests can be simplified and can essentially play the role of a dispatcher for the UI thread.

The way services are mocked depends on the asynchronous event pattern used to implement their operations. If a method-based pattern is used, mocks for the service interface created by using a standard mocking framework are usually enough, but if the event-based pattern is used, mocks based on a custom class that implements the methods to add and remove handlers for the service events are usually preferred.

The following code example shows a test for the appropriate behavior on the successful completion of an asynchronous operation notified in the UI thread using mocks for services. In this example, the test code captures the callback supplied by the view model when it makes the asynchronous service call. The test then simulates the completion of that call later in the test by invoking the callback. This approach allows you to test a component that uses an asynchronous service without the complexity of making your tests asynchronous.

C#

```
questionnaireRepositoryMock
    .Setup(
        r =>
            r.SubmitQuestionnaireAsync(
                It.IsAny<Questionnaire>(),
                It.IsAny<Action<IOperationResult>>()))
    .Callback<Questionnaire, Action<IOperationResult>>(
        (q, a) => callback = a);

uiServiceMock
    .Setup(svc => svc.ShowView(ViewNames.QuestionnaireTemplatesList))

    .Callback<string>(viewName => requestedViewName = viewName);
submitResultMock
    .Setup(sr => sr.Error)
    .Returns<Exception>(null);
CompleteQuestionnaire(viewModel);
viewModel.Submit();
// Simulate callback posted to the UI thread.
callback(submitResultMock.Object);
// Check expected behavior - request to navigate to the list view.
Assert.AreEqual(ViewNames.QuestionnaireTemplatesList, requestedViewName);
```

Note: *Using this testing approach only exercises the functional capabilities of the objects under test; it does not test that the code is thread safe.*

More Information

For more information about the logical tree, see "Trees in WPF" on MSDN:
http://msdn.microsoft.com/en-us/library/ms753391.aspx.
For more information about attached properties, see "Attached Properties Overview" on MSDN:
http://msdn.microsoft.com/en-us/library/cc265152(VS.95).aspx.
For more information about MEF, see "Managed Extensibility Framework Overview" on MSDN:
http://msdn.microsoft.com/en-us/library/dd460648.aspx.
For more information about Unity, see "Unity Application Block" on MSDN:
http://www.msdn.com/unity.
For more information about **DelegateCommand**, see Chapter 5, "Implementing the MVVM Pattern."
For more information about using Microsoft Expression Blend behaviors, see "Working with built-in behaviors" on MSDN:
http://msdn.microsoft.com/en-us/library/ff724013(v=Expression.40).aspx.
For more information about creating custom behaviors with Expression Blend, see "Creating Custom Behaviors" on MSDN:
http://msdn.microsoft.com/en-us/library/ff724708(v=Expression.40).aspx.
For more information about creating custom triggers and actions with Microsoft Expression Blend, see "Creating Custom Triggers and Actions" on MSDN:
http://msdn.microsoft.com/en-us/library/ff724707(v=Expression.40).aspx.
For more information about using the dispatcher in WPF and Silverlight, see "Threading Model" and "The Dispatcher Class" on MSDN:
http://msdn.microsoft.com/en-us/library/ms741870.aspx.
http://msdn.microsoft.com/en-us/library/ms615907(v=VS.95).aspx.
For more information about unit testing in Silverlight, see "Unit Testing with Silverlight 2":
http://www.jeff.wilcox.name/2008/03/silverlight2-unit-testing.
For more information about region navigation, see the section, "View-Based Navigation" in Chapter 8, "Navigation."
For more information about the Event-based Asynchronous pattern, see "Event-based Asynchronous Pattern Overview" on MSDN:
http://msdn.microsoft.com/en-us/library/wewwczdw.aspx.
For more information about the IAsyncResult design pattern, see "Asynchronous Programming Overview" on MSDN:
http://msdn.microsoft.com/en-us/library/ms228963.aspx.
To access web resources more easily, see the online version of the bibliography on MSDN:
http://msdn.microsoft.com/en-us/library/gg405487(PandP.40).aspx.

7   Composing the User Interface

An application user interface (UI) can be built by using one of the following paradigms:

- All required controls for a form are contained in a single Extensible Application Markup Language (XAML) file, composing the form at design time.

- Logical areas of the form are separated into distinct parts, typically user controls. The parts are referenced by the form, and the form is composed at design time.

- Logical areas of the form are separated into distinct parts, typically user controls. The parts are unknown to the form and are dynamically added to the form at run time. Applications that use this methodology are known as composite applications.

A composite application UI is composed from loosely coupled visual components known as *views* that are typically contained in the application modules, although they do not need to be. If you divide your application into modules, you need some way to loosely compose the UI, but you might choose a loosely coupled approach even if the views are not in modules. To the user, the application presents a seamless user experience and delivers a fully integrated application.

To compose the UI, you need an architecture that allows you to create a layout composed of loosely coupled visual elements generated at run time. Additionally, the architecture should provide strategies for these visual elements to communicate in a loosely coupled fashion.

The Stock Trader Reference Implementation (Stock Trader RI) is composed by loading multiple views that come from different modules into regions exposed by the shell, as shown in the following illustration.

Stock Trader RI regions and views

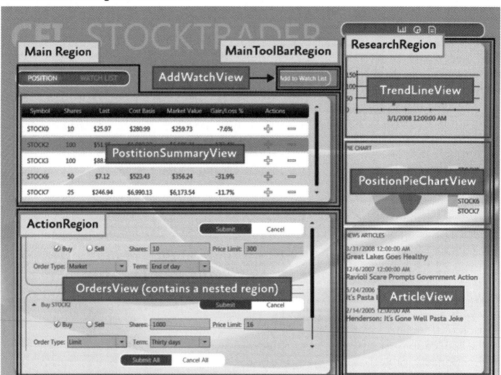

This chapter points to articles that you should review. Links are provided at the end of the chapter and in the online bibliography on MSDN at:

http://www.microsoft.com/prism.

UI Layout Concepts

The root object in a composite application is known as the *shell*. The shell acts as a master page for the application. The shell contains one or more regions. Regions are placeholders for content that will be loaded at run time. A region is attached to a UI element such as a **ContentControl**, **ItemsControl**, **TabControl**, or custom control, and manages the UI element's content. Region content can be loaded automatically or on demand, depending on the application requirements.

Typically, a region's content is a view. A view encapsulates a portion of the UI that you would like to keep as decoupled as possible from other parts of the application. You can define a view as a user control, data template, or even a custom control.

A region manages the display and layout of views and supports dynamically adding or removing views. A region can be accessed in a decoupled way by using its name. Regions support dynamically adding or removing views. Think of regions as containers into which views are dynamically loaded.

The following sections introduce the high-level core concepts for composite application development.

SHELL

The shell is the application root object that contains the primary UI content. In a Windows Presentation Foundation (WPF) application, the shell is the **Window** object. In a Silverlight application, the shell is the **RootVisual UserControl**.

The shell plays the role of a master page that provides the layout structure for the application. The shell contains one or more named regions in which modules can specify the views that will appear. It can also define certain top-level UI elements, such as the background, main menu, and toolbar.

The shell defines the overall appearance of the application. It might define styles and borders that are present and visible in the shell layout itself, and it might also define styles, templates, and themes that will be applied to the views that are plugged into the shell.

Typically, the shell is a part of the WPF application project or primary Silverlight project. The assembly that contains the shell might or might not reference the assemblies that contain the views to be loaded in the shell's regions.

VIEWS

Views are the main unit of UI construction in a composite application. You can define a view as a user control, page, data template, or custom control. A view encapsulates a portion of the UI that you would like to keep as decoupled as possible from other parts of the application. You can choose what goes in a view based on encapsulation or a piece of functionality, or you can choose to define something as a view because you will have multiple instances of that view in your application.

Because of the content model of WPF and Silverlight, there is nothing specific to the Prism Library required to define a view. The easiest way to define a view is to define a user control. To add a view to the UI, you simply need a way to construct it and add it to a container. WPF and Silverlight provide mechanisms to do this. The Prism Library adds the ability to define a region into which a view can be dynamically added at run time.

Composite Views

A view that supports specific functionality can become complicated. In that case, you might want to divide the view into several child views and have the parent view handle constructing itself by using the child views as parts. The application might do this statically at design time, or it might support having modules add child views through a contained region at run time. When you have a view that is not fully defined in a single view class, you can refer to it as a composite view. In many situations, a composite view is responsible for constructing the child views and for coordinating the interactions between them. You can design child views that are more loosely coupled from their sibling views and their parent composite view by using the Prism Library commands and the event aggregator.

Views and Design Patterns

Although the Prism Library does not require that you use them, you should consider using one of several UI design patterns when implementing a view. The Stock Trader RI and QuickStarts demonstrate the Model-View-ViewModel (MVVM) pattern as a way to implement a clean separation between the view layout and the view logic.

The MVVM UI design pattern is recommended because it is a natural fit for the Microsoft XAML platforms, WPF, Silverlight, and Silverlight for Windows Phone 7. The dependency property system and rich data binding stack of these platforms enable the view and view model to communicate in a loosely coupled manner.

Separating the logic from the view is important for testability and maintainability, and it improves the developer-designer workflow.

If you create a view with a user control or custom control and put all the logic in the code-behind file, your view can be difficult to test because you have to create an instance of the view to unit test the logic. This is a problem particularly if the view derives from, or depends on, running WPF or Silverlight components as part of its execution context. To make sure that you can unit test the view logic in isolation without these dependencies, you need to be able to create a mockup of the view to remove the dependencies on the execution context, which requires separate classes for the view and the logic.

If you define a view as a data template, there is no code associated with the view itself. Therefore, you have to put the associated logic somewhere else. The same clean separation of logic from layout that is required for testability also helps make the view easier to maintain.

Note: *Unit testing and UI automation testing are two different types of testing with different coverage.*

Unit testing best practices recommend that the object be tested in isolation. To achieve object isolation, you need a mockup or stub for each external dependency. Then granular unit tests are run against the object.

UI automation testing runs the application, applies gestures to the UI, and then tests for the expected results. This type of test verifies that UI elements are correctly connected to the application logic.

Separating the logic from the view provides a clean separation of concerns. In addition to testability considerations, this separation enables the designer to work on the UI independently of the developer. For more information about MVVM, see Chapter 5, "Implementing the MVVM Pattern."

Commands, UI Triggers, Actions, and Behaviors

When a view is implemented with its logic in the code-behind file, you add event handlers to service UI interactions. However, when you use MVVM, the view model cannot directly handle events raised by the UI. To route UI gesture events to the view model, you can use commands or UI triggers, actions, and behaviors.

Commands

Commands separate the semantics and the object that invokes a command from the logic that executes the command. Built into each command is the ability to indicate whether an action is available. Commands in the UI are data bound to **ICommand** properties in the view model. For more information about commands, see "Commands" in Chapter 5, "Implementing the MVVM Pattern."

UI Triggers, Actions, and Behaviors

Triggers, actions, and behaviors are part of the **Microsoft.Expression.Interactivity** namespace and are shipped with Expression Blend. They are also part of the Expression SDK. Triggers, actions, and behaviors provide a comprehensive API for handling UI events or commands, and then routing them to the **ICommand** properties methods exposed by the **DataContext**. For more information about UI triggers, actions, and behaviors, see sections "Invoking Command Objects from the View" and "Invoking Command Methods from the View" in Chapter 5, "Implementing the MVVM Pattern."

Data Binding

Data binding is one of the most important framework features of the XAML platforms. To successfully develop applications on the XAML platforms, you need a solid understanding of data binding.

Data binding takes full advantage of the intrinsic change notification provided by the dependency property system. When combined with the Common Language Runtime (CLR) class implementation of the **INotifyPropertyChanged** interface, change notification enables codeless interaction between the target and source objects participating in the data binding.

Data binding enables dissimilar target and source types to bind by using a value converter to convert one type of data to the other type. A data binding pipeline contains multiple validation hooks that you can use to validate user input.

You are strongly encouraged to read the "Dependency Properties Overview" and "Data Binding Overview" topics on MSDN. A full understanding of these two topics is critical to successfully developing applications on the Microsoft XAML platforms. For more information about data binding, see "Data Binding" in Chapter 5, "Implementing the MVVM Pattern."

REGIONS

Regions are enabled in the Prism Library through a region manager, regions, and region adapters. The next sections describe how they work together.

Region Manager

The **RegionManager** class is responsible for creating and maintaining a collection of regions for the host controls. The **RegionManager** uses a control-specific adapter that associates a new region with the host control. The following illustration shows the relationship between the region, control, and adapter set up by the **RegionManager**.

Region, control, and adapter relationship

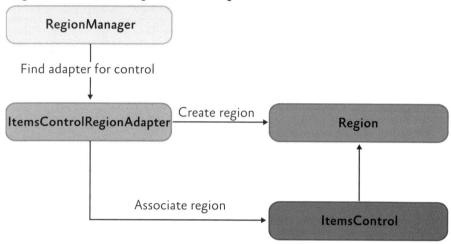

The **RegionManager** can create regions in code or in XAML. The **RegionManager. RegionName** attached property is used to create a region in XAML by applying the attached property to the host control.

Applications can contain one or more instances of a **RegionManager.** You can specify the **RegionManager** instance into which you want to register the region. This is useful if you want to move the control around in the visual tree and do not want the region to be cleared when the attached property value is removed.

The **RegionManager** provides a **RegionContext** attached property that permits its regions to share data.

Region Implementation

A region is a class that implements the **IRegion** interface. The term *region* represents a container that can hold dynamic data that is presented in a UI. A region allows the Prism Library to place dynamic content contained in modules in predefined placeholders in a UI container.

Regions can hold any type of UI content. A module can contain UI content presented as a user control, a data type that is associated with a data template, a custom control, or any combination of these. This lets you define the appearance for the UI areas and then have modules place content in these predetermined areas.

A region can contain zero or more items. Depending on the type of host control the region is managing, one or more of the items could be visible. For example, a **Content-Control** can display only a single object. However, the region in which it is located can contain many items, and an **ItemsControl** can display multiple items. This allows each item in the region to be visible on the UI.

In the following illustration, the Stock Trader RI shell contains four regions: **Main Region, MainToolbarRegion, ResearchRegion,** and **ActionRegion.** These regions are populated by the various modules in the application—the content can be changed at any time.

Stock Trader RI regions

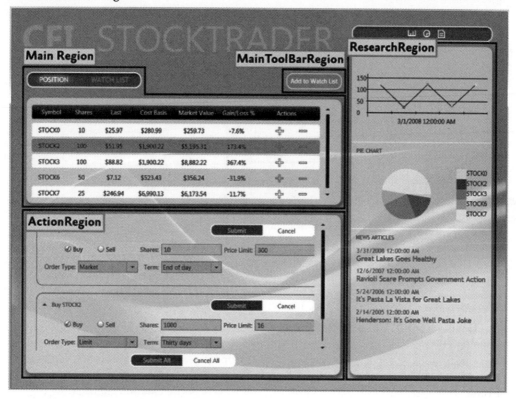

Module User Control to Region Mapping

To demonstrate how modules and content are associated with regions, see the following illustration. It shows the association of **WatchModule** and the **NewsModule** with the corresponding regions in the shell.

The **MainRegion** contains the **WatchListView** user control, which is contained in the **WatchModule**. The **ResearchRegion** also contains the **ArticleView** user control, which is contained in the **NewsModule**.

In applications created with the Prism Library, mappings like this are part of the design process because designers and developers use them to determine what content should be in a specific region. This allows designers to determine the overall space needed and any additional items that must be added to ensure that the content will be viewable in the allowable space.

Module user control to region mapping

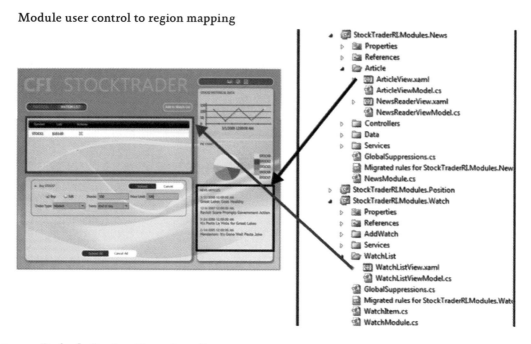

Default Region Functionality

While you do not need to fully understand region implementations to use them, it might be useful to understand the default region functionality and how controls and regions are associated: for example, how a region locates and instantiates views, how views can be notified when they are the active view, or how view lifetime can be tied to activation.

The following sections describe the region adapter and region behaviors.

Region Adapter

To expose a UI control as a region, it must have a region adapter. Region adapters are responsible for creating a region and associating it with the control. This allows you to use the **IRegion** interface to manage the UI control contents in a consistent way. Each region adapter adapts a specific type of UI control. The Prism Library provides the following three region adapters:

* **ContentControlRegionAdapter**. This adapter adapts controls of type **System. Windows.Controls.ContentControl** and derived classes.
* **SelectorRegionAdapter**. This adapter adapts controls derived from the class **System.Windows.Controls.Primitives.Selector**, such as the **System.Windows. Controls.TabControl** control.
* **ItemsControlRegionAdapter**. This adapter adapts controls of type **System. Windows.Controls.ItemsControl** and derived classes.

Note: *The Silverlight version of the Prism Library contains a fourth region adapter named* **TabControlRegionAdapter**. *This is because the* **TabControl** *control in Silverlight 4 does not extend the* **Selector** *class and behaves differently from its WPF counterpart.*

Region Behaviors

The Prism Library introduces the concept of region behaviors. These are pluggable components that give a region most of its functionality. Region behaviors were introduced to support view discovery and region context (described later in this chapter), and to create an API that is consistent across both WPF and Silverlight. Additionally, behaviors provide an effective way to extend a region's implementation.

A region behavior is a class that is attached to a region to give the region additional functionality. This behavior stays attached to the region and remains active for the lifetime of the region. For example, when an **AutoPopulateRegionBehavior** is attached to a region, it automatically instantiates and adds any **ViewTypes** that are registered for regions with that name. For the lifetime of the region, it keeps monitoring the **Region ViewRegistry** for new registrations. It is easy to add custom region behaviors or replace existing behaviors, either on a system-wide or a per-region basis.

The next sections describe the default behaviors that are automatically added to all regions. One behavior, the **SelectorItemsSourceSyncBehavior**, is only attached to controls that derive from the **Selector**.

Registration Behavior

The **RegionManagerRegistrationBehavior** is responsible for making sure that the region is registered with the correct **RegionManager**. When a view or control is added to the visual tree as a child of another control or region, any region defined in the control should be registered in the **RegionManager** of the parent control. When the child control is removed, the registered region is unregistered.

Auto-Population Behavior

There are two classes responsible for implementing view discovery. One of them is the **AutoPopulateRegionBehavior**. When it is attached to a region, it retrieves all view types that are registered under the name of the region. It then creates instances of those views and adds them to the region. After the region is created, the **AutoPopulateRegionBehavior** monitors the **RegionViewRegistry** for any newly registered view types for that region name.

If you want to have more control over the view discovery process, consider creating your own implementation of the **IRegionViewRegistry** and the **AutoPopulateRegion Behavior**.

Region Context Behaviors

The region context functionality is contained within two behaviors: the **SyncRegionContext WithHostBehavior** and the **BindRegionContextToDependencyObjectBehavior**. These behaviors are responsible for monitoring changes to the context that were made on the region, and then synchronizing the context with a context dependency property attached to the view.

Activation Behavior

The **RegionActiveAwareBehavior** is responsible for notifying a view if it is active or inactive. The view must implement **IActiveAware** to receive these change notifications. This active aware notification is one-directional (it travels from the behavior to the view). The view cannot affect its active state by changing the active property on the **IActiveAware** interface.

Region Lifetime Behavior

The **RegionMemberLifetimeBehavior** is responsible for determining if an item should be removed from the region when it is deactivated. The **RegionMemberLifetimeBehavior** monitors the region's **ActiveViews** collection to discover items that transition into a deactivated state. The behavior checks the removed items for **IRegionMemberLifetime** or the **RegionMemberLifetimeAttribute** (in that order) to determine if it should be kept alive after removal.

If the item in the collection is a **System.Windows.FrameworkElement**, the behavior will also check its **DataContext** for **IRegionMemberLifetime** or the **RegionMember LifetimeAttribute**.

The region items are checked in the following order:

1. IRegionMemberLifetime.KeepAlive value

2. DataContext's IRegionMemberLifetime.KeepAlive value

3. RegionMemberLifetimeAttribute.KeepAlive value

4. DataContext's RegionMemberLifetimeAttribute.KeepAlive value

Control-Specific Behaviors

The **SelectorItemsSourceSyncBehavior** is used only for controls that derive from **Selector**, such as tab controls in WPF. It is responsible for synchronizing the views in the region with the items of the selector, and then synchronizing the active views in the region with the selected items of the selector.

The **TabControlRegionSyncBehavior** is used for Silverlight only, and provides behavior that is similar to **SelectorItemsSourceSyncBehavior** for the Silverlight tab control.

Extending the Region Implementation

The Prism Library provides extension points that allow you to customize or extend the default behavior of the provided APIs. For example, you can write your own region adapters, region behaviors, change the way the Navigation API parses URIs, or extend the Navigation API to work with Silverlight Frame Navigation. For more information about extending the Prism Library, see "Extending Prism" on MSDN.

VIEW COMPOSITION

View composition is the constructing of a view. In composite applications, views from multiple modules have to be displayed at run time in specific locations on the application UI. To achieve this, you need to define the locations where the views will appear and how the views will be created and displayed in those locations.

Views can be created and displayed in the locations either automatically through view discovery, or programmatically through view injection. These two techniques determine how individual views are mapped to named locations on the application UI.

View Discovery

In view discovery, you set up a relationship in the **RegionViewRegistry** between a region's name and the type of a view. When a region is created, the region looks for all the **View Types** associated with the region and automatically instantiates and loads the corresponding views. Therefore, with view discovery, you do not have explicit control over when the views that correspond to a region are loaded and displayed.

View Injection

In view injection, your code obtains a reference to a region, and then programmatically adds a view into it. Typically, this is done when a module initializes or as a result of a user action. Your code will query a **RegionManager** for a specific region by name and then inject views into it. With view injection, you have more control over when views are loaded and displayed. You also have the ability to remove views from the region. However, with view injection, you cannot add a view to a region that has not yet been created.

Navigation

The Prism Library 4.0 contains Navigation APIs. The Navigation APIs simplify the view injection process by allowing you to navigate a region to an URI. The Navigation API instantiates the view, adds it to the region, and then activates it. Additionally, the Navigation API allows navigating back to a previously created view contained in a region. For more information about the Navigation APIs, see the next chapter, "Navigation."

When to Use View Discovery vs. View Injection

Choosing which view loading strategy to use for a region depends on the application requirements and the function of the region.

Use view discovery in the following situations:

- Automatic view loading is desired or required.

- Single instances of a view will be loaded into the region.

Use view injection in the following situations:

- Your application uses the Navigation APIs.

- You need explicit or programmatic control over when a view is created and displayed, or you need to remove a view from a region; for example, as a result of application logic or navigation.

- You need to display multiple instances of the same views in a region, and each view instance is bound to different data.

- You need to control which instance of a region a view is added to. For example, you want to add a customer detail view to a specific customer detail region. (This scenario requires implementing scoped regions as described later in this chapter.)

UI Layout Scenarios

In composite applications, views from multiple modules are displayed at run time in specific locations on the application UI. To achieve this, you need to define the locations in which the views will appear and you need to specify how the views will be created and displayed in those locations.

The decoupling of the view and the UI location in which it will be displayed allows the appearance and layout of the application to evolve independently of the views that appear within the region.

The next sections describe the core scenarios that you will encounter when you develop a composite application. When appropriate, examples from the Stock Trader RI will be used to demonstrate a solution for the scenario.

IMPLEMENTING THE SHELL

The shell is the application root object in which the primary UI content is contained. In a Windows Presentation Foundation (WPF) application. The shell is the **Window** object. In a Silverlight application, the shell is the **RootVisual UserControl**.

A shell can contain named regions in which modules can specify the views that will appear. It can also define certain top-level UI elements, such as the main menu and toolbar. The shell defines the overall structure and appearance for the application, and is similar to an ASP.NET master page control. It could define styles and borders that are present and visible in the shell layout itself, and it could also define styles, templates, and themes that are applied to the views that are plugged into the shell.

You do not need to have a distinct shell as part of your application architecture to use the Prism Library. If you are building a completely new composite application, implementing a shell provides a well-defined root and initialization pattern for setting up the main UI of your application. However, if you are adding Prism Library features to an existing application, you do not have to change the basic architecture of your application to add a shell. Instead, you can alter your existing window definitions or controls to add regions that can pull in views as needed.

You can also have more than one shell in your application. If your application is designed to open more than one top-level window for the user, each top-level window acts as shell for the content it contains.

Stock Trader RI Shell

The WPF Stock Trader RI has a shell as its main window. In the following illustration, the shell and views are highlighted. The shell is the main window that appears when the Stock Trader RI starts and which contains all the views. It defines the regions into which modules add their views and a couple of top-level UI items, including the CFI Stock Trader title and the Watch List tear-off banner.

Stock Trader RI shell window, regions, and views

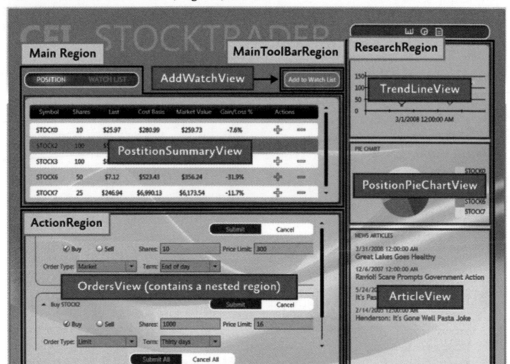

The shell implementation in the Stock Trader RI is provided by Shell.xaml, its code-behind file, Shell.xaml.cs, and its view model, ShellViewModel.cs. Shell.xaml includes the layout and UI elements that are part of the shell, including definitions of regions to which modules add their views.

The following XAML shows the structure and main XAML elements that define the shell. Notice that the **RegionName** attached property is used to define the four regions and that the window background image provides a background for the shell.

```
XAML Shell.xaml (WPF)
<Window x:Class="StockTraderRI.Shell">

<!—shell background -->
<Window.Background>
 <ImageBrush ImageSource="Resources/background.png" Stretch="UniformToFill"/>
</Window.Background>

<Grid>
```

```xml
<!-- logo -->
<Canvas x:Name="Logo">
<TextBlock Text="CFI" ... />
<TextBlock Text="STOCKTRADER" .../>
</Canvas>

<!-- main bar -->
<ItemsControl
 x:Name="MainToolbar"
 cal:RegionManager.RegionName="{x:Static inf:RegionNames.MainToolBarRegion}">
</ItemsControl>

<!-- content -->
<Grid>
 <Controls:AnimatedTabControl
  x:Name="PositionBuySellTab"
  cal:RegionManager.RegionName="{x:Static inf:RegionNames.MainRegion}"/>
</Grid>

<!-- details -->
<Grid>
 <ContentControl
  x:Name="ActionContent"
  cal:RegionManager.RegionName="{x:Static inf:RegionNames.ActionRegion}">
 </ContentControl>
</Grid>

<!-- sidebar -->
<Grid x:Name="SideGrid">
 <Controls:ResearchControl
  cal:RegionManager.RegionName="{x:Static inf:RegionNames.ResearchRegion}">
 </Controls:ResearchControl>
</Grid>

</Grid>
</Window>
```

The implementation of the **Shell** code-behind file is very simple. The **Shell** is exported so that when the bootstrapper creates it; its dependencies will be resolved by the Managed Extensibility Framework (MEF). The shell has its single dependency—the **ShellViewModel**—injected during construction, as shown in the following examples.

C# Shell.xaml.cs

```csharp
[Export]
public partial class Shell : Window
```

```
{
public Shell()
{
 InitializeComponent();
}


[Import]
ShellViewModel ViewModel
{
 set
 {
  this.DataContext = value;
 }
}
}
```

C# ShellViewModel.cs
```
[Export]
public class ShellViewModel : NotificationObject
{
// This is where any view model logic for the shell would go.
}
```

The minimal code in the code-behind file illustrates the power and simplicity of the composite application architecture and loose coupling between the shell and its constituent views.

Defining Regions

You define where views will appear by defining a layout with named locations known as regions. Regions act as placeholders for one or more views that will be displayed at run time. Modules can locate and add content to regions in the layout without knowing how and where the regions are displayed. This allows the layout to change without affecting the modules that add the content to the layout.

Regions are defined by assigning a region name to a WPF or Silverlight control, either in XAML as shown in the previous Shell.xaml file or in code. Regions can be accessed by their region name. At run time, views are added to the named **Region** control, which then displays the view or views according to the layout strategy that the views implement. For example, a tab control region will lay out its child views in a tabbed arrangement. Regions support the addition or removal of views. Views can be created and displayed in regions either programmatically or automatically. In the Prism Library, the former is achieved through view injection and the latter through view discovery. These two techniques determine how individual views are mapped to the named regions on the application UI.

The shell of the application defines the application layout at the highest level; for example, by specifying the locations for the main content and the navigation content, as shown in the following illustration. Layout within these high-level views is similarly defined, allowing the overall UI to be recursively composed.

A template shell

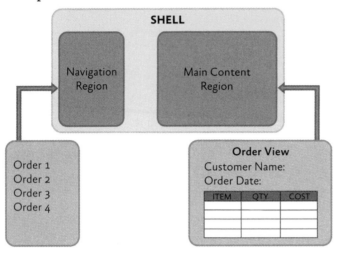

Regions are sometimes used to define locations for multiple views that are logically related. In this scenario, the region control is typically an **ItemsControl**-derived control that will display the views according to the layout strategy that it implements, such as in a stacked or tabbed layout arrangement.

Regions can also be used to define a location for a single view; for example, by using a **ContentControl**. In this scenario, the region control displays only one view at a time, even if more than one view is mapped to that region location.

Stock Trader RI Shell Regions

The Stock Trader RI shows the use of both the single view and the multiple view layout approaches. You can see both in the shell for the application, which defines locations for the application's high-level views. The following illustration shows the regions defined by the Stock Trader RI shell.

Stock Trader RI shell regions

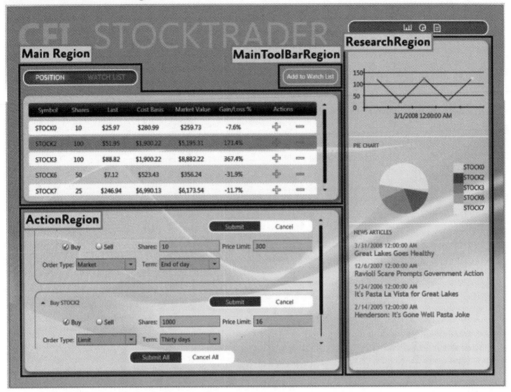

A multiple-view layout is also demonstrated in the Stock Trader RI when the application is buying or selling a stock. The Buy/Sell area is a list-style region that shows multiple buy/sell views (**OrderCompositeView**) as part of its list, as shown in the following illustration.

ItemsControl region

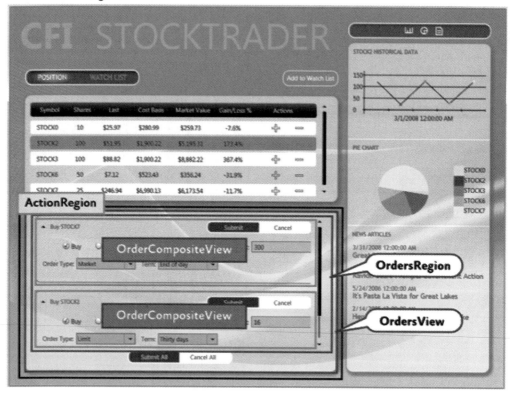

The shell's **ActionRegion** contains the **OrdersView**. The **OrdersView** contains the **Submit All** and **Cancel All** buttons as well as the **OrdersRegion**. The **OrdersRegion** is attached to a **ListBox** control which displays multiple **OrderCompositeViews**.

IRegion

A region is a class that implements the **IRegion** interface. The region is the container that holds content to be displayed by a control. The following code shows the **IRegion** interface.

```C#
public interface IRegion : INavigateAsync, INotifyPropertyChanged
{
    IViewsCollection Views { get; }
    IViewsCollection ActiveViews { get; }
    object Context { get; set; }
    string Name { get; set; }
    Comparison<object> SortComparison { get; set; }
    IRegionManager Add(object view);
```

```
IRegionManager Add(object view, string viewName);
IRegionManager Add(object view, string viewName, bool createRegionManagerScope);
void Remove(object view);
void Deactivate(object view);
object GetView(string viewName);
IRegionManager RegionManager { get; set; }
IRegionBehaviorCollection Behaviors { get; }
IRegionNavigationService NavigationService { get; set; }
}
```

Using XAML to Add a Region

The **RegionManager** supplies an attached property that you can use for simple region creation in XAML. To use the attached property, you must load the Prism Library namespace into the XAML file and then use the **RegionName** attached property. The following example shows how to use the attached property in a window with an **Animated TabControl.**

Notice the use of the **x:Static** markup extension to reference the **MainRegion** string constant. This practice eliminates magic strings in the XAML.

```
XAML (WPF)
<Controls:AnimatedTabControl
  x:Name="PositionBuySellTab"
  cal:RegionManager.RegionName="{x:Static inf:RegionNames.MainRegion}"/>
```

Silverlight 4 does not support **x:Static**. Therefore, you need to use string values for the region names or, optionally, define an application-level string resource for each region name. The **RegionName** attached property could then data binding to the string resource to resolve the region name.

```
XAML (Silverlight)
<Controls:AnimatedTabControl
  Regions:RegionManager.RegionName="MainRegion" />
```

Using Code to Add a Region

The **RegionManager** can register regions directly without using XAML. The following code example shows how to add a region to a control from the code-behind file. First a reference to the region manager is obtained. Then, using the **RegionManager** static methods **SetRegionManager** and **SetRegionName**, the region is attached to the UI's **ActionContent** control, and that region is named **ActionRegion**.

```
C#
IRegionManager regionManager = ServiceLocator.Current.GetInstance<IRegionManager>();
RegionManager.SetRegionManager(this.ActionContent, regionManager);
RegionManager.SetRegionName(this.ActionContent, "ActionRegion");
```

DISPLAYING VIEWS IN A REGION WHEN THE REGION LOADS

With the view discovery approach, modules can register views (view models or presentation models) for a specific named location. When that location is displayed at run time, any views that have been registered for that location will be created and displayed within it automatically.

Modules register views with a registry. The parent view queries this registry to discover the views that were registered for a named location. After they are discovered, the parent view places those views on the screen by adding them to the placeholder control.

After the application is loaded, the composite view is notified to handle the placement of new views that have been added to the registry.

The following illustration shows the view discovery approach.

View discovery

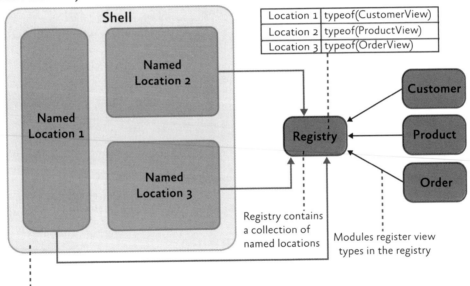

The Prism Library defines a standard registry, **RegionViewRegistry**, to register views for these named locations.

To show a view in a region, register the view with the region manager, as shown in the following code example. You can directly register a view type with the region, in which case the view will be constructed by the dependency injection container and added to the region when the control that hosts the region is loaded.

```
C#
// View discovery
this.regionManager.RegisterViewWithRegion("MainRegion", typeof(EmployeeView));
```

Optionally, you can provide a delegate that returns the view to be shown, as shown in the next example. The region manager will display the view when the region is created.

```C#
// View discovery
this.regionManager.RegisterViewWithRegion("MainRegion", () =>
this.container.Resolve<EmployeeView>());
```

The UI Composition QuickStart has a walkthrough in the EmployeeModule Module-Init.cs file that demonstrates how to use the **RegisterViewWithRegion** method.

DISPLAYING VIEWS IN A REGION PROGRAMMATICALLY

In the view injection approach, views are programmatically added or removed from a named location by the modules that manage them. To enable this, the application contains a registry of named locations that appear on the UI. A module can use the registry to look up one of the locations and then programmatically inject views into it. To make sure that locations in the registry can be accessed similarly, each of the named locations adheres to a common interface used to inject the view. The following illustration shows the view injection approach.

View injection

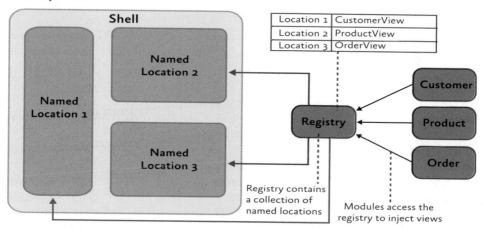

The Prism Library defines a standard registry, **RegionManager**, and a standard interface, **IRegion**, for accessing these locations.

To use view injection to add a view to a region, get the region from the region manager, and then call the **Add** method, as shown in the following code. With view injection, the view is displayed only after the view is added to a region, which can happen when the module is loaded or when a user action completes a predefined action.

```C#
// View injection
IRegion region = regionManager.Regions["MainRegion"];
```

```
var ordersView = container.Resolve<OrdersView>();
region.Add(ordersView, "OrdersView");
region.Activate(ordersView);
```

In addition to the Stock Trader RI, the UI Composition QuickStart has a walkthrough for implementing view injection.

Navigation

The Prism Library 4.0 includes Navigation APIs that provide a rich and consistent API for implementing navigation in a WPF or Silverlight application.

Region navigation is a form of view injection. When a navigation request is processed, it will attempt to locate a view in the region that can fulfill the request. If it cannot find a matching view, it calls the application container to create the object, and then injects the object into the target region and activates it.

The following code example from the Stock Trader RI **ArticleViewModel** illustrates how to initiate a navigation request.

```
C#
this.regionManager.RequestNavigate(RegionNames.SecondaryRegion,
 new Uri("/NewsReaderView", UriKind.Relative));
```

For more information about region navigation, see Chapter 8, "Navigation." The View-Switching Navigation QuickStart and State-Based Navigation QuickStart are also examples of implementing application navigation.

ORDERING VIEWS IN A REGION

Whether it uses view discovery or view Injection, an application might need to order how views appear in a **TabControl**, **ItemsControl**, or any other control that displays multiple active views. By default, views appear in the order that they were registered and added to the region.

When a composite application is built, views are often registered from different modules. Declaring dependencies between modules can help alleviate the problem, but when modules and views do not have any real interdependencies, declaring an artificial dependency couples modules unnecessarily.

To allow views to participate in ordering themselves, the Prism Library provides the **ViewSortHint** attribute. This attribute contains a string **Hint** property that allows a view to declare a hint of how it should be ordered in the region.

When displaying views, the **Region** class uses a default view sorting routine that uses the hint to order the views. This is a simple case-sensitive ordinal sort. Views that have the sort hint attribute are ordered ahead of those without it. Also, those without the attribute appear in the order in which they were added to the region.

If you want to change how views are ordered, the **Region** class provides a **Sort Comparison** property that you can set with your own **Comparison<*object*>** delegate method. It is important to note that the ordering of the region's **Views** and **ActiveViews** properties are reflected on the UI because adapters such as the **ItemsControlRegion-Adapter** bind directly to these properties. A custom region adapter could implement its own sorting and filter that will override how the region orders views.

The View Switching QuickStart demonstrates a simple numbering scheme to order the views on the left navigation region. The following code examples show **ViewSortHint** applied to each of the navigation item views.

```C#
[Export]
[ViewSortHint("01")]
public partial class EmailNavigationItemView

[Export]
[ViewSortHint("02")]
public partial class CalendarNavigationItemView

[Export]
[ViewSortHint("03")]
public partial class ContactsDetailNavigationItemView

[Export]
[ViewSortHint("04")]
public partial class ContactsAvatarNavigationItemView
```

SHARING DATA BETWEEN MULTIPLE REGIONS

The Prism Library provides multiple approaches to communicating between views, depending on your scenario. The region manager provides the **RegionContext** property as one of these approaches.

RegionContext is useful when you want to share context between a parent view and child views that are hosted in a region. **RegionContext** is an attached property. You set the value of the context on the region control so that it can be made available to all child views that are displayed in that region control. The region context can be any simple or complex object and can be a data-bound value. The **RegionContext** can be used with either view discovery or view injection.

Note: *The* **DataContext** *property in Silverlight and WPF is used to set the local data context for the view. It allows the view to use data binding to communicate with a view model, local presenter, or model.* **RegionContext** *is used to share context between multiple views and is not local to a single view. It provides a simple mechanism for sharing context between multiple views.*

The following code shows how the **RegionContext** attached property is used in XAML.

```xaml
XAML
<TabControl AutomationProperties.AutomationId="DetailsTabControl"
  cal:RegionManager.RegionName="{x:Static local:RegionNames.TabRegion}"
  cal:RegionManager.RegionContext="{Binding Path=SelectedEmployee.EmployeeId}"
  ...>
```

You can also set the **RegionContext** in code, as shown in the following example.

```csharp
C#
RegionManager.Regions["Region1"].Context = employeeId;
```

To retrieve the **RegionContext** in a view, the **GetObservableContext** static method of the **RegionContext** class is used. It passes the view as a parameter and then accesses its **Value** property, as shown in the following code example.

```csharp
C#
private void GetRegionContext()
{
  this.Model.EmployeeId = (int)RegionContext.GetObservableContext(this).Value;
}
```

The value of the **RegionContext** can be changed from within a view by simply assigning a new value to its **Value** property. Views can opt to be notified of changes to the **RegionContext** by subscribing to the **PropertyChanged** event on the **ObservableObject** that is returned by the **GetObservableContext** method. This allows multiple views to be kept in synchronization when their **RegionContext** is changed. The following code example demonstrates subscribing to the **PropertyChanged** event.

```csharp
C#
ObservableObject<object> viewRegionContext =
                RegionContext.GetObservableContext(this);
viewRegionContext.PropertyChanged += this.ViewRegionContext_OnPropertyChangedEvent;

private void ViewRegionContext_OnPropertyChangedEvent(object sender,
                PropertyChangedEventArgs args)
{
  if (args.PropertyName == "Value")
  {
    var context = (ObservableObject<object>) sender;
    int newValue = (int)context.Value;
  }
}
```

Note: *The* **RegionContext** *is set as an attached property on the content object hosted in the region. This means that the content object has to derive from* **Dependency Object**. *In the preceding example, the view is a visual control, which ultimately derives from* **DependencyObject**.

If you choose to use WPF or Silverlight data templates to define your view, the content object will represent the **ViewModel** *or* **PresentationModel**. *If your view model or presentation model needs to retrieve the* **RegionContext***, it will need to derive from the* **DependencyObject** *base class.*

CREATING MULTIPLE INSTANCES OF A REGION

Scoped regions are available only with view injection. You should use them if you need a view to have its own instance of a region. Views that define regions with attached properties automatically inherit their parent's **RegionManager**. Usually, this is the global **RegionManager** that is registered in the shell window. If the application creates more than one instance of that view, each instance would attempt to register its region with the parent **RegionManager**. **RegionManager** allows only uniquely named regions; therefore, the second registration would produce an error.

Instead, use scoped regions so that each view will have its own **RegionManager** and its regions will be registered with that **RegionManager** rather than the parent **Region Manager**, as shown in the following illustration.

Parent and scoped RegionManagers

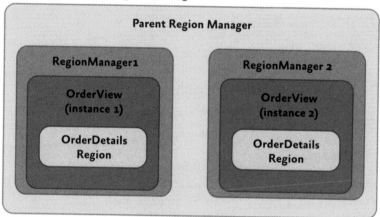

To create a local **RegionManager** for a view, specify that a new **RegionManager** should be created when you add your view to a region, as shown in the following code example.

```
C#
IRegion detailsRegion = this.regionManager.Regions["DetailsRegion"];
View view = new View();
bool createRegionManagerScope = true;
IRegionManager detailsRegionManager = detailsRegion.Add(view, null,
                        createRegionManagerScope);
```

The **Add** method will return the new **RegionManager** that the view can retain for further access to the local scope.

CREATING VIEWS

The visual representation of your application can take many forms, including user controls, custom controls, and data templates, to name a few. In the case of the Stock Trader RI, user controls are typically used to represent distinct sections on the main window, but this is not a standard. In your application, you should use an approach that you are most familiar with and that fits into how you work as a designer. Regardless of the predominating visual representation in your application, you will inevitably use a combination of user controls, custom controls, and data templates in your overall design. The following figure shows where the Stock Trader RI uses these various items. This illustration also serves as a reference for the following sections, which describe each of the items.

Stock Trader RI usage of user controls, custom controls, and data templates

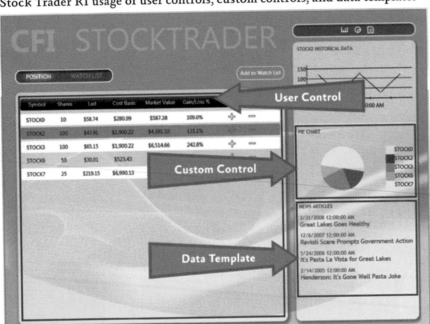

User Controls

Both Expression Blend and Visual Studio 2010 provide rich support for creating user controls. User controls created with these tools are therefore recommended for creating UI content with the Prism Library. As mentioned earlier, the Stock Trader RI uses them extensively to create content that will be inserted into regions. The **WatchListView.xaml** user control is a good example of a simple UI representation that is contained inside the **WatchModule**. This control is a very simple control that is straightforward to create using this model.

Custom Controls

In some situations, a user control is too limiting. In these cases, custom layout or extensibility is more important than ease of creation. This is where custom controls are useful. In the Stock Trader RI, the pie chart control is a good example of this. This control is composed from data derived from the positions and shows a chart of the overall portfolio. This type of control is a little more challenging to create than a user control, and it has limited visual design support in Expression Blend and Visual Studio 2010, compared to a user control.

Data Templates

Data templates are an important part of most types of data-driven applications. The use of data templates for list-based controls is prevalent throughout the Stock Trader RI. In many cases, you can use a data template to create complete visual representations without needing to create any type of control. The **ResearchRegion** uses a data template to show articles and, in conjunction with an **Items** style, provides an indication of which item was selected.

Expression Blend has full visual design support for data templates. Visual Studio 2010 only provides support for using the XAML editor to edit data templates.

Resources

Resources such as styles, resource dictionaries, and control templates can be scattered throughout an application. This is especially true with a composite application. When you consider where to place resources, pay special attention to dependencies between UI elements and the resources they need. The Stock Trader RI solution, shown in the following figure, contains labels that indicate the various areas where resources can live.

Resource distribution across a solution

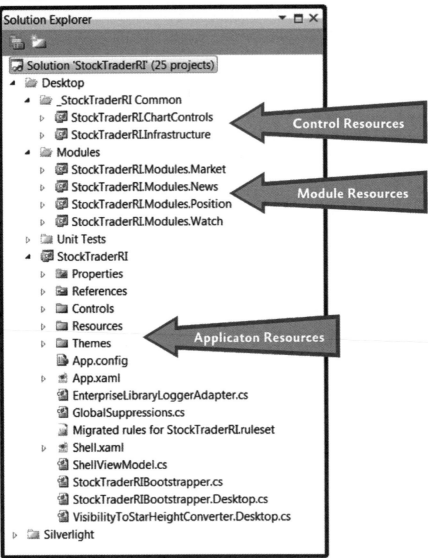

Application Resources

Typically, application resources are resources that are available to an application as a whole. These resources tend to be focused on the root application, but they can also provide default styling on a type basis for modules or controls. An example of this is a text box style that is applied to the text box type in the root application. This style will be available to all text boxes in the application unless the style is overridden at the module or control level.

Module Resources

Module resources play the same role as root application resources in that they can apply to all items in a module. Using resources at this level can provide a consistent appearance across the entire module and can also allow for reuse in more specific instances that span one or more visual components. The use of resources at the module level should be contained within the individual module. Creating dependencies between modules can lead to issues that are difficult to locate when UI elements appear incorrectly.

Control Resources

Control resources are usually contained in control libraries and can be used by all the controls in the control library. These resources tend to have the most limited scope because control libraries typically contain very specific controls and do not contain user controls. (In an application created with the Prism Library, user controls are typically placed in the modules in which they are used.)

UI Design Guidance

The goal of this section is to provide some high-level guidance to the XAML designer and developer who are building an application with the Prism Library and WPF or Silverlight. This section describes UI layout, visual representation, data binding, resources, and the presentation model. After reading this, you should have a high-level understanding of how to approach designing the UI of an application based on the Prism Library and some of the techniques that can help you create a maintainable UI for a composite application.

GUIDELINES FOR DESIGNING USER INTERFACES

The layout of composite applications created with the Prism Library builds on the standard principals of WPF and Silverlight—the layout uses the concepts of panels that contain related items. However, with composite applications, the content inside the various panels is dynamic and is not known during design time. This forces designers and developers to create page structures that can contain layout content and then design each of the elements that fit into the layout separately. As a designer or developer, this means that you have to think about two main layout concepts in the Prism Library: container composition and regions.

Container Composition

Container composition is really just an extension of the containment model that WPF and Silverlight inherently provide. The term *container* can mean any element, including a window, page, user control, panel, custom control, control template, or data template, that can contain other elements.

How you visualize your UI can vary from implementation to implementation, but you will find recurring themes that stand out. You will create a window, page, or user control that contains both fixed content and dynamic content. The fixed content will consist of the overall structure of the containing UI element, and the dynamic content will be what is placed inside a region.

For example, the WPF Stock Trader RI has a startup window named Shell.xaml that contains the overall structure for the application. The next illustration shows the shell loaded in Expression Blend. Notice that only the fixed portion of the UI is visible. The remaining sections of the shell are dynamically inserted into the various regions by the modules as the application loads.

The design-time experience is a little limited in this type of application, but you know that content will be placed in the various regions at run time, and you need to design for that fact. To see an example of this, compare the designer view of the main page in the next illustration to the run-time view in the illustration that follows it. In the designer view, the page is mostly empty. Contrast that with the run-time view, where there is a position area that contains a tab control with position data, and a trend line, pie chart, and news area pertaining to the selected stocks. The differences between the designer view and run-time view demonstrate the challenges designers and developers face when they create applications built with the Prism Library.

The items cannot be seen during design time; therefore, determining how big they are and how they fit into the overall appearance of the application is a little difficult. Consider the following as you create the layout for your containers:

- Are there any size constraints that will limit how large content can be? If there are, consider using containers that support scrolling.

- Consider using an expander and **ScrollViewer** combination for situations in which a large amount of dynamic content needs to fit into a confined area.

- Pay close attention to how content enlarges as the screen content grows to ensure that the appearance of your application is appealing in any resolution.

Stock Trader RI main window in Expression Blend

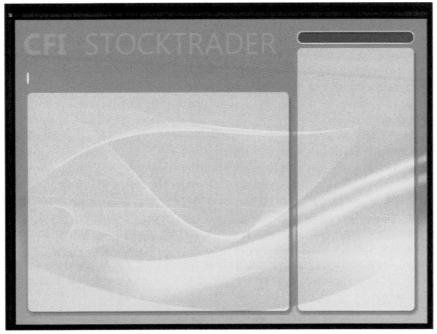

Stock Trader RI main window during run time

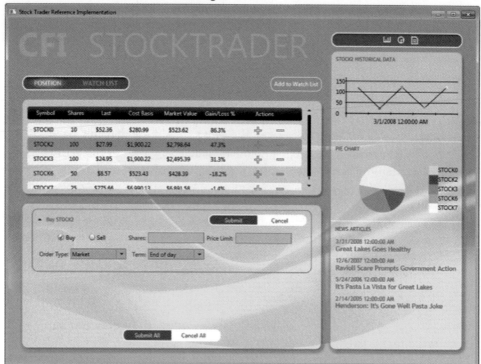

Viewing Composite Application at Design Time

The two previous figures illustrate one of the challenges of working with high-level views that are composed at run time. Each UI element in a composite application must be designed separately. This makes it hard to visualize how the composite page or window will look at run time. To visualize the composite view in its composed state, you can create a test project with a page or window that contains all the UI elements for the view you want to test.

- Additionally, consider using the design-time sample data features in Expression Blend and Visual Studio 2010 to populate UI elements with data. Design-time data is very helpful when you work with data templates, list controls, charts, or graphs. For more information, see the section "Guidelines for Design-Time Sample Data."

Layout

Consider the following when you design the layout of a composite application:

- The shell defines the main layout of the application. Each area of the layout is a region and should be kept as an empty container. Do not place content inside regions at design time because content will be loaded there at run time.
- The shell should contain the background, titles, and the footer. Think of the shell as an ASP.NET master page.

- Control containers that act as regions are decoupled from the views that they contain. Therefore, you should be able to change the size of the views without modifying the controls, and you should be able to change the size of the controls without modifying the views. You should consider the following when defining the size of a view:
    - If a view will be used in several regions or if it is uncertain where it will be used, design it with dynamic width and height.
    - If the views have fixed sizes, the regions of the shell should use dynamic sizes.
    - If the shell regions have fixed sizes, the views should use dynamic sizes.
    - Views might require a fixed height and dynamic width. An example of this is the **PositionPieChart** view located in the sidebar of the Stock Trader RI.
    - Other views might require a dynamic height and width. For example, the **NewsReader** views in the sidebar of the Stock Trader RI. The height itself depends on the title's length, and the width should always adapt to the region's size (sidebar width). The same applies to the **PositionSummaryView** view, where the grid's width should adapt to the screen size and the height should adapt to the number of rows in the grid.
- Views should generally have transparent backgrounds, allowing the shell background to provide the application visual background.
- Always use named resources for assigning colors, brushes, fonts and font sizes, rather than directly assigning the property value in XAML. This makes application maintenance much easier over time. It also allows an application to respond to changes in resource dictionaries at run time.

Animation

Consider the following when you use animation in the shell or views:

- You can animate the layout of the shell, but you will have to animate its contents and views separately.
- Design and animate each view separately.
- Use soft or gentle animations to provide a visual clue that a UI element is being brought into view or being removed from view. This gives an application a polished look and feel.

Expression Blend offers a rich set of behaviors, easing functions, and an outstanding editing experience for animating and transitioning UI elements based on visual state changes or events. For more information, see the "VisualStateManager Class" topic on MSDN.

Run-Time Optimization

Consider the following tips for performance optimization:

- Place any common resources in the App.xaml file or a merged dictionary to avoid duplicating the styles.

- In Silverlight, avoid using non-system fonts for specific static text that should be styled differently from the rest of the application (for example, the application title). In this case, determine if it is better to convert the text to a path or to embed the font.

Embedding a font can affect the size of the downloaded .xap file because some font files are rather large. To minimize the size of the downloaded .xap file, Expression Blend allows you to download a subset of the font characters instead of the entire font.

For more information about this, see "Using Custom Fonts in Silverlight" on the Silverlight Developer Center.

Design-Time Optimizations

The following sections describe design-time scenarios and provide solutions for making the most of the design-time experience.

Large Solutions with Many XAML Resources

In large applications with many XAML resources that are part of the solution, visual designer load time can be affected, sometimes significantly. This performance slowdown exists because the visual designer must parse all merged XAML resources. The solution to this problem is to move all XAML resources to another solution, compile that solution, and then reference the new XAML resource DLL from the large solution. Because the XAML resources are in a binary referenced assembly, the visual designer does not parse the XAML resources, thus improving design-time performance. When moving XAML resources to an external assembly, you might want to consider exposing **Component ResourceKeys** for your resources. For more information, see the "Component ResourceKey Markup Extension" topic on MSDN.

XAML Assets

XAML is a powerful and expressive language for creating assets such as images, diagrams, drawings, and 3-D scenes. Some developers and designers prefer creating XAML assets instead of using .ico, .jpg, or .png image files. One reason that they prefer the XAML approach is to take advantage of the resolution independence of XAML rendering. Another is that they can use one tool set, the Expression Suite, to create all the required assets and design their applications.

If the solution has many of these assets, design-time visual designer loading can be affected. Moving assets to a separate DLL solves the performance problem. Moving the assets also enables reuse across multiple solutions.

Visual Designers and Referenced Assemblies

An unfortunate side-effect of moving XAML resources and assets to a binary referenced assembly is that the Expression Blend and Visual Studio 2010 property editors do not list resources located in binary referenced assemblies. This means that you will not be able to pick a named resource from one of the resource pickers provided by the tools. Instead, you will need to type the name of the resource.

Silverlight Design-Time App.xaml Resources

Silverlight composite applications can be structured in several ways to allow run-time delayed loading of assemblies or to reduce initial .xap download size. One strategy that you can use is to create your main Silverlight application, and then create a satellite assembly for each module. When you add the satellite project assembly, you can choose one of the Silverlight application project templates or the Silverlight class library project template.

Choosing a Silverlight application project template for a satellite assembly provides a deployment benefit: the assembly will be packaged as a .xap file when built. However, there is a side effect that affects the visual designers when more than one Silverlight application is present in a single solution. The main Silverlight application will have its application resources merged in App.xaml. The problem is that the visual designer consumes resources exposed in App.xaml. Because there is more than one Silverlight application in the solution, the visual designer does not attempt to use resources from another Silverlight application; instead, it uses only those resources from the active Silverlight application.

Expression Blend 4 provides a solution to this problem. When Expression Blend detects this condition, it displays a dialog box that allows you to select a design time resource dictionary that will be used across all projects in the solution.

Visual Studio 2010 does not have this feature; therefore, satellite Silverlight application assemblies will not have the normal rich visual design-time experience unless you merge application-level resources in the local assembly. If you choose to merge application-level resources for a better visual design experience, you must remember to remove them before deploying your application.

GUIDELINES FOR CREATING DESIGNER FRIENDLY VIEWS

The following are some of the characteristics of a designer friendly (also known as a *blendable* or *tool-able*) application:

- It provides a productive editing experience by using the Visual Studio and Expression Blend designers.
- It is tooling-enabled. For example, it allows you to use the binding builder.
- It provides design-time sample data when required.
- It allows code to be executed at design time without causing unhandled exceptions.

The following actions are performed many times during an editing session. User code that is not designer friendly will cause one or more of these actions to fail, thus reducing the productivity and creativity of a developer or designer.

- Design surface actions:
  - Constructing objects
  - Loading objects
  - Setting property values
  - Performing design surface gestures
  - Using a control as the root element
  - Hosting a control inside another control

- Repeatedly opening, closing, and reopening a XAML file
- Rebuilding the project
- Reloading the designer
- Binding builder actions:
  - Discovering the **DataContext**
  - Listing the available data sources
  - Listing data source type properties
- Design-time sample data actions:
  - Using controls on the design surface to correctly display sample data

Coding for Design Time

To give you a rich design-time experience, the Visual Studio and Expression Blend designers instantiate objects and run code at design time. However, null reference exceptions caused by code that attempts to access a reference type before it has been instantiated cause a high percentage of loading failures and unnecessary design time exceptions.

The following table lists the main causes of poor design-time experiences. By avoiding the following issues and using the techniques to mitigate these problems, your design-time experience and productivity will be greatly enhanced, and the developer-to-designer workflow will be much smoother.

Avoid This in User Code	Visual Studio 2010	Blend 4
Spinning multiple threads at design time. For example, instantiating and starting a **Timer** in a constructor or **Loaded** event at design time.	∅	∅
Using controls that cause stack overflows at design time. Using controls that attempt to recursively load themselves.	∅	∅
Throwing null reference exceptions in converters or data template selectors.	∅	∅
Throwing null reference or other exceptions in constructors. These are caused by: • Using code that calls into the business or data layers to return data from a database or over the network at design time. • Attempting to resolve dependencies by using MEF, inversion of control (IoC), or a Service Locator before bootstrapping or container initialization code has run.	∅	∅
Throwing null reference or other exceptions inside the **Loaded** events of controls or user controls. This happens when you make assumptions about the state of the control that might be true at run time but are not true at design time.	∅	∅
Attempting to access the **Application** or **Application.Current** object at design time.	∅	∅
Consuming a **StaticResource** in WPF **UserControls**.	✓	∅
Creating very large projects.	✓	∅

Mitigating Problems in Design-Time User Code

A few defensive coding practices will eliminate most of the issues described in the preceding table. However, before you can mitigate problems in design-time user code, you must understand that your application controls and code are being executed by the designer in isolation, inside an uninitialized application domain. *Uninitialized* in this case means that the usual startup, bootstrapping, or initialization code has not run.

When your application executes at run time, the startup code in App.xaml.cs or App.xaml.vb is run. If you have code in there that the rest of your application depends on, this code will not have been executed at design time. If you have not anticipated this in your code, unwanted exceptions will occur. (This is why attempting to access the **Application** or **Application.Current** object in user code at design time will result in exceptions.) To mitigate these issues:

- Never assume that referenced objects will be instantiated in design-time code. In code that can be executed at design time, always perform a null check before accessing any reference object.

- If your code accesses the **Application** or **Application.Current** objects, perform a null reference check before accessing the object.

- If your constructors or **Loaded** event handlers need to run complex code or code that accesses a database or calls out to the network, consider one of the following solutions:

  - Wrap the code inside a check that determines if the code is running at design time by calling one of the below **System.ComponentModel DesignerProperties** methods:

    - **WPF**: DesignerProperties.GetIsInDesignMode
    - **Silverlight**: DesignerProperties.IsInDesignTool

  - Instead of running the code directly in the constructor or **Loaded** event handler, abstract the calls to a class behind an interface, and then use one of many techniques to resolve that dependency differently at design time, run time, and test time.

For example, instead of calling out to a data service directly to retrieve data, wrap the data service calls in a class that exposes the methods through an interface. Then, at design time, resolve the interface with a mock or design-time object.

Understanding when User Control Code Executes at Design-Time

Both Expression Blend and Visual Studio use mockups of the root object displayed in a designer pane. This is necessary to provide the required design experience. Because the root object is mocked, its constructor and **Loaded** event code are not executed at design time. However, the remaining controls in the scene are constructed normally, and their **Loaded** event is raised just like at run time.

In the following illustration, the root **Windows** constructor and **Loaded** event code will not be executed. The child user controls constructor and **Loaded** event code will be executed.

Relationship of a window and its child user controls

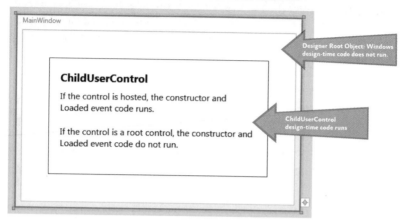

These concepts are important, especially if you are building composite applications or applications that are built dynamically at run time.

Most application views are coded and designed independently. Because they are designed independently, they are typically root objects in the designer, which means that their constructor and **Loaded** event code never executes.

However, if you take that same user control and place it on a design surface as a child of another control, the once isolated user control code is now executing at design time. If you have not followed the above practices for mitigating design-time code problems, the now hosted user control could cause designer load issues.

Design-Time Properties

The built-in "d:" design-time properties provide a smooth road to a successful design-time tooling experience.

The problem we need to solve is how to provide a shape to the Binding Builder tools at design-time. In this case, the shape is an instantiated **Type** that the Binding Builder can reflect on, and then list those properties for selection when building a binding.

Shape is also provided by design-time sample data. Sample data is covered in the section, "Guidelines for Design-Time Sample Data."

The following sections describe how to use the **d:DataContext** property and the **d:DesignInstance** markup extension.

The "d:" in the property and markup extension is the alias for the design namespace that the design properties are members of. The following are MSDN topics that cover the "d:" properties and markup extensions:

- "Design-Time Attributes in the WPF Designer"
- "Design-Time Attributes in the Silverlight Designer"

The "d:" properties and markup extensions cannot be created or extended in user code; they can only be used in XAML. The "d:" properties and markup extensions are not compiled into your application; they are used only by the Visual Studio and Expression Blend tooling.

d:DataContext Property

d:DataContext, specifies a design-time data context for a control and its children. When specifying **d:DataContext**, you should always provide the same shape to the design-time **DataContext** as the run-time **DataContext**.

If both a **DataContext** and a **d:DataContext** are specified for a control, the tooling will use the **d:DataContext**.

d:DesignInstance Markup Extension

If markup extensions are new to you, read the "Markup Extensions and WPF XAML" topic on MSDN.

d:DesignInstance returns an instantiated Type ("shape") that you will want to assign as the data source for binding to controls in the designer. The type does not need to be creatable to be used for establishing shape. The following table explains the **d:DesignInstance** markup extension properties.

Markup Extension Property	Definition
Type	Name of the Type that will be created. Type is the default parameter in the constructor.
IsDesignTimeCreatable	Can the specified Type be created? If false, a faux Type will be created rather than the real Type. The default is false.
CreateList	If true, returns a generic list of the specified Type. The default is false.

Typical d:DataContext Scenario

The following three code examples demonstrate a repeatable pattern for connecting and configuring views and view models and enabling the designer's tooling.

The **PersonViewModel** is a dependency that the **PersonView** has at run time. While the view model in the example is incredibly simple, real-world view models typically have one or more external dependencies that must be resolved, and those dependencies are typically injected into their constructor.

When the **PersonView** is constructed, its dependency **PersonViewModel** will be built and its dependencies resolved by MEF or a dependency injection container.

> **Note:** *If the view model has no external dependencies that need to be resolved, the view model can be instantiated in the view's XAML, and its **DataContext** and the **d:DataContext** are not required.*

```
C# PersonViewModel.cs
[Export]
public class PersonViewModel {

  public String FirstName { get; set; }
  public String LasName { get; set; }


}
```

```csharp
C# PersonView.xaml.cs
[Export]
public partial class PersonView : UserControl
{
 public PersonView()
 {
  InitializeComponent();
 }

 [Import]
 public PersonViewModel ViewModel
 {
  get { return this.DataContext as PersonViewModel; }
  set { this.DataContext = value; }
 }
}
```

This is a good pattern for connecting and configuring a view and view model; however, it leaves the view unaware of its **DataContext**'s shape (view model) at design time.

In the following XAML example, you can see the **d:DesignInstance** markup extension used on the **Grid** to return a faux instance of **PersonViewModel** that is then exposed by the **d:DataContext**. As a result, all child controls of the **Grid** will inherit the **d:DataContext**, enabling the designer tooling to discover and use its types and properties, resulting in a more productive design experience for developers and designers.

```xml
XAML PersonView.xaml
<UserControl
 xmlns:local="clr-namespace:WpfApplication1"
 x:Class="WpfApplication1.PersonView"
 xmlns="http://schemas.microsoft.com/winfx/2006/xaml/presentation"
 xmlns:x="http://schemas.microsoft.com/winfx/2006/xaml"
 xmlns:mc="http://schemas.openxmlformats.org/markup-compatibility/2006"
 xmlns:d="http://schemas.microsoft.com/expression/blend/2008"
 mc:Ignorable="d"
 d:DesignHeight="300" d:DesignWidth="300">

<Border BorderBrush="LightGray" BorderThickness="1" CornerRadius="10" Padding="10">

  <Grid d:DataContext="{d:DesignInstance local:PersonViewModel}">
   <Grid.RowDefinitions>
    <RowDefinition Height="Auto" />
    <RowDefinition Height="Auto" />
   </Grid.RowDefinitions>
   <Grid.ColumnDefinitions>
    <ColumnDefinition Width="100" />
    <ColumnDefinition Width="Auto" />
```

```
   </Grid.ColumnDefinitions>

   <Label Grid.Column="0" Grid.Row="0" Content="First Name" />
   <Label Grid.Column="0" Grid.Row="1" Content="Las Name" />

   <TextBox
     Grid.Column="1" Grid.Row="0" Width="150" MaxLength="50"
     HorizontalAlignment="Left" VerticalAlignment="Top"
     Text="{Binding Path=FirstName, Mode=TwoWay}" />
   <TextBox
     Grid.Column="1" Grid.Row="1" Width="150" MaxLength="50"
     HorizontalAlignment="Left" VerticalAlignment="Top"
     Text="{Binding Path=LasName, Mode=TwoWay}" />

   </Grid>
  </Border>

</UserControl>
```

Attached Property and ViewModel Locator Solution

*There are several alternative techniques for associating a view and view model available from the developer community. One of the challenges is that solutions that work well at run time do not always work at design time. One such solution is the use of attached properties and view model locators to assign a view's **DataContext**. The view model locator is required so that the view model can be constructed and have its dependencies resolved.*

*The problem with this solution is that you must also include the **d:DataContext** – **d:DesignInstance** combination because the visual designer tooling cannot be reflected in the results of the attached property the way that it can with the **d:DesignInstance**.*

Regardless of which technique you implement in your applications for resolving shape at design time, the most important goal is to be consistent throughout your application. Consistency will make application maintenance much easier and will lead to a successful designer-developer workflow.

GUIDELINES FOR DESIGN-TIME SAMPLE DATA

The WPF and Silverlight Designer team published an in-depth, scenario-based training article that discusses the use of sample data in WPF and Silverlight projects. The article, "Sample Data in the WPF and Silverlight Designer," is available on MSDN.

Using Design-Time Sample Data

If you use a visual design tool, such as Expression Blend or Visual Studio 2010, design-time sample data becomes very important. The views can be populated with data and images, making the design task easier and quicker to accomplish. This results in improved productivity and creativity.

Empty list controls that contain data templates will not be visible unless they are populated with data, making the task of editing the empty controls more time consuming because you need to run the application to see how the last edit will look at run time.

Sample Data Sources

You can use sample data from any of the following sources:

* Expression Blend XML sample data
* Expression Blend 4 and Visual Studio 2010 XAML sample data
* XAML resources
* Code

The data from each of these sources is described in the following subsections.

Expression Blend XML Sample Data

Expression Blend gives you the capability to quickly create an XML schema and populate a corresponding XML file. This is accomplished without any dependency on any project classes.

The purpose of this type of sample data is to let designers start their projects quickly, without waiting for a developer or before application classes are available for consumption.

While most sample data is supported in both the Expression Blend and Visual Studio designers, XML sample data is an Expression Blend feature and does not render in the Visual Studio designer.

Note: *XML sample data file is not compiled or added to the assembly when built; however, the XML schema is compiled into the built assembly.*

Expression Blend 4 and Visual Studio 2010 XAML Sample Data

Beginning in Expression Blend 4 and Visual Studio 2010, the **d:DesignData** markup extension was added to enable the design-time loading of XAML sample data.

Sample data XAML files contain XAML that instantiates one or more types and assigns values to properties.

d:DesignData has a **Source** property that takes a uniform resource identifier (URI) to the sample data XAML file located in the project. The **d:DesignData** markup extension loads the XAML file, parses it, and then returns an object graph. The object graph can be consumed by the **d:DataContext** property, **CollectionViewSource d:DesignSource** property, or **DomainDataSource d:DesignData** property.

One of the challenges that the **d:DesignData** markup extension overcomes is that it can create sample data for non-creatable user types. For example, WCF Rich Internet Application (RIA) Services entity–derived objects cannot be created in code. In addition, developers might have their own types that are not creatable, but would still like to have sample data for these types.

You can change how **d:DesignData** processes your sample data file by setting the **Build Action** property for the sample data file in Solution Explorer, as follows:

- **Build Action = DesignData** – faux types will be created.
- **Build Action = DesignDataWithDesignTimeCreatableTypes** – real types will be created.

When you use Expression Blend to create sample data for a class, it creates a XAML sample data file with the **Build Action** set to **DesignData**. If you require real types, open the solution in Visual Studio and change the **Build Action** for the sample data file to **DesignDataWithDesignTimeCreatableTypes**.

> **Note:** *In the next illustration, the* **Custom Tool** *property is empty. This is required for sample data to work correctly. By default, Expression Blend correctly sets this property to empty.*
>
> *When you use Visual Studio 2010 to add a sample data file, you typically add a new resource dictionary item and edit from there. In this case, you must set the* **Build Action** *and clear the* **Custom Tool** *property.*

Sample data file properties

Faux type sample data property settings

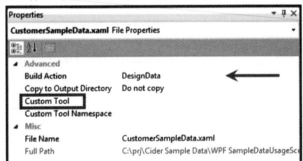

Real type sample data property settings

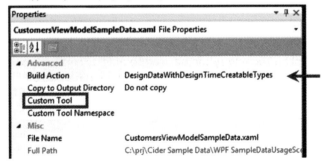

Expression Blend provides tooling for quickly creating and binding XAML sample data. The XAML sample data can be used and viewed in the Visual Studio 2010 designer, as shown in the following illustration.

Defining sample data in Expression Blend 4

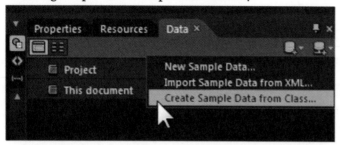

After it generates the sample data, the data will appear in the Data pane, as shown in the following illustration.

Data pan

You can then drag it onto the root element of the view, such as the **UserControl**, and have it set the **d:DataContext** property. You can also drop sample data collections onto items controls, and Expression Blend will configure the sample data and connect it to the control.

Note: *XAML sample data files are not compiled into or included in built assemblies.*

XAML Resource

You can create a resource in XAML that instantiates the desired types, and then bind that resource to a **DataContext** or list control.

This technique can be used to quickly create throw-away sample data that is used for editing a data template that would take longer to edit without the sample data.

Code

If you prefer creating sample data in code, you can write a class that exposes properties or methods that return sample data to their consumer. For example, you could write a **Customers** class that in its default empty constructor populated itself with multiple instances of the **Customer** class. Each of the **Customer** instances would have the appropriate property values set also.

One technique that you can use to consume the sample data class described previously is to use the **d:DataContext**, **d:DesignInstance** combination, ensuring that you set the **d:DesignInstance IsDesignTimeCreatable** property to **True**. The reason **IsDesign TimeCreatable** must be **True** is that you want the customers constructor to be executed so that the code to populate the class will run. If **Customers** is treated as a faux type, the **Customers** code will never be run and only the "shape" will be discoverable by the tooling.

The following XAML example instantiate the **Customers** class, and then sets it as the **d:DataContext**. Child controls of this **Grid** can consume data exposed by the **Customers** class.

XAML
```
<Grid d:DataContext="{d:DesignInstance local:Customers,
IsDesignTimeCreatable=True}">
```

UI Layout Key Decisions

When you begin a composite application project, there are some UI design decisions that you need to make that will be difficult to change later. Generally, these decisions are application-wide, and their consistency helps developers and designer productivity.

The following are the important UI layout decisions:
- Decide on application flow, and define regions accordingly.
- Decide which type of view loading each region will use.
- Decide if you want to use the Region Navigation APIs.
- Decide which UI Design pattern you will use (MVVM, presentation model, and so on).
- Decide on a sample data strategy.

More Information

For more information about extending the Prism Library, see "Extending Prism" on MSDN:

http://msdn.microsoft.com/en-us/library/gg430866(PandP.40).aspx.

For more information about commands, see "Commands" in Chapter 5, "Implementing the MVVM Pattern."

For more information about data binding, see "Data Binding" in Chapter 5, "Implementing the MVVM Pattern."

For more information about region navigation, see Chapter 8, "Navigation."

For more information about the guidelines discussed in this chapter, see the following:

- "Dependency Properties Overview" on MSDN:
  http://msdn.microsoft.com/en-us/library/ms752914.aspx.

- Data binding; see:
  - "Data Binding Overview" on MSDN:
    http://msdn.microsoft.com/en-us/library/ms742521.aspx.
  - "Data Binding in WPF" in *MSDN Magazine*:
    http://msdn.microsoft.com/en-us/magazine/cc163299.aspx.

- "Data Templating Overview" on MSDN:
  http://msdn.microsoft.com/en-us/library/ms742521.aspx.

- "Resources Overview" on MSDN:
  http://msdn.microsoft.com/en-us/library/ms750613.aspx.

- "UserControl Class" on MSDN:
  http://msdn.microsoft.com/en-us/library/system.windows.forms.usercontrol.aspx.

- "VisualStateManager Class" on MSDN:
  http://msdn.microsoft.com/en-us/library/cc626338(v=VS.95).aspx.

- "Customizing Controls For Windows Presentation Foundation" in *MSDN Magazine*:
  http://msdn.microsoft.com/en-us/magazine/cc163421.aspx.

- "ComponentResourceKey Markup Extension" MSDN topic:
  http://msdn.microsoft.com/en-us/library/ms753186.aspx.

- "Design-Time Attributes in the WPF Designer" on MSDN:
  http://msdn.microsoft.com/en-us/library/ee839627.aspx.

- "Design-Time Attributes in the Silverlight Designer" on MSDN:
  http://msdn.microsoft.com/en-us/library/ff602277(VS.95).aspx.

- "Markup Extensions and WPF XAML" on MSDN:
  http://msdn.microsoft.com/en-us/library/ms747254.aspx.

- "Using Custom Fonts in Silverlight":
  http://silverlight.net/learn/learnvideo.aspx?video=69800.

- "Sample Data in the WPF and Silverlight Designer" on MSDN:
  http://blogs.msdn.com/b/wpfsldesigner/archive/2010/06/30/sample-data-in-the-wpf-and-silverlight-designer.aspx.

- Learning the Visual Studio WPF and Silverlight Designer

This contains tutorials and articles on layout, resources, data binding, sample data, debugging data bindings, object data sources, and master-detail forms.

- http://blogs.msdn.com/b/wpfsldesigner/archive/2010/01/15/learn.aspx.

To access web resources more easily, see the online version of the bibliography on MSDN:

http://msdn.microsoft.com/en-us/library/gg405487(PandP.40).aspx.

8   Navigation

As the user interacts with a rich client application, the user interface (UI) will be continuously updated to reflect the current task and data that the user is working on. The UI may undergo considerable changes over time as the user interacts with and completes various tasks in the application. The process by which the application coordinates these UI changes is often referred to as *navigation*.

Typically, navigation means that certain controls on the UI are removed, while other controls are added. In other cases, navigation may mean that the visual state of one or more existing controls is updated—for example, some controls may be simply hidden or collapsed, while other controls are shown or expanded. Similarly, navigation may mean that the data being displayed by a control is updated to reflect the current state of the application—for example, in a master-detail scenario, the data displayed in the detail view will be updated based on the currently selected item in the master view. All of these scenarios can be considered navigation because the user interface is updated to reflect the user's current task and the application's current state.

Navigation in an application can result from the user's interaction with the UI (via mouse events or other UI gestures) or from the application itself as a result of internal logic-driven state changes. In some cases, navigation may involve very simple UI updates that require no custom application logic. In other cases, the application may implement complex logic to programmatically control navigation so that certain business rules are enforced—for example, the application might not allow the user to navigate away from a certain form without first verifying that the data entered is correct.

Implementing the required navigation behavior in a Windows Presentation Foundation (WPF) or Silverlight application can often be relatively straightforward because they both provide direct support for navigation. However, navigation can be more complex to implement in applications that use the Model-View-ViewModel (MVVM) pattern or in composite applications that use multiple loosely-coupled modules. Prism provides guidance on implementing navigation in these situations.

Navigation in Prism

Navigation is defined as the process by which the application coordinates changes to its UI as a result of the user's interaction with the application or as a result of internal application state changes.

UI updates can be accomplished by adding or removing elements from the application's visual tree, or by applying state changes to existing elements in the visual tree. WPF and Silverlight are very flexible platforms, and it is often possible to implement a particular navigation scenario by using either of these two approaches. However, the approach that will be most appropriate for your application depends on multiple factors.

Prism differentiates between the two styles of navigation described earlier. Navigation accomplished via state changes to existing controls in the visual tree is referred to as *state-based navigation*. Navigation accomplished via the addition or removal of elements from the visual tree is referred to as *view-based navigation*. Prism provides guidance on implementing both styles of navigation, focusing on situations in which the application is using the Model-View-ViewModel (MVVM) pattern to separate the UI (encapsulated in the view) from the presentation logic and data (encapsulated in the view model).

STATE-BASED NAVIGATION

In state-based navigation, the view that represents the UI is updated either through state changes in the view model or through the user's interaction within the view itself. In this style of navigation, instead of replacing the view with another view, the view's state is changed. Depending on how the view's state is changed, the updated UI may appear to the user like navigation.

This style of navigation is suitable in the following situations:

- The view needs to display the same data or functionality in different styles or formats.
- The view needs to change its layout or style based on the underlying state of the view model.
- The view needs to initiate limited modal or non-modal interaction with the user in the context of the view.

This style of navigation is not suitable for situations in which the UI has to present different data to the user or when the user has to perform a different task. In these situations, it is better to implement separate views (and view models) to represent the data or task, and then use view-based navigation to navigate between them, as described later in this chapter. Similarly, this style of navigation is not suitable if the UI state changes required to implement the navigation are overly complex because the view's definition can become large and difficult to maintain. In this case, it is better to implement the navigation across separate views by using view-based navigation.

The following sections describe the typical situations in which state-based navigation can be used. Each of these sections refers to the State-Based Navigation QuickStart, which implements an instant messaging–style application that allows users to manage and chat with their contacts.

Displaying Data in Different Formats or Styles

Your application may often need to present the same data to the user, but in different formats or styles. In this scenario, you can use a state-based navigation in the view to switch between the different styles, possibly using an animated transition between them. For example, the State-Based Navigation QuickStart allows users to choose how their contacts are displayed—either as a simple text list or as avatars (icons). Users can switch between these visual representations by clicking the **List** button or the **Avatars** button. The view provides an animated transition between the two representations, as shown in the following illustration.

Contact view navigation in the State-Based Navigation QuickStart

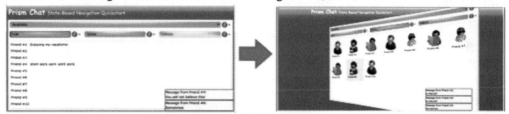

Because the view is presenting the same data in a different visual representation, the view model does not need to be involved in the navigation between representations. In this case, navigation is entirely handled within the view itself. This approach gives the UI designer the flexibility to design a compelling user experience without requiring changes to the application's code.

Microsoft Expression Blend behaviors provide a good way to implement this style of navigation in a view. The State-Based Navigation QuickStart application uses Expression Blend's **DataStateBehavior** and binds it to a radio button to switch between two visual states that are defined by the visual state manager: one button to show the contacts as a list and one button to show the contacts as icons. The following example demonstrates this usage.

```
XAML
<DataStateBehavior
        Binding="{Binding IsChecked, ElementName= ShowAsListButton}"
        TrueState="ShowAsList" FalseState="ShowAsIcons"/>
```

As the user clicks the **Contacts** or **Avatar** radio buttons, the visual state is toggled between the **ShowAsList** visual state and the **ShowAsIcons** visual state. The flip transition animation between these states is also defined by the visual state manager.

Another example of this style of navigation is shown in the State-Based Navigation QuickStart application when the user switches to the details views for the currently selected contact. The following illustration shows an example of this.

The Contact Details view in the State-Based Navigation QuickStart

Again, this can be easily implemented by using the Expression Blend **DataState Behavior;** however, this time the behavior is bound to the **ShowDetails** property on the view model, which uses a flip transition animation to toggle between the **ShowDetails** and **ShowContacts** visual states.

Reflecting Application State

Similarly, the view in an application may sometimes need to change its layout or style based on changes to an internal application state, which in turn is represented by a property on a view model. An example of this is shown in the State-Based Navigation QuickStart, where the user's connection status is represented on the **Chat** view model class by a **ConnectionStatus** property. As the user's connection status changes, the view is informed (via a property change notification event) allowing the view to visually represent the current connection state appropriately, as shown in the following illustration.

Connection state representation in the State-Based Navigation QuickStart

To implement this, the view defines a **DataStateBehavior** and binds it to the view model's **ConnectionStatus** property to toggle between the appropriate visual states, as shown in the following example.

```
XAML
<DataStateBehavior Binding="{Binding ConnectionStatus}"
        TrueState="Available" FalseState="Unavailable"/>
```

Note that the connection state can be changed by the user via the UI or by the application according to some internal logic or event. For example, the application might move to an unavailable state if the user does not interact with the view within a certain time period or when the user's calendar indicates that he or she is in a meeting. The State-Based Navigation QuickStart simulates this scenario by using a timer to switch the connection status randomly. When the connection status is changed, the property on the view model is updated, and the view is informed via a property changed event. The UI is then updated to reflect the current connection status.

All the preceding examples involve defining visual states in the view and switching between them as a result of the user's interaction with the view or via changes in properties defined by the view model. This approach allows the UI designer to implement navigation-like visual behavior in the view without requiring the view to be replaced or requiring any changes to the application's code. This approach is suitable when the view is required to render the same data in different styles or layouts. It is not suitable for situations in which the user is to be presented with different data or application functionality or when navigating to a different part of the application.

Interacting with the User

Frequently, an application will need to interact with the user in a limited way. In these situations, it is often more appropriate to interact with the user in the context of the current view, instead of navigating to a new view. For example, in the State-Based Navigation QuickStart, the user is able to send a message to a contact by clicking the **Send Message** button. The view then displays a pop-up window that allows the user to type the message, as shown in the following illustration. Because this interaction with the user is limited and logically takes place in the context of the parent view, it can be easily implemented as state-based navigation.

Using a pop-up window to interact with the user in the State-Based Navigation QuickStart

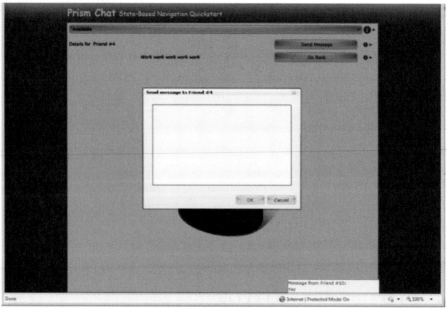

To implement this behavior, the State-Based Navigation QuickStart implements a **SendMessage** command, which is bound to the **Send Message** button. When this command is invoked, the view model interacts with the view to display the pop-up window. This is achieved by using the Interaction Request pattern described in Chapter 5, "Implementing the MVVM Pattern."

The following code example shows how the view in the State-Based Navigation QuickStart application responds to the **SendMessageRequest** interaction request object provided by the view model. When the request event is received, the **SendMessageChild Window** is displayed as a popup window.

```XAML
<prism:InteractionRequestTrigger SourceObject="{Binding SendMessageRequest}">
    <prism:PopupChildWindowAction>
        <prism:PopupChildWindowAction.ChildWindow>
            <vs:SendMessageChildWindow />
        </prism:PopupChildWindowAction.ChildWindow>
    </prism:PopupChildWindowAction>
</prism:InteractionRequestTrigger>
```

VIEW-BASED NAVIGATION

Although state-based navigation can be useful for the scenarios outlined earlier, navigation in an application will most often be accomplished by replacing one view on the application's UI with another. In Prism, this style of navigation is referred to as view-based navigation.

Depending on the requirements of the application, this process can be fairly complex and require careful coordination. The following are common challenges that you may have to address when implementing view-based navigation:

- The target of the navigation (the container or host control of the views to be added or removed) may handle navigation differently as views are added or removed from it, or it may visually represent navigation in different ways. In many cases, the navigation target will be a simple **Frame** or **ContentControl**, and navigated views will simply be displayed in these controls. However, there are many scenarios where the target for the navigation operation is a different type of container control, such as a **TabControl** or a **ListBox** control. In these cases, navigation might require the activation or selection of an existing view or the addition of a new view in a specific way.

- Often, the application will also have to define how the view to be navigated to is identified. For example, in a web application, the page to be navigated to is often directly identified by a Uniform Resource Identifier (URI). In a client application, the view can be identified by type name, resource location, or in a variety of other different ways. In a composite application, which is composed from loosely coupled modules, the views will often be defined in separate modules. Individual views will need to be identified in a way that does not introduce tight coupling and dependencies between modules.

- After the view is identified, the process by which the new view is instantiated and initialized has to be carefully coordinated. This can be particularly important when you use the MVVM pattern. In this case, the view and view model may need to be instantiated and associated with each other via the view's data context during the navigation operation. If the application uses a dependency injection container, such as the Unity Application Block (Unity) or the Managed Extensibility Framework (MEF), you may need to use a specific construction mechanism to instantiate the views and/or view models (and other dependent classes).

- The MVVM pattern provides a separation between the application's UI and its presentation and business logic. However, the navigational behavior of the application will often span UI and presentation logic parts of the application. Frequently, the user will initiate navigation from inside the view, and the view will be updated as a result of that navigation, but navigation will also need to be initiated or coordinated from within the view model. The ability to cleanly separate the navigational behavior of the application across the view and view model is an important aspect to consider.

- Additionally, an application will often need to pass parameters or context to the view so that it can be initialized properly. For example, if the user navigates to a view to update the details of a specific customer, the customer's ID or data will have to be passed to the view so that it can display the correct information.

- Many applications must carefully coordinate navigation to ensure that certain business rules are followed. For example, users may be prompted before navigating away from a view so that they can correct any invalid data or be prompted to submit or discard any data changes that they have made in that view. This process requires careful coordination between the previous view and the new view.

- Lastly, most modern applications allow the user to easily navigate backward (or forward) to previously displayed views. Similarly, some applications implement their workflows by using a sequence of views or forms and allow users to navigate forward or backward through them, adding or updating data as they go, before completing the task and submitting all their changes at one time. These scenarios require some kind of journaling (or history) mechanism so that the sequence of navigation can be stored, replayed, or pre-defined.

Prism provides support and guidance for these challenges by extending its region mechanism to support navigation. The following sections provide a brief summary of Prism regions and describe how they have been extended to support view-based navigation.

Prism Region Overview

Prism regions are designed to support the development of composite applications (that is, applications that consist of multiple modules) by allowing the application's overall UI to be constructed in a loosely-coupled way. Regions allow views defied in a module to be displayed on the application's UI without requiring the module to have explicit knowledge of the application's overall UI structure. They allow the layout of the application's UI to be changed easily, thereby allowing the UI designer to choose the most appropriate UI design and layout for the application without requiring changes in the modules themselves.

Essentially, Prism regions are named placeholders that views can be displayed in. Any control in the application's UI can be a declared a region by simply adding a **RegionName** attached property to it, as shown in the following example.

XAML
```xaml
<ContentControl prism:RegionManager.RegionName="MainRegion" ... />
```

For each control specified as a region, Prism creates a **Region** object to represent the region and a **RegionAdapter** object, which manages the placement and activation of views in the specified control. The Prism Library provides **RegionAdapter** implementations for most of the common Silverlight and WPF controls. You can create a custom **RegionAdapter** to support additional controls or when you need to define a custom behavior. The **RegionManager** class provides access to the **Region** objects in the application.

In many cases, the region control will be a simple control, such as a **ContentControl**, that can display one view at a time. In other cases, the **Region** control will be a control that is able to display multiple views at the same time, such as a **TabControl** or a **ListBox** control.

The region adapter manages a list of views in the associated region. One or more of these views will be displayed in the region control according to its defined layout strategy. Views can be assigned a name that can be used to retrieve that view later on. The region adapter manages the active state of the views in the region. The active view is the view that is the selected or top-most view—for example, in a **TabControl**, the active view is the one displayed in the selected tab; in a **ContentControl**, the active view is the view that is currently displayed as the control's content.

Note: *The active state of a view is important to consider during navigation. Frequently, you will want the active view to participate in navigation so that it can save data before the user navigates away from it, or so that it can confirm or cancel the navigation operation.*

Previous versions of Prism allowed views to be displayed in a region in two ways. The first, called *view injection*, allows views to be programmatically displayed in a region. This approach is useful for dynamic content, where the view to be displayed in the region changes frequently, according to the application's presentation logic.

View injection is supported by using the **Add** method on the **Region** class. The following code example shows how you can use the **RegionManager** class to obtain a reference to a **Region** object, and then programmatically add a view to it. In this example, a dependency injection container is used to create the view.

C#
```csharp
IRegionManager regionManager = ...;
IRegion mainRegion = regionManager.Regions["MainRegion"];
InboxView view = this.container.Resolve<InboxView>();
mainRegion.Add(view);
```

The second method, called *view discovery*, allows a module to register a view type for a region name. Whenever a region with the specified name is displayed, an instance of the specified view will be created automatically and displayed in the region. This approach is useful for relatively static content, where the view to be displayed in a region does not change.

View discovery is supported by using the **RegisterViewWithRegion** method on the **RegionManager** class. This method allows you to specify a callback method that will be called when the named region is shown. The following code example shows how you can use the dependency injection container to create a view when the main region is first shown.

```C#
IRegionManager regionManager = ...;
regionManager.RegisterViewWithRegion("MainRegion", () =>
                    container.Resolve<InboxView>());
```

For a detailed overview of Prism's region support and information about how to use regions, view injection, and discovery to compose the application's UI, see Chapter 7, "Composing the User Interface." The rest of this chapter describes how regions have been extended to support view-based navigation, and how this addresses the various challenges described earlier.

Basic Region Navigation

Both view injection and view discovery can be considered to be limited forms of navigation—view injection is a form of explicit, programmatic navigation, and view discovery is a form of implicit or deferred navigation. However, in Prism 4.0, regions have been extended to support a more general notion of navigation based on URIs and an extensible navigation mechanism.

Navigation within a region means that a new view is to be displayed in that region. The view to be displayed is identified via a URI, which, by default, refers to the name of the view to be created. You can programmatically initiate navigation by using the **RequestNavigate** method defined by the **INavigateAsync** interface.

> **Note:** *Despite its name, the **INavigateAsync** interface does not support asynchronous navigation that's carried out on a separate background thread. Instead, the **INavigate Async** interface gives you the ability to perform pseudo-asynchronous navigation. The **RequestNavigate** method may return synchronously following the completion of navigation operation, or it may return while a navigation operation is still pending, as in the case where the user needs to confirm the navigation. By allowing you to specify callbacks and continuations during navigation, Prism provides a mechanism to enable these scenarios without requiring the complexity of navigating on a background thread.*

The **INavigateAsync** interface is implemented by the **Region** class, allowing you to initiate navigation within the region.

```C#
IRegion mainRegion = ...;
mainRegion.RequestNavigate(new Uri("InboxView", UriKind.Relative));
```

You can also call the **RequestNavigate** method on the **RegionManager**, which allows you to specify the name of the region to be navigated. This method obtains a reference to the specified region and then calls the **RequestNavigate** method, as shown in the preceding code example.

```C#
IRegionManager regionManager = ...;
regionManager.RequestNavigate("MainRegion",
                            new Uri("InboxView", UriKind.Relative));
```

By default, the navigation URI specifies the name of a view that is registered in the container. The code below illustrates the relationship of the view registration name in the container and the use of the name when navigating the view when using the Unity container.

```C#
container.RegisterType<object, InboxView>("InboxView");
regionManager.Regions[Constants.MainRegion].RequestNavigate(new Uri("InboxView",
UriKind.Relative));
```

Important: *When the region navigation service creates a view, it requests a type of* **Object** *from the container with a name that matches the one supplied in the navigation URI. Various containers provide different registration mechanisms to support this. For instance, in Unity you will need to register your views against the* **Object** *type, map it to your view type, and provide a name that matches the one used in the navigation URI.*

In MEF, it is implemented differently and only the contract name is used. Therefore, as long as the view is exported with a contract name that matches the name in the URI request, the view can be successfully constructed.

Example: When using Unity to register your view for navigation:

Do not use:

```
container.RegisterType<InboxView>("InboxView");
```

Instead you must use:

```
container.RegisterType<object,InboxView>("InboxView");
```

Note: *The name used to register the view in the container and to navigate does not have to be associated with the type name; any string will suffice. For example, you can use the full type name instead of a quoted string:*

```
typeof(InboxView).FullName
```

If you use MEF, you can simply export the view type with the specified name, as shown in the following code example.

```C#
[Export("InboxView")]
public partial class InboxView : UserControl
```

During navigation, the specified view is instantiated, via the container or MEF, along with its corresponding view model and other dependent services and components. After the view is instantiated, it is added to the specified region and activated (activation is described in more detail later in this chapter).

Note: *The preceding description illustrates view-first navigation, where the URI refers to the name of the view type, as it is exported or registered with the container. With view-first navigation, the dependent view model is created as a dependency of the view. An alternative approach is to use view model–first navigation, where the navigation URI refers to the name of the view model type, as it is exported or registered with the container. View model–first navigation is useful when the view is defined as a data template, or when you want your navigation scheme to be defined independently of the views.*

The **RequestNavigate** method also allows you to specify a callback method, or a delegate, which will be called when navigation is complete, as shown in the following example.

```C#
private void SelectedEmployeeChanged(object sender, EventArgs e)
{
    ...

    regionManager.RequestNavigate(RegionNames.TabRegion,
                    "EmployeeDetails", NavigationCompleted);
}
private void NavigationCompleted(NavigationResult result)
{
    ...
}
```

The **NavigationResult** class defines properties that provide information about the navigation operation. The **Result** property indicates whether or not navigation succeeded. If navigation failed, the **Error** property provides a reference to any exception that was thrown during navigation. The **Context** property provides access to the navigation URI and any parameters it contains, and a reference to the navigation service that coordinated the navigation operation.

View and View Model Participation in Navigation

Frequently, you will want the views and view models in your application to participate in navigation. The **INavigationAware** interface enables this. You can implement this interface on the view or (more commonly) the view model. By implementing this interface, your view or view model can choose to participate in the navigation process.

Note: *In the description that follows, although a reference is made to calls to this interface during navigation between views, the **INavigationAware** interface will be called during navigation whether it is implemented by the view or by the view model.*

*During navigation, Prism checks to see whether the view implements the **INavigation Aware** interface, and if it does, it calls the required methods during navigation. Prism also checks to see whether the object set as the view's **DataContext** implements this interface, and if it does, it calls the required methods during navigation.*

This interface allows the view or view model to participate in a navigation operation. The **INavigationAware** interface defines three methods, as shown in the following example.

```C#
public interface INavigationAware
{
    bool IsNavigationTarget(NavigationContext navigationContext);
    void OnNavigatedTo(NavigationContext navigationContext);
    void OnNavigatedFrom(NavigationContext navigationContext);
}
```

The **IsNavigationTarget** method allows an existing (displayed) view or view model to indicate whether it is able to handle the navigation request. This is useful in cases in which you can reuse an existing view to handle the navigation operation or when you navigate to a view that already exists. For example, a view displaying customer information can be updated to display a different customer's information. For more information about using this method, see the section, "Navigating to Existing Views," later in this chapter.

The **OnNavigatedFrom** and **OnNavigatedTo** methods are called during a navigation operation. If the currently active view in the region implements this interface (or its view model), its **OnNavigatedFrom** method is called before navigation takes place. The **OnNavigatedFrom** method allows the previous view to save any state or to prepare for its deactivation or removal from the UI, for example, to save any changes that the user has made to a web service or database.

If the newly created view implements this interface (or its view model), its **On NavigatedTo** method is called after navigation is complete. The **OnNavigatedTo** method allows the newly displayed view to initialize itself, potentially using any parameters passed to it on the navigation URI. For more information, see the next section, "Passing Parameters During Navigation."

After the new view is instantiated, initialized, and added to the target region, it becomes the active view, and the previous view is deactivated. In some situations, you may want the deactivated view to be removed from the region. Prism provides the **IRegion MemberLifetime** interface, which allows you to control the lifetime of views in regions by letting you specify whether deactivated views are to be removed from the region or simply marked as deactivated. The following code example uses the **IRegionMember Lifetime** interface used to determine if a view should be removed.

```C#
public class EmployeeDetailsViewModel : IRegionMemberLifetime
{
    public bool KeepAlive
    {
        get { return true; }
    }
}
```

The **IRegionMemberLifetime** interface defines a single read-only property, **Keep Alive**. If this property returns **false**, the view is removed from the region when it is deactivated. Because the region no longer has a reference to the view, it then becomes eligible for garbage collection (unless some other component in your application maintains a reference to it). You can implement this interface in your view or your view model classes. Although the **IRegionMemberLifetime** interface is primarily intended to allow you to manage the lifetime of views in regions during activation and deactivation, the **KeepAlive** property is also evaluated during navigation after the new view is activated in the target region.

Note: *Regions that can display multiple views, such as those that use an* **ItemsControl** *or a* **TabControl***, will display both inactive and active views. Removal of an inactive view from these types of regions will result in the view being removed from the UI.*

Passing Parameters During Navigation

To implement the required navigational behavior in your application, you will often need to specify additional data during a navigation request than just the target view name. The **NavigationContext** object provides access to the navigation URI and to any parameters that were specified in it. You can access the **NavigationContext** from within the **Is NavigationTarget**, **OnNavigatedFrom**, and **OnNavigatedTo** methods.

Prism provides the **UriQuery** class to help specify and retrieve navigation parameters. You can use this class to add navigation parameters to the navigation URI before you initiate navigation and to access individual parameters during navigation. The **UriQuery** class maintains a list of name-value pairs, one for each parameter.

The following code example shows how to add individual parameters to the **UriQuery** instance so that it can be appended to the navigation URI.

```csharp
C#
Employee employee = Employees.CurrentItem as Employee;
if (employee != null)
{
    UriQuery query = new UriQuery();
    query.Add("ID", employee.Id);
    _regionManager.RequestNavigate(RegionNames.TabRegion,
        new Uri("EmployeeDetailsView" + query.ToString(), UriKind.Relative));
}
```

You can retrieve the navigation parameters by using the **Parameters** property on the **NavigationContext** object, as shown in the following example. This property returns an instance of the **UriQuery** class, which provides an indexer property to allow easy access to individual parameters.

```csharp
C#
public void OnNavigatedTo(NavigationContext navigationContext)
{
    string id = navigationContext.Parameters["ID"];
}
```

Navigating to Existing Views

It may be more appropriate for the views in your application to be reused, updated, or activated during navigation, instead of being replaced by a new view. This is often the case when you are navigating to the same type of view but need to display different information or state to the user, or when the appropriate view is already available on the UI but needs to be activated (that is, selected or made top-most).

For an example of the first scenario, imagine that your application allows the user to edit customer records by using the **EditCustomer** view, and the user is currently using that view to edit customer ID 123. If the customer decides to edit the customer record for customer ID 456, the user can simply navigate to the **EditCustomer** view and enter the new customer ID. The **EditCustomer** view can then retrieve the data for the new customer and update its UI accordingly.

An example of the second scenario is where the application allows the user to edit more than one customer record at a time. In this case, the application displays multiple **EditCustomer** view instances in a tab control—for example, one for customer ID 123 and another for customer ID 456. When the user navigates to the **EditCustomer** view and enters customer ID 456, the corresponding view will be activated (that is, its corresponding tab will be selected). If the user navigates to the **EditCustomer** view and enters customer ID 789, a new instance will be created and displayed in the tab control.

The ability to navigate to an existing view is useful for a variety of reasons. It is often more efficient to update an existing view instead of replacing it with a new instance of the same type. Similarly, activating an existing view, instead of creating a duplicate view, provides a more consistent user experience. In addition, the ability to handle these situations seamlessly without requiring much custom code means that the application is easier to develop and maintain.

Prism supports the two existing view scenarios described here via the **IsNavigation Target** method on the **INavigationAware** interface. This method is called during navigation on all views in a region that are of the same type as the target view. In the preceding examples, the target type of the view is the **EditCustomer** view; therefore, the **IsNavigation Target** method will be called on all existing **EditCustomer** view instances currently in the region. Prism determines the target type from the view URI, which it assumes is the short type name of the target type.

> **Note:** *For Prism to determine the type of the target view, the view's name in the navigation URI should be the same as the actual target type's short type name. For example, if your view is implemented by the* **MyApp.Views.EmployeeDetailsView** *class, the view name specified in the navigation URI should be* **EmployeeDetailsView**. *This is the default behavior provided by Prism. You can customize this behavior by implementing a custom content loader class. You can do this by implementing the* **IRegionNavigation- ContentLoader** *interface or by deriving from the* **RegionNavigationContentLoader** *class.*

The implementation of the **IsNavigationTarget** method can use the **Navigation Context** parameter to determine whether it can handle the navigation request, as shown in the next code example. The **NavigationContext** object provides access to the navigation

URI and the navigation parameters. In the preceding examples, the implementation of this method in the **EditCustomer** view model compares the current customer ID to the ID specified in the navigation request, and it returns **true** if they match.

```C#
public bool IsNavigationTarget(NavigationContext navigationContext)
{
    string id = navigationContext.Parameters["ID"];
    return _currentCustomer.Id.Equals(id);
}
```

If the **IsNavigationTarget** method always returns **true**, regardless of the navigation parameters, that view instance will always be reused. This allows you to make sure that only one view of a particular type will be displayed in a particular region.

Confirming or Canceling Navigation

You will often find that you will need to interact with the user during a navigation operation, so that the user can confirm or cancel navigation. In many applications, for example, the user might try to navigate while in the middle of entering or editing data. In these situations, you may want to ask the user whether he or she wants to save or discard the data that has been entered before navigating away from the page, or whether the user wants to cancel the navigation operation altogether. Prism supports these scenarios via the **IConfirmNavigationRequest** interface.

The **IConfirmNavigationRequest** interface derives from the **INavigationAware** interface and adds the **ConfirmNavigationRequest** method. By implementing this interface on your view or view model class, you allow them to participate in the navigation sequence in a way that allows them to interact with the user so that the user can confirm or cancel the navigation. You will often use an **Interaction Request** object, as described in "Using Interaction Request Objects" in Chapter 6, "Advanced MVVM Scenarios," to display a confirmation pop-up window.

Note: *The* **ConfirmNavigationRequest** *method is called on the active view or view model, similar to the* **OnNavigatedFrom** *method described earlier.*

The **ConfirmNavigationRequest** method provides two parameters: a reference to the current navigation context, as described earlier, and a callback method that you can call when you want navigation to continue. For this reason, the callback is known as a continuation callback. You can store a reference to the continuation callback so the application can call it after it finishes interacting with the user. If your application interacts with the user through an **Interaction Request** object, you can chain the call to the continuation callback to the callback from the interaction request. The following diagram illustrates the overall process.

Using an InteractionRequest object to confirm navigation

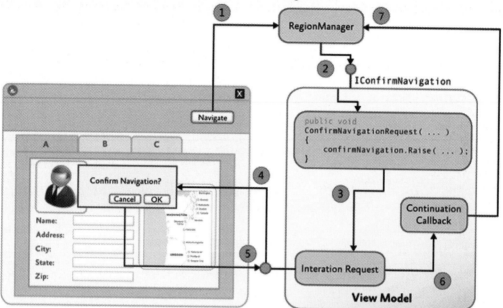

The following steps summarize the process of using an **InteractionRequest** object to confirm navigation:

1. Navigation operation is initiated via a **RequestNavigate** call.

2. If the view or view model implements **IConfirmNavigation**, call **Confirm NavigationRequest**.

3. The view model raises the interaction request event.

4. The view displays the confirmation pop-up window and awaits the user's response.

5. The interaction request callback is invoked when the user closes the pop-up window.

6. Continuation callback is invoked to continue or cancel the pending navigation operation.

7. The navigation operation is completed or canceled.

To illustrate this, look at the View-Switching Navigation QuickStart. The QuickStart application enables the user use the **ComposeEmailView** and **ComposeEmailView Model** classes to compose a new email message. The view model class implements the **IConfirmNavigation** interface. If the user navigates, such as by clicking the **Calendar** button, when he or she is composing email, the **ConfirmNavigationRequest** method will be called so that the view model can confirm the navigation with the user. To support this, the view model class defines an interaction request, as shown in the following code example.

C#
```csharp
public class ComposeEmailViewModel : NotificationObject, IConfirmNavigationRequest
{
    private readonly InteractionRequest<Confirmation>
                                        confirmExitInteractionRequest;

    public ComposeEmailViewModel(IEmailService emailService)
    {
        this.confirmExitInteractionRequest = new
                                InteractionRequest<Confirmation>();
    }

    public IInteractionRequest ConfirmExitInteractionRequest
    {
        get { return this.confirmExitInteractionRequest; }
    }
}
```

In the **ComposeEmailVew** class, an interaction request trigger is defined, and data is bound to the **ConfirmExitInteractionRequest** property on the view model. When the interaction request is made, a simple pop-up window will be displayed to the user, as shown in the following example.

XAML
```xml
<UserControl.Resources>
    <DataTemplate x:Name="ConfirmExitDialogTemplate">
        <TextBlock HorizontalAlignment="Center" VerticalAlignment="Center"
                Text="{Binding}"/>
    </DataTemplate>
</UserControl.Resources>

<Grid x:Name="LayoutRoot" Background="White">
    <ei:Interaction.Triggers>
        <prism:InteractionRequestTrigger
                SourceObject="{Binding ConfirmExitInteractionRequest}">
            <prism:PopupChildWindowAction
                ContentTemplate="{StaticResource ConfirmExitDialogTemplate}"/>
        </prism:InteractionRequestTrigger>
    </ei:Interaction.Triggers>
...
```

The **ConfirmNavigationRequest** method on the **ComposeEmailVewModel** class is called if the user attempts to navigate while an email is being composed. The implementation of this method invokes the interaction request defined earlier so that the user can confirm or cancel the navigation operation. The following example shows the use of the **ConfirmNavigationRequest** method.

```C#
void IConfirmNavigationRequest.ConfirmNavigationRequest(
        NavigationContext navigationContext, Action<bool> continuationCallback)
{
    this.confirmExitInteractionRequest.Raise(
            new Confirmation {Content = "...", Title = "..."},
            c => {continuationCallback(c.Confirmed);});
}
```

The callback for the interaction request is called when the user clicks a button in the confirmation pop-up window to confirm or cancel the operation. This callback simply calls the continuation callback, passing the value of the **Confirmed** flag, and causing the navigation to continue or be canceled.

> **Note:** *After the interaction request event is raised, the* **ConfirmNavigationRequest** *method immediately returns so that the user can continue to interact with the application UI. When the user clicks the* **OK** *or* **Cancel** *buttons in the pop-up window, the callback method of the interaction request is made, which in turn calls the continuation callback to complete the navigation operation. All the methods are called on the UI thread. This technique requires no background threads.*

By using this mechanism, you can control whether the navigation request is carried out immediately or deferred pending an interaction with the user or some other asynchronous interaction (for example, as a result of a web service request). To enable navigation to proceed, you can simply call the continuation callback method, passing **true** to indicate that it can continue, as shown in the following example. Similarly, you can pass **false** to indicate that the navigation should be canceled.

```C#
void IConfirmNavigationRequest.ConfirmNavigationRequest(
        NavigationContext navigationContext, Action<bool> continuationCallback)
{
    continuationCallback(true);
}
```

If you want to defer navigation, you can store a reference to the continuation callback that you can then call when the interaction with the user (or web service) is completed. The navigation operation will be pending until you call the continuation callback.

If the user initiates another navigation operation while this operation is pending, the original navigation request will be canceled. In this case, calling the continuation callback has no effect because the navigation operation to which it relates no longer exists. Similarly, if you decide not to call the continuation callback, the navigation operation will be pending until it is replaced by a new navigation operation.

Using the Navigation Journal

The **NavigationContext** class provides access to the region navigation service, which is responsible for coordinating the sequence of operations during navigation in a region. It provides access to the region in which navigation is taking place and to the navigation journal associated with that region. The region navigation service implements the **IRegion NavigationService**, which is defined as shown in the following example.

```C#
public interface IRegionNavigationService : INavigateAsync
{
    IRegion Region {get; set;}
    IRegionNavigationJournal Journal {get;}
    event EventHandler<RegionNavigationEventArgs> Navigating;
    event EventHandler<RegionNavigationEventArgs> Navigated;
    event EventHandler<RegionNavigationFailedEventArgs> NavigationFailed;
}
```

Because the region navigation service implements the **INavigateAsync** interface, you can initiate navigation in the parent region by calling its **RequestNavigate** method. The **Navigating** event is raised when a navigation operation is initiated. The **Navigated** event is raised when navigation in a region is completed. The **NavigationFailed** is raised if an error was encountered during navigation.

The **Journal** property provides access to the navigation journal associated with the region. The navigation journal implements the **IRegionNavigationJournal** interface, which is defined as shown in the following example.

```C#
public interface IRegionNavigationJournal
{
    bool CanGoBack {get;}
    bool CanGoForward {get;}
    IRegionNavigationJournalEntry CurrentEntry {get;}
    INavigateAsync NavigationTarget {get; set;}
    void Clear();
    void GoBack();
    void GoForward();
    void RecordNavigation(IRegionNavigationJournalEntry entry);
}
```

During navigation, you can use an **OnNavigatedTo** method call to obtain a reference to the region navigation service and store it in a view. By default, Prism provides a simple stack-based journal that allows you to navigate forward or backward within a region.

You can use the navigation journal to allow the user to navigate from inside the view itself. In the following example, the view model implements a **GoBack** command, which uses the navigation journal within the host region. Therefore, the view can display a **Back** button that allows the user to easily navigate back to the previous view in the region. Similarly, you can implement a **GoForward** command to implement a wizard style workflow.

```csharp
C#
public class EmployeeDetailsViewModel : INavigationAware
{
    ...
    private IRegionNavigationService navigationService;

    public void OnNavigatedTo(NavigationContext navigationContext)
    {
        navigationService = navigationContext.NavigationService;
    }

    public DelegateCommand<object> GoBackCommand {get; private set;}

    private void GoBack(object commandArg)
    {
        if (navigationService.Journal.CanGoBack)
        {
            navigationService.Journal.GoBack();
        }
    }

    private bool CanGoBack(object commandArg)
    {
        return navigationService.Journal.CanGoBack;
    }
}
```

You can implement a custom journal for a region if you need to implement a specific workflow pattern in that region.

Note: *The navigation journal can only be used for region-based navigation operations that are coordinated by the region navigation service. If you use view discovery or view injection to implement navigation in a region, the navigation journal will not be updated during navigation and cannot be used to navigate forward or backward within that region.*

Using the WPF and Silverlight Navigation Frameworks

Prism region navigation was designed to address a wide range of common scenarios and challenges that you may face when implementing navigation in a loosely-coupled, modular application that uses the MVVM pattern and a dependency injection container, such as Unity, or the Managed Extensibility Framework (MEF). It also was designed to support navigation confirmation and cancelation, navigation to existing views, navigation parameters, and navigation journaling.

By supporting navigation within Prism regions, it also supports navigation within a wide range of layout controls, as well as the ability to change the layout of the application's UI without affecting its navigation structure. In addition, it supports pseudo-synchronous navigation, which allows for rich user interaction during navigation.

However, the Prism region navigation was not designed to replace the Silverlight navigation framework (introduced in Silverlight 3.0) or the WPF navigation framework. Instead, Prism region navigation was designed to be used side-by-side with the Silverlight and WPF navigation frameworks.

The Silverlight navigation framework provides support for deep linking, browser integration, and navigation URI mapping. Navigation takes place with a **Frame** control. The **Frame** can optionally display a navigation bar that allows the user to navigate forward or backward through the views displayed in the **Frame**. It is common to use the Silverlight navigation framework to implement top-level navigation in the application's shell and then to use Prism regions to implement navigation in the rest of the application. In this way, your application can support deep linking and be integrated with the browser's journal and address bar, but it still takes advantage of Prism region navigation.

By default, the Silverlight navigation framework does not directly support the use of the MVVM pattern or the user of a dependency injection container or MEF. However, you can implement a custom content loader—the component used by the frame to load the content associated with a specific URI—which can instantiate and initialize the view and its associated view model as appropriate and display it in the **Frame**. You can also implement a custom content loader to more fully integrate Silverlight's navigation framework with the Prism region navigation mechanisms.

The WPF navigation framework is not as extensible as the one in Silverlight; therefore, it is difficult for it to support the MVVM pattern and dependency injection. It is also based on a **Frame** control that provides similar functionality in terms of journaling and navigation UI. You can use the WPF navigation framework alongside Prism region navigation, although it might be easier and more flexible to implement navigation by using only Prism regions.

The Region Navigation Sequence

The following illustration provides an overview of the sequence of operations during a navigation operation. It is provided for reference so that you can see how the various elements of the Prism region navigation work together during a navigation request.

Prism region navigation sequence

Async Navigation Request
INavigateAsync.Request.Navigate

- - - -Error during- - - -
Navigation Request

If the currently active view (or its view model) implements the **IConfirmNavigationRequest** interface, then the **ConfirmationNavigationRequest** method is called to determine whether the currently active view wishes to confirm navigation.

If callback was provided, invoke **INavigateASync NavigationRequest** callback.

Region.NavigationService raises **IRegionNavigationService NavigationFailed** event.

Yes

If the currently active view (or its view model) implements the **INavigationAware** interface, then the **OnNavigatedFrom** method is called for each active view.

For each view of the correct type that implements **INavigationAware**, the **IsNavigationTarget** method is called to determine whether the view (or its view model) instance can handle the specific navigation request. If this method returns true, then the view is activated.

No → Stop

Can't Locate

Located

Using the service locator, the Navigation service asks the registered container to create the new view / view model.

Unity: View type must be registered with a container.

MEF: View must be exported.

Navigation service adds the constructed object to the region and activates it.

Navigation service activates target object.

If the previously active view (or its view model) implements the **IRegionMemeberLifeTime** interface, then the region manager calls the **KeepAlive** method to determine whether the previously active view should be removed from the region.

Region Navigation service raises the **IRegionNavigationService** navigated event.

If the target view (or its view model) implements the **INavigationAware** interface, then the **OnNavigatedTo** method is called to allow the view to intialize itself.

If the navigation callback was specified in the navigation request, it is invoked, passing in a **NavigationResult** object.

Region Navigation service raises the **IRegionNavigationService** navigated event.

Navigation complete.

More Information

For more information about Prism regions, see Chapter 7, "Composing the User Interface."

For more information about the MVVM pattern and Interaction Request pattern, see Chapter 5, "Implementing the MVVM Pattern" and Chapter 6, "Advanced MVVM Scenarios."

For more information about the **Interaction Request** object, see "Using Interaction Request Objects" in Chapter 6, "Advanced MVVM Scenarios."

For more information about the Visual State Manager, see "VisualStateManager Class" on MSDN:
    http://msdn.microsoft.com/en-us/library/cc626338(v=VS.95).aspx.

For more information about using Microsoft Expression Blend behaviors, see "Working with built-in behaviors" on MSDN:
    http://msdn.microsoft.com/en-us/library/ff724013(v=Expression.40).aspx.

For more information about creating custom behaviors with Microsoft Expression Blend, see "Creating Custom Behaviors" on MSDN:
    http://msdn.microsoft.com/en-us/library/ff724708(v=Expression.40).aspx.

For more information about the Silverlight Navigation Framework, see "Navigation Overview" on MSDN:
    http://msdn.microsoft.com/en-us/library/cc838245(VS.95).aspx.

For more information about integrating Silverlight's Navigation Framework with Prism, see "Integrating Prism v4 Region Navigation with Silverlight Frame Navigation" on Karl Schifflett's blog:
    http://blogs.msdn.com/b/kashiffl/archive/2010/10/05/integrating-prism-v4-region-navigation-with-silverlight-frame-navigation.aspx.

To access web resources more easily, see the online version of the bibliography on MSDN:
    http://msdn.microsoft.com/en-us/library/gg405487(PandP.40).aspx.

9

Communication Between Loosely Coupled Components

It is important to maintain a loose coupling between the various components in your application to ensure that it remains flexible and easy to maintain. There are various ways to implement loose coupling. The most appropriate choice depends on the components involved and the required communication between them. In all cases, your goal should be to minimize static dependencies on specific implementations of components while allowing them to communicate efficiently.

To determine how to achieve this goal, it is important for you to understand the differences between the various approaches so that you can best determine which one to use in your particular scenario. In some cases, you may have two components or classes that interact very closely with each other—for example, a view and a view model—and can achieve loose coupling and communication by using data binding, commands, interaction requests, and so on. In other cases, the components involved may be much more coarse-grained.

For example, a common and effective approach to building large complex applications is to divide the functionality into discrete modules. It is desirable to minimize the use of static references between these modules so that the modules can be independently developed, tested, deployed, and updated. However, these modules will often be required to communicate in a loosely coupled fashion with other modules, and with the hosting application itself.

The Prism Library supports the following loosely coupled communication approaches:

- **Commanding**. Use this when there is an expectation of immediate action from the user interaction.

- **Region context**. Use this to provide contextual information between the host and views in the host's region. This approach is somewhat similar to the **DataContext**, but it does not rely on it.

- **Shared services**. Callers can call a method on the service, which raises an event to the receiver of the message. Use this if none of the preceding is applicable.

- **Event aggregation**. Use this for communication across view models, presenters, or controllers when there is not a direct action-reaction expectation.

Commanding

If you need to respond to a user gesture, such as clicking on a command invoker (for example, a button or menu item), and if you want the invoker to be enabled based on business logic, use commanding.

Windows Presentation Foundation (WPF) provides **RoutedCommand**, which connects command invokers, such as menu items and buttons, with command handlers that are associated with the current item in the visual tree that has keyboard focus.

However, in a composite scenario, the command handler is often a view model that does not have any associated elements in the visual tree or is not the focused element. To support this scenario, the Prism Library provides **DelegateCommand**, which allows you to call a delegate method when the command is executed, and **CompositeCommand**, which allows you to combine multiple commands. These commands are different from the built-in **RoutedCommand**, which will route command execution and handling up and down the visual tree. This allows you to trigger a command at a point in the visual tree and handle it at a higher level.

The **CompositeCommand** is an implementation of **ICommand** so that it can be bound to invokers. **CompositeCommands** can be connected to several child commands. When the **CompositeCommand** is invoked, the child commands are also invoked.

CompositeCommands support enablement. **CompositeCommands** listen to the **CanExecuteChanged** event of each one of its connected commands. It then raises this event notifying its invoker(s). The invoker(s) reacts to this event by calling **CanExecute** on the **CompositeCommand**. The **CompositeCommand** then polls all its child commands again by calling **CanExecute** on each child command. If any call to **CanExecute** returns **false**, the **CompositeCommand** will return **false**, thus disabling the invoker(s).

How does this help you with cross module communication? Applications based on the Prism Library may have global **CompositeCommands** that are defined in the shell and have meaning across modules, such as **Save**, **Save All**, and **Cancel**. Modules can then register their local commands with these global commands and participate in their execution.

About WPF Routed Events and Routed Commands

A routed event is a type of event that can invoke handlers on multiple listeners in an element tree, instead of notifying only the object that directly subscribed to the event. WPF-routed commands deliver command messages through UI elements in the visual tree, but the elements outside the tree will not receive these messages because the messages only bubble up or down from the focused element or an explicitly stated target element. Routed events can be used to communicate through the element tree, because the event data for the event is perpetuated to each element in the route. One element could change something in the event data, and that change would be available to the next element in the route.

Therefore, you should use WPF routed events when you define common handlers at a common root or when you define a custom control class.

CREATING A DELEGATE COMMAND

To create a delegate command, instantiate a **DelegateCommand** field in the constructor of your view model, and then expose it as an **ICommand** property, as shown in the following example.

```csharp
C# ArticleViewModel.cs
public class ArticleViewModel : NotificationObject
{
    private readonly ICommand showArticleListCommand;

    public ArticleViewModel(INewsFeedService newsFeedService,
                            IRegionManager regionManager,
                            IEventAggregator eventAggregator)
    {
        this.showArticleListCommand = new DelegateCommand(this.ShowArticleList);
    }

    public ICommand ShowArticleListCommand
    {
        get { return this.showArticleListCommand; }
    }
}
```

CREATING A COMPOSITE COMMAND

To create a composite command, instantiate a **CompositeCommand** field in the constructor, add commands to it, and then expose it as an **ICommand** property, as shown in the following example.

```csharp
C#
public class MyViewModel : NotificationObject
{
    private readonly CompositeCommand saveAllCommand;

    public ArticleViewModel(INewsFeedService newsFeedService,
                            IRegionManager regionManager,
                            IEventAggregator eventAggregator)
    {
```

```
        this.saveAllCommand = new CompositeCommand();
        this.saveAllCommand.RegisterCommand(new SaveProductsCommand());
        this.saveAllCommand.RegisterCommand(new SaveOrdersCommand());
    }

    public ICommand SaveAllCommand
    {
        get { return this.saveAllCommand; }
    }
}
```

MAKING A COMMAND GLOBALLY AVAILABLE

Typically, to create a globally available command, create an instance of the **Delegate Command** or the **CompositeCommand** and expose it through a static class, as the next example demonstrates.

C#
```
public static class GlobalCommands
{
    public static CompositeCommand MyCompositeCommand = new CompositeCommand();
}
```

In your module, associate child commands to the globally available command, as shown in the next example.

C#
```
GlobalCommands.MyCompositeCommand.RegisterCommand(command1);
GlobalCommands.MyCompositeCommand.RegisterCommand(command2);
```

Note: *To increase the testability of your code, you can use a proxy class to access the globally available commands and mock that proxy class in your tests.*

BINDING TO A GLOBALLY AVAILABLE COMMAND

The following code example shows how to bind a button to the command in WPF.

XAML
```
<Button Name="MyCompositeCommandButton" Command="{x:Static local:GlobalCommands.
MyCompositeCommand}">Execute My Composite Command </Button>
```

Silverlight does not provide support for **x:static**. Therefore, use the following steps to bind a button to a command in Silverlight.

To bind a button to a command

1. On the view's model, create a public property to obtain the command from the static class. This is shown in the following code example.

```C#
public ICommand MyCompositeCommand
{
    get { return GlobalCommands.MyCompositeCommand; }
}
```

2. Typically, models are passed to the view through its **DataContext** (this is done in the view's code-behind file). The following code example shows how to set the model as the **DataContext** of the view. By doing this, you can declaratively bind the command to a control in your view in the XAML code.

```C#
view.DataContext = model;
```

3. Make sure that the following XML namespace is added to root element of the view's XAML file.

```XAML
xmlns:prism="clr-namespace:Microsoft.Practices.Prism.Commands;
assembly=Microsoft.Practices.Prism"
```

4. Use the **Click.Command** attached property to bind a button to the command in Silverlight, as shown in the following code example.

```XAML
<Button Name="MyCommandButton" prism:Click.Command="{Binding
MyCompositeCommand}"/>Execute MyCommand</Button>
```

Note: *Another approach is to store the command as a resource inside the App.xaml file in the* **Application.Resources** *section. Then, in the view—which must be created after setting that resource—you can set* **prism: Click.Command="{Binding MyComposite Command, Source={StaticResource GlobalCommands}}"** *to add an invoker to the command.*

Region Context

There are many scenarios in which you might want to share contextual information between the view that is hosting a region and a view that is inside a region. For example, a master detail–like view shows a business entity and exposes a region to show additional detail information for that business entity. The Prism Library uses the **RegionContext** to share an object between the host of the region and any views that are loaded inside the region, as shown in the following illustration.

Using RegionContext

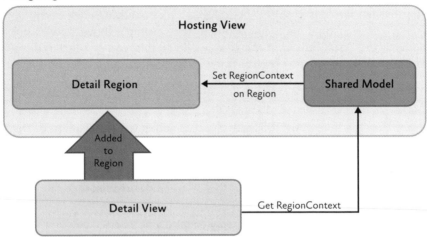

Depending on the scenario, you can choose to share a single piece of information (such as an identifier) or a shared model. The view can retrieve the **RegionContext**, and then sign up for change notifications. The view can also change the **RegionContext**'s value. There are several ways of exposing and consuming the **RegionContext**:

- You can expose **RegionContext** to a region in Extensible Application Markup Language (XAML).
- You can expose **RegionContext** to a region in code.
- You can consume **RegionContext** from a view inside a region.

> **Note:** *The Prism Library currently only supports consuming the **RegionContext** from a view inside a region if that view is a **DependencyObject**. If your view is not a **DependencyObject** (for example, you are using WPF automatic data templates and adding your view model directly in the region), consider creating a custom **RegionBehavior** to forward the **RegionContext** to your view objects.*

About the DataContext Property

Data context is a concept that allows elements to inherit information from their parent elements about the data source that is used for binding. Child elements automatically inherit the **DataContext** *of their parent element. The data flows down the visual tree.*

The best method for binding a view model to a view in Silverlight is by using the **DataContext** *property; that is why, in most cases, the* **DataContext** *is used to store the view's model.*

Because of this, unless you have very simple views, it is not recommended that you use the **DataContext** *property as a communication mechanism between different loosely coupled views.*

Shared Services

Another method of cross-module communication is through shared services. When the modules are loaded, modules add their services to the service locator. Typically, services are registered and retrieved from a service locator by common interface types. This allows modules to use services provided by other modules without requiring a static reference to the module. Service instances are shared across modules; therefore, you can share data and pass messages between modules.

In the Stock Trader Reference Implementation (Stock Trader RI), the Market module provides an implementation of **IMarketFeedService**. The Position module consumes these services by using the shell application's dependency injection container, which provides service location and resolution. The **IMarketFeedService** is meant to be consumed by other modules; therefore, it can be found in the **StockTraderRI.Infrastructure** common assembly. However, the concrete implementation of this interface does not need to be shared; therefore, it is defined directly in the Market module and can be updated independently of other modules.

To see how these modules register their services in the Unity Application Block (Unity) dependency injection container, see the MarketModule.cs file. The following code example is an excerpt from this file. The Position module's **ObservablePosition** receives the **IMarketFeedService** service through constructor dependency injection.

```
C# MarketModule.cs
protected void RegisterViewsAndServices()
{
   _container.RegisterType<IMarketFeedService, MarketFeedService>(new
ContainerControlledLifetimeManager());
   //...
}
```

This helps with cross-module communication because service consumers do not need a static reference to modules providing the service. This service can be used to send or receive data between modules.

Event Aggregation

The Prism Library provides an event mechanism that enables communication between loosely coupled components in the application. This mechanism, based on the event aggregator service, allows publishers and subscribers to communicate through events without having a direct reference to each other.

The **EventAggregator** provides multicast publish/subscribe functionality. This means there can be multiple publishers that raise the same event and there can be multiple subscribers listening to the same event. Consider using the **EventAggregator** to publish an event across modules and when sending a message between business logic code, such as controllers and presenters.

One example of this, from the Stock Trader RI, is when the **Process Order** button is clicked and the order successfully processes. In this case, other modules need to know that the order is successfully processed so that they can update their views.

Events created with the Prism Library are typed events. This means that you can take advantage of compile-time type checking to detect errors before you run the application. In the Prism Library, the **EventAggregator** allows subscribers or publishers to locate a specific **EventBase**. The event aggregator service also allows for multiple publishers and multiple subscribers, as shown in the following illustration.

Event aggregator service

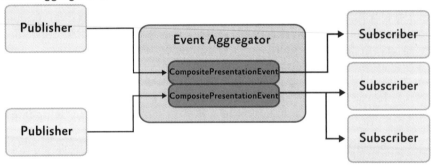

About .NET Framework Events

Using .NET Framework events is the most simple and straightforward approach for communication between components if loose coupling is not a requirement. Events in the .NET Framework implement the Publish-Subscribe pattern. However, to subscribe to an object, you need a direct reference to that object, which, in composite applications, typically resides in another module. This results in a tightly coupled design. Therefore, in a loosely coupled application, .NET Framework events are used for communication within modules instead of between modules.

If you use .NET Framework events, you have to be very careful of memory leaks, especially if you have a non-static or short-lived component that subscribes to an event in a static or longer-lived component. If you do not unsubscribe the subscriber, it will be kept alive by the publisher, and this will prevent it from being garbage-collected.

IEventAggregator

The **EventAggregator** class is offered as a service in the container and can be retrieved through the **IEventAggregator** interface. The event aggregator is responsible for locating or building events and for keeping a collection of the events in the system.

```
C#
public interface IEventAggregator
{
    TEventType GetEvent<TEventType>() where TEventType : EventBase;
}
```

The **EventAggregator** constructs the event during its first access if it has not already been constructed. This relieves the publisher or subscriber from needing to determine whether the event is available.

CompositePresentationEvent

The real work of connecting publishers and subscribers is done by the **CompositePresentationEvent** class. This is the only implementation of the **EventBase** class that is included in the Prism Library. This class maintains the list of subscribers and handles event dispatching to the subscribers.

The **CompositePresentationEvent** class is a generic class that requires the payload type to be defined as the generic type. This helps enforce, at compile time, that publishers and subscribers provide the correct methods for successful event connection. The following code shows a partial definition of the **CompositePresentationEvent** class.

```
C# CompositePresentationEvent.cs
public class CompositePresentationEvent<TPayload> : EventBase
{
    ...
    public SubscriptionToken Subscribe(Action<TPayload> action);
    public SubscriptionToken Subscribe(Action<TPayload> action, ThreadOption
threadOption);
    public SubscriptionToken Subscribe(Action<TPayload> action, bool
keepSubscriberReferenceAlive)
    public virtual SubscriptionToken Subscribe(Action<TPayload> action, ThreadOption
threadOption, bool keepSubscriberReferenceAlive);
    public virtual SubscriptionToken Subscribe(Action<TPayload> action, ThreadOption
threadOption, bool keepSubscriberReferenceAlive, Predicate<TPayload> filter);
    public virtual void Publish(TPayload payload);
    public virtual void Unsubscribe(Action<TPayload> subscriber);
    public virtual bool Contains(Action<TPayload> subscriber)
    ...
}
```

CREATING AND PUBLISHING EVENTS

The following sections describe how to use the **IEventAggregator** interface to create, publish, and subscribe to **CompositePresentationEvent**.

Creating an Event

The **CompositePresentationEvent<TPayload>** is intended to be the base class for application- or module-specific events. **TPayLoad** is the type of the event's payload. The payload is the argument that will be passed to subscribers when the event is published.

For example, the following code shows the **TickerSymbolSelectedEvent** in the Stock Trader Reference Implementation (Stock Trader RI). The payload is a string containing the company symbol. Notice how the implementation for this class is empty.

```C#
public class TickerSymbolSelectedEvent : CompositePresentationEvent<string>{}
```

> **Note:** *In a composite application, the events are frequently shared between multiple modules; therefore, they are defined in a common place. In the Stock Trader RI, this is done in the StockTraderRI.Infrastructure project.*

Publishing an Event

Publishers raise an event by retrieving the event from the **EventAggregator** and calling the **Publish** method. To access the **EventAggregator**, you can use dependency injection by adding a parameter of type **IEventAggregator** to the class constructor.

For example, the following code demonstrates publishing the **TickerSymbolSelected Event**.

```C#
this.eventAggregator.GetEvent<TickerSymbolSelectedEvent>().Publish("STOCK0");
```

SUBSCRIBING TO EVENTS

Subscribers can use one of the **Subscribe** method overloads available on the **CompositePresentationEvent** class to subscribe to an event. There are several ways to subscribe to **CompositePresentationEvents**. Use the following criteria to help determine which option best suits your needs:

- If you need to be able to update UI elements when an event is received, subscribe to receive the event on the UI thread.
- If you need to filter an event, provide a filter delegate when subscribing.
- If you have performance concerns with events, consider using strongly referenced delegates when subscribing and then manually unsubscribe from the **Composite PresentationEvent**.
- If none of the preceding is applicable, use a default subscription.

   The following sections describe these options.

Subscribing on the UI Thread

Frequently, subscribers will need to update UI elements in response to events. In WPF and Silverlight, only a UI thread can update UI elements.

By default, the subscriber receives the event on the publisher's thread. If the publisher sends the event from the UI thread, the subscriber can update the UI. However, if the publisher's thread is a background thread, the subscriber may be unable to directly update UI elements. In this case, the subscriber would need to use the **Dispatcher** class to schedule the updates on the UI thread.

The **CompositePresentationEvent** provided with the Prism Library can assist by allowing the subscriber to automatically receive the event on the UI thread. The subscriber indicates this during subscription, as shown in the following code example.

```csharp
C#
public void Run()
{
   ...
   this.eventAggregator.GetEvent<TickerSymbolSelectedEvent>().Subscribe(ShowNews,
ThreadOption.UIThread);
);
}


public void ShowNews(string companySymbol)
{
   this.articlePresentationModel.SetTickerSymbol(companySymbol);
}
```

The following options are available for **ThreadOption**:

- **PublisherThread**. Use this setting to receive the event on the publishers' thread. This is the default setting.

- **BackgroundThread**. Use this setting to asynchronously receive the event on a .NET Framework thread-pool thread.

- **UIThread**. Use this setting to receive the event on the UI thread.

Subscription Filtering

Subscribers may not need to handle every instance of a published event. In these cases, the subscriber can use the **filter** parameter. The **filter** parameter is of type **System. Predicate<TPayLoad>** and is a delegate that is executed when the event is published to determine if the payload of the published event matches the criteria for having the subscriber callback invoked. If the payload does not meet the specified criteria, the subscriber callback is not executed.

Frequently, this filter is supplied as a lambda expression, as shown in the following code example.

```C#
FundAddedEvent fundAddedEvent = this.eventAggregator.GetEvent<FundAddedEvent>();

fundAddedEvent.Subscribe(FundAddedEventHandler, ThreadOption.UIThread, false,
fundOrder => fundOrder.CustomerId == this.customerId);
```

Silverlight does not support weak references to lambda expressions or anonymous delegates. For Silverlight, you need to call a separate public method, as shown in the following code example.

```C#
public bool FundOrderFilter(FundOrder fundOrder)
{
    return fundOrder.CustomerId == this.customerId;
}
...

FundAddedEvent fundAddedEvent = this.eventAggregator.GetEvent<FundAddedEvent>();

subscriptionToken = fundAddedEvent.Subscribe(FundAddedEventHandler,
ThreadOption.UIThread, false, FundOrderFilter);
```

Note: *The **Subscribe** method returns a subscription token of type **Microsoft.Practices. Prism.Events.SubscriptionToken** that can be used to remove a subscription to the event later. This token is particularly useful when you are using anonymous delegates or lambda expressions as the callback delegate or when you are using the same subscription event handler with different filters.*

Note: *You should not modify the payload object from within a callback delegate because several threads could be accessing the payload object simultaneously. You could configure the payload to be immutable to avoid concurrency errors.*

Subscribing Using Strong References

If you are raising multiple events in a short amount of time and have noticed performance issues with them, you may need to subscribe with strong delegate references. If you do that, you will then need to manually unsubscribe from the event when you dispose of the subscriber.

By default, **CompositePresentationEvent** maintains a weak delegate reference to the subscriber's handler and filter on the subscription. This means that the reference that **CompositePresentationEvent** holds on to will not prevent garbage collection of the subscriber. Using a weak delegate reference relieves the subscriber from the need to unsubscribe and allows for proper garbage collection.

However, maintaining this weak delegate reference is slower than using a strong reference. For most applications, the performance degradation will not be noticeable, but if your application publishes a large number of events in a short time period, you may need to use strong references with **CompositePresentationEvent**. If you do use strong delegate references, your subscriber should unsubscribe to enable proper garbage collection of your subscribing object when it is no longer used.

To subscribe with a strong reference, use the **keepSubscriberReferenceAlive** parameter on the **Subscribe** method, as shown in the following code example.

```C#
FundAddedEvent fundAddedEvent = eventAggregator.GetEvent<FundAddedEvent>();

bool keepSubscriberReferenceAlive = true;

fundAddedEvent.Subscribe(FundAddedEventHandler, ThreadOption.UIThread,
keepSubscriberReferenceAlive, fundOrder => fundOrder.CustomerId == _customerId);
```

The **keepSubscriberReferenceAlive** parameter is of type **bool**:
- When set to **true**, the event instance keeps a strong reference to the subscriber instance, thereby not allowing it to be garbage collected. For information about how to unsubscribe, see the section "Unsubscribing from an Event" later in this chapter.
- When set to **false** (the default value when this parameter omitted), the event maintains a weak reference to the subscriber instance, thereby allowing the garbage collector to dispose of the subscriber instance when there are no other references to it. When the subscriber instance is collected, the event is automatically unsubscribed.

Default Subscriptions

For a minimal or default subscription, the subscriber must provide a callback method with the appropriate signature that receives the event notification. For example, the handler for the **TickerSymbolSelectedEvent** requires the method to take a string parameter, as shown in the following code example.

```C#
public void Run()
{
    ...

    this.eventAggregator.GetEvent<TickerSymbolSelectedEvent>().Subscribe(ShowNews);
}

public void ShowNews(string companySymbol)
{
    articlePresentationModel.SetTickerSymbol(companySymbol);
}
```

Unsubscribing from an Event

If your subscriber no longer wants to receive events, you can unsubscribe by using your subscriber's handler or you can unsubscribe by using a subscription token.

The following code example shows how to directly unsubscribe to the handler.

```csharp
C#
FundAddedEvent fundAddedEvent = this.eventAggregator.GetEvent<FundAddedEvent>();

fundAddedEvent.Subscribe(FundAddedEventHandler, ThreadOption.PublisherThread);

fundAddedEvent.Unsubscribe(FundAddedEventHandler);
```

The following code example shows how to unsubscribe with a subscription token. The token is supplied as a return value from the **Subscribe** method.

```csharp
C#
FundAddedEvent fundAddedEvent = this.eventAggregator.GetEvent<FundAddedEvent>();

subscriptionToken = fundAddedEvent.Subscribe(FundAddedEventHandler,
ThreadOption.UIThread, false, fundOrder => fundOrder.CustomerId == this.customerId);

fundAddedEvent.Unsubscribe(subscriptionToken);
```

More Information

For more information about weak references, see "Weak References" on MSDN:
    http://msdn.microsoft.com/en-us/library/ms404247.aspx.
To access web resources more easily, see the online version of the bibliography on MSDN:
    http://msdn.microsoft.com/en-us/library/gg405487(PandP.40).aspx.

10   Sharing Code Between Silverlight and WPF

This chapter helps you understand how you can use Prism to create applications that can run on both WPF and Silverlight by using a common code base. These kinds of applications are called multi-targeted applications. Multi-targeted applications are designed to share as much code as possible by cleanly separating common application code from any WPF or Silverlight-specific code. Prism supports the development of multi-targeted applications by using design patterns that support this separation, and by providing tools and techniques to help you share code between your WPF and Silverlight projects. This chapter describes common challenges that you might face when developing a multi-targeted application and how to use Prism to help you overcome those challenges.

Goal and Benefits

When you write applications for WPF and Silverlight that have similar features and capabilities, it makes sense to strive for a single code base. Although the WPF and Silverlight platforms are very similar, they have limited binary compatibility. Only Silverlight 4 assemblies that reference a certain set of core, portable framework assemblies can be loaded into the .NET Framework 4 runtime.

Because Prism offers largely the same capabilities for both WPF and Silverlight, much of your code can be built to target both of these technologies. Supporting multi-targeted applications is primarily about implementing the patterns and infrastructure that maximize the possibility of sharing code and components between the two environments, and allowing an application to integrate environment-specific functionality so that it can take full advantage of desktop or browser-specific features. By using Prism to create your multi-targeting composite application, you can reuse source code across WPF and Silverlight applications.

Out of Scope

If you can structure your assemblies to take advantage of the binary compatibility support between Silverlight and WPF, you should do so. For more information about this, see the CLR Team Blog post, "Sharing Silverlight Assemblies with .NET Apps" at http://blogs.msdn.com/b/clrteam/archive/2009/12/01/sharing-silverlight-assemblies-with-net-apps.aspx.

This chapter is not intended to address this scenario. Instead, it describes challenges and solutions for building multi-targeted applications that share source code.

Multi-Targeting Scenarios

Multi-targeting is useful primarily for applications that must deliver both a feature-rich desktop experience and a wide-reach Internet application experience. In this scenario, you may want to develop an application that has the same features and workflow on WPF and Silverlight or one that offers different features and workflows. Multi-targeting is particularly beneficial in the following scenarios:

- You need to provide users with a full-featured application while they are in the office and a scaled-down, browser-based version for when they are traveling.
- You need to provide internal users with a desktop-based application and external customers or partners with a browser-hosted application.

For example, a business might have both a call center application for customers who want to place their orders over the phone and an online order application for customers who want to place their orders online. However, the forms are not exactly the same. The call center desktop order form offers more information and expanded functionality than the online order form. Nonetheless, because they accomplish similar things, there will be certain parts of the order form and business logic that can be reused for both scenarios.

Service-oriented applications are easier to multi-target because Silverlight is inherently service-oriented. Silverlight does not have support for local storage or database access because of its targeted feature set and security restrictions. Additionally, connected applications are also easier to multi-target because of Silverlight's connected nature.

Multi-Targeted Considerations

If you choose to make your solution multi-targetable, you should also consider the following:

- Silverlight offers limited, isolated storage on the local client computer.
- You may lose simplicity and readability of code in a multi-targetable solution. Because some features of WPF are not available in Silverlight, you will need to work around these issues, and your code may not be as elegant or readable.
- By default, Silverlight applications execute in a secure sandbox, so there are a several things that you cannot do outside of the sandbox context. These applications have restricted access to the local computer and are constrained to help prevent malicious behavior. These restrictions prevent a sandboxed application from accessing devices and interacting with other running programs.

> **Note:** *If you need access to some of these items, you can create an out-of-browser Silverlight application with elevated trust. For more information, see "Trusted Applications" on MSDN.*

- Silverlight supports only asynchronous communications; therefore, you cannot multi-target applications that use synchronous communications.

Multi-Targeted Elements

Typical applications contain a significant amount of code that is unrelated to the presentation technology it uses. Because the Silverlight and .NET Framework runtimes are so similar, they can share the bulk of this code. The key is to cleanly separate code that can run unmodified on both runtimes from code that is WPF or Silverlight-specific. This separation allows you to maximize the amount of code that can be shared while keeping WPF or Silverlight-specific code encapsulated. Generally, you can share much of the application's code, including the following:

- **Application presentation and business logic**. The use of Separated Presentation patterns can help to isolate the underlying application logic from its visual presentation, which in turns helps to maximize the separation between UI-specific and UI-independent code. Using patterns such as the Model-View-ViewModel (MVVM), Model-View-Presenter (MVP), or Model-View-Controller (MVC) patterns can help you share presentation and business logic code between WPF and Silverlight while encapsulating WPF or Silverlight-specific functionality in view classes.

- **Application Services**. Service classes that encapsulate non-UI application functionality, such as logging, exception handling, authentication, or data/service access, can often be multi-targeted.

- **Simple views**. In some cases, code sharing doesn't need to be limited to UI-independent code. Because Silverlight uses a subset of the Extensible Application Markup Language (XAML) defined by WPF, you can create application UI elements that can be shared unmodified. Typically, this is possible if the XAML used is supported by both Silverlight and WPF and if a view consists of basic controls and simple data binding only.

- **Unit tests**. Many unit tests can be used for both WPF and Silverlight if you use tools, such as the Silverlight Unit Test Framework, that have the same attribute structure as MSTest.

For the most part, the Silverlight API is a subset of the .NET Framework API. Therefore, it may make sense to develop your application with the smaller Silverlight API to reduce the chance of using a feature that isn't available for both platforms. Because of the differences between the XAML in Silverlight and WPF, the following elements are difficult to reuse:

- Complex views (XAML)
- Controls
- Styling
- Animation
- Expression Blend behaviors and triggers

A Solution to Multi-Targeting: Multiple Linked Projects

Silverlight and WPF have only limited binary compatibility. Therefore, some code and components have to be recompiled for each target environment. The approach Prism takes is to provide guidance on structuring application and module code into multiple linked projects. Each project manages all the references, resources, and code specific to the WPF or Silverlight target environment. Code that is shared is linked between two projects so that it is automatically compiled into each target. Unit tests can similarly be shared between the two environments, so that they can be written once and run against the target code in either of the two target environments. The Prism team created a tool named Project Linker to help create and maintain these links. The Project Linker was used to link projects in the Prism Library, QuickStarts, and reference implementations.

Note: *You can download Project Linker from Visual Studio Gallery or open Visual Studio, click* **Extension Manager** *on the* **Tools** *menu, click* **Online Gallery** *in the* **Extension Manager** *dialog box, and then search for* **Project Linker**.

Non-UI code and components are typically the easiest to share. Therefore, you should make sure that you carefully adhere to separate UI patterns so that the UI and non-UI pieces of the application or modules are also cleanly separated.

Core Application

The overall pattern is based on defining the core application in shared code and then augmenting that with extensions that implement WPF (desktop) or Silverlight (browser)–specific functionality. The core application defines the overall structure of the application and contains the application code and components that are common to the two environments. Silverlight is largely a subset of WPF; therefore, developing the core application in Silverlight reduces the risk of relying on an API or feature that is available in WPF, but not in Silverlight.

Note: *Many solutions in the Prism source tree actually have their core source files in the WPF projects, and the Silverlight projects link to the files in the WPF projects. This is usually because of historical reasons because the first version of Prism was built before the first Silverlight release.*

The following illustration shows the Solution Explorer view for the Multi-Targeted QuickStart. Most files in the WPF version of the QuickStart are linked files because the core application was developed in Silverlight. The shared files found in the QuickStart are images, models, services, interfaces, and resources. The shared (linked) files are high-lighted.

Shared files in the Multi-Targeting QuickStart

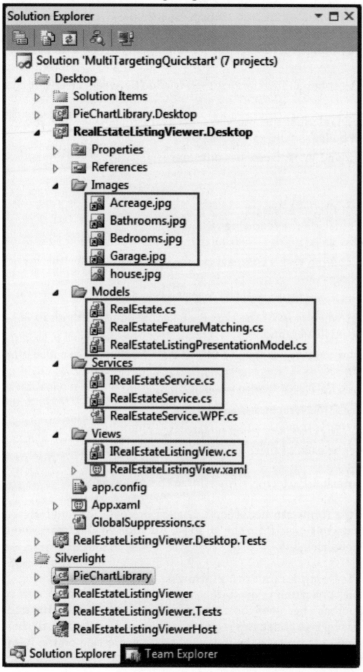

Creating Multi-Targeted Applications

This section contains the following subsections, which describe areas to consider when you develop a multi-targeted application:

- **Design and Code Guidelines**. Describes considerations for sharing code between Silverlight and WPF.
- **Process Guidelines**. Describes approaches for sharing code between Silverlight and WPF.
- **Team Build Guidelines**. Describes specific Microsoft Team Build issues that you might encounter when building multi-targeted applications.
- **Contrasting Silverlight and WPF**. Describes differences between Silverlight 4 and WPF.

DESIGN AND CODE GUIDELINES

Design and code guidelines include the following:

- Use Separated Presentation patterns to maximize the amount of shared code.
- Where possible, write code so that it compiles on both platforms. When this is not possible, do the following:
  - Use **#if** statements if you have simple or single line constructs.
  - Use partial classes when most of the class is similar but some methods have platform-specific implementations.
  - Use partial methods only if you need to call an extra method on one platform but not the other.
  - Build platform-specific classes with a single responsibility.
- Create a solution folder for Silverlight and another for WPF.
- Check Silverlight and WPF references when refactoring code.

  The next sections describe each of these guidelines in more detail.

Use Separated Presentation Patterns to Maximize the Amount of Shared Code

Sharing view-code across platforms can be difficult. Sharing presentation and business logic is easier if you separate this logic from the UI logic. Additionally, this makes your code easier to understand and maintain.

Write Code So That It Compiles on Both Platforms

Where possible, write your application code so that it compiles on both platforms to enable reuse. When this approach becomes too complicated, you have to make the trade-off to see if the cost of having two codebases is less than having a less elegant solution. For example, in Silverlight you can execute the following LINQ expression on the **Items** property of an **ItemsControl**.

```
C#
ItemsControl someItemsControl = new ItemsControl();
someItemsControl.Items.Add(new TextBox());
bool hasDependencyObjects = someItemsControl.Items.Any(item => item is
DependencyObject);
```

However, because the **Items** property is not **IEnumerable<T>** in WPF, this approach does not work. Instead of creating a different version for WPF and Silverlight, opt for a less-preferable single source solution, as shown in the following code.

```
C#
ItemsControl someItemsControl = new ItemsControl();
someItemsControl.Items.Add(new TextBox());
bool hasDependencyObjects = false;
foreach (var item in someItemsControl.Items)
{
    if (item is DependencyObject)
    {
        hasDependencyObjects = true;
        break;
    }
}
```

The easiest approach is to begin writing your code in Silverlight, because it is a more constrained version of the .NET Framework.

Use #if statements if you have simple or single line constructs
Sometimes it is not possible to create a single code base because of incompatibility between WPF and Silverlight. In this case, you can use **#if SILVERLIGHT** constructs to create conditional compiled sections. The following code example shows a **#if SILVERLIGHT** statement.

```
C#
#if SILVERLIGHT
        System.Windows.Application.Current.RootVisual = shell;
#else
        Application.Current.MainWindow = shell;
        shell.Show();
#endif
```

However, **#if** statements have several drawbacks:
- The code is less readable and maintainable. If code is scattered with #if constructs, it becomes hard to read and a lot harder to maintain.
- Debugging becomes harder. If there is a compiler error within a construct, when you try to open the file, Visual Studio selects the solution that has the physical file instead of the solution that has the error. This means you either have to manually close the file and open the correct solution or edit the code without using IntelliSense.

Use partial classes if most of the class is similar but some methods
have platform-specific implementations

When the changes between Silverlight and WPF become more complex, you can create partial classes. Mark the shared class files as **partial** and then create a partial class for the specific platforms. This also applies to unit tests. The following are some additional recommendations:

- Try to keep the platform-specific methods private. This way, the unit tests will not need to contain specific logic for specific platforms.
- Make sure your class has a single, clear responsibility. Any partial methods for platform-specific code should change the implementation details only.

Note: *If the differences between the two platforms become very extensive, and the classes for both platforms become very different, consider creating platform-specific classes instead of partial classes.*

The following code example shows a partial class, **RealEstateService**, that is shared between the Silverlight and WPF projects in the Multi-Targeting QuickStart.

```
C# RealEstateService.cs
namespace RealEstateListingViewer.Services
{
    public partial class RealEstateService: IRealEstateService
    {
        public RealEstate GetRealEstate ()
        {
            ...
            return property;
        }
    }
}
```

The following code example shows the Silverlight-specific partial class for retrieving images for the **RealEstateService** class in the Multi-Targeting QuickStart.

```
C# RealEstateService.silverlight.cs
namespace RealEstateListingViewer.Services
{
    public partial class RealEstateService
    {
        /// <summary>
        /// Return the images. In Silverlight, you want to download the image
        /// from a web server.
        /// You can either store the images on the server or build an
```

```
            /// HTTP handler to retrieve the images.
            /// </summary>
            private static BitmapImage GetImage()
            {
                Uri imageUri;
                Uri source = App.Current.Host.Source;

                if (source.ToString().StartsWith("file://",
StringComparison.OrdinalIgnoreCase))
                {
                    imageUri = new Uri("../Images/House.jpg", UriKind.Relative);
                }
                else
                {
                    source = new Uri(string.Format(CultureInfo.InvariantCulture,
"{0}://{1}:{2}/", source.Scheme, source.Host, source.Port));
                    imageUri = new Uri(source, "Images/house.jpg");
                }
                return new BitmapImage(imageUri);
            }
        }
    }
}
```

The following code example shows the WPF-specific partial class for retrieving images for the **RealEstateService** class in the Multi-Targeting QuickStart.

C# RealEstateService.WPF.cs

```
namespace RealEstateListingViewer.Services
{
    public partial class RealEstateService
    {
        /// <summary>
        /// Return the images. In a windows application, normally you
        /// retrieve the image from a database.
        /// But for simplicity, it is just being retrieved from the file system.
        /// </summary>
        private static BitmapImage GetImage()
        {
            return new BitmapImage(new Uri("../Images/house.jpg", UriKind.Relative));
        }
    }
}
```

*Use partial methods only if you need to call an extra method
on one platform but not the other*

If some work needs to be performed for only one platform (Silverlight or WPF), you could also use partial methods. This means that you can put an interface for the method in the parent class and put an implementation of that interface in only one of the platform-specific classes. For the other platform, the compiler will remove the method call. However, there are several limitations to partial methods:

- Partial method declarations must begin with the contextual keyword **partial** and the method must return **void**.
- Partial methods can have **ref** parameters but not **out** parameters.
- Partial methods are implicitly **private**; therefore, they cannot be **virtual**.
- Partial methods cannot be **extern**, because the presence of the body determines whether they are defining or implementing.
- Partial methods can have **static** and **unsafe** modifiers.
- Partial methods can be generic. Constraints are put on the defining partial method declaration and may optionally be repeated on the implementing one. Parameter and type parameter names do not have to be the same in the implementing declaration as in the defining one.
- You cannot make a **delegate** to a partial method.

Build platform-specific classes with a single responsibility

Frequently, it makes more sense to factor all platform-specific code into a separate class (for example, services or service agents). This can happen if most of the logic differs between the platforms. This way, you can create platform-specific implementations for services, such as caching, data access, or authentication. This approach also works for providing functionality that is present in only one platform. The following are some additional recommendations:

- Use a common interface to share code between the different platforms. For example, in the Prism Library, there are several platform specific classes for loading module types, such as the **XapModuleTypeLoader** for Silverlight and the **File ModuleTypeLoader** for desktop applications. They both implement the **IModule TypeLoader** interface.
- When there is some shared functionality between the different platforms, favor composition over inheritance (for example, by using the strategy pattern). In other words, see if it makes sense to factor out the shared code and place it in a shared class with a specific responsibility. In some scenarios, inheritance makes sense.

Create a Solution Folder for Silverlight and Another for WPF

Use solution folders to keep your solution organized. Typically, you do this by using two solution folders: one for the Silverlight code and the other for WPF code. For an example of how to structure your solution, see the Multi-Targeting QuickStart.

Check Silverlight and WPF References When Refactoring Code

Sometimes a Silverlight reference might slip into a WPF project or vice versa. This is caused by using refactoring tools. If you get unexpected compiler errors about Silverlight assemblies not being referenced in your WPF project, check the references.

PROCESS GUIDELINES

Process guidelines include the following:

- Develop the core application in Silverlight.
- Link the shared code between the source project and the target project.
- Use the same namespace for Silverlight and WPF projects.

The next sections describe each of these guidelines in more detail.

Develop the Core Application in Silverlight

Because Silverlight is a subset of WPF, the same code will work on WPF without major modifications; therefore, you should develop your core application in Silverlight.

Link the Shared Code Between the Source Project and the Target Project

For files that are common to both Silverlight and WPF but need different references, you should link the files. One of the ways to do this is to use the Project Linker tool to link the shared code between the source project and the target project.

Use the Same Namespace for Silverlight and WPF Projects

Keep the namespaces the same between projects because the shared code requires the same namespaces.

TEAM BUILD GUIDELINES

This section describes Team Build guidelines.

Configure Team Build to Build in Place

If you use Team Build to build a solution that holds both WPF and Silverlight projects, you might run into file collision problems. By default, Team Build copies the output from the projects to a single output folder. Because the output of the WPF and Silverlight projects should have the same name, there is a file name collision problem that will prevent you from compiling the projects or running unit tests.

By setting the property **CustomizableOutDir** to **true**, you are telling Team Build to build in place instead of copying the output to a single location. This prevents the collision name problem.

Additionally, if you set this property and want to run unit tests in your build, you need to specify where the **TestContainers** are located, as shown in the following example.

```XML
<PropertyGroup>
<!--Build in place-->
    <CustomizableOutDir>true</CustomizableOutDir>
</PropertyGroup>

  <!—Override the BeforeTestConfiguration target to specify where the testcontainers
live. -->
  <Target Name="BeforeTestConfiguration">

  <!--
    Change the outdir, because the testtoolstask needs this to execute all the
tests
  -->
    <PropertyGroup>
      <OutDir>$(SolutionRoot)\Source\</OutDir>
    </PropertyGroup>

    <!--Create a list of all tests dll's to run (test only the desktop versions) -->
    <CreateItem Include="$(SolutionRoot)\**\Desktop\**\Bin\Debug\%2a.Tests.dll">
      <Output ItemName="TestContainer" TaskParameter="Include" />
    </CreateItem>

  </Target>
```

Note: *This example assumes that your desktop projects are located in a folder named Desktop. MSTest.exe is only able to run unit tests that target the desktop version of the .NET Framework; therefore, Silverlight test assemblies are excluded.*

Contrasting Silverlight and WPF

Silverlight and WPF both allow you to develop rich user experiences based on XAML and the .NET Framework. However, there are some differences between these platforms, and you need to consider these differences carefully when you transition an application between Silverlight and WPF or when you build an application that targets both WPF and Silverlight.

Note: *This section describes differences between Silverlight 4 and the version of WPF that is part of the .NET Framework 4.0. These differences are expected to be reduced in future versions of Silverlight and WPF.*

Silverlight and WPF Architectural Overview

WPF provides developers with a unified programming model for building rich Windows applications that incorporate UI, media, and documents. WPF enables software developers to deliver a new level of user experience (UX) by providing a declarative-based language (XAML) for specifying vector-based graphics that can scale and take advantage of hardware acceleration.

Silverlight is a cross-browser, cross-platform implementation of the .NET Framework for delivering next-generation rich interactive media and content over the web, in desktop business applications, and in browser-hosted Rich Internet Applications (RIAs) that can integrate data and services from many sources. Silverlight enables developers to build applications that significantly enhance the typical end user experience, compared with traditional web applications. Like WPF, Silverlight provides a XAML-based language to specify user interfaces.

Silverlight and WPF share many of the same features and capabilities, but they are built on different run-time stacks, as illustrated in the following image. WPF makes use of the full .NET Framework and executes on the common language runtime (CLR). Silverlight is based on a subset of XAML and the full .NET Framework, and it executes on a different version of the CLR.

WPF and Silverlight

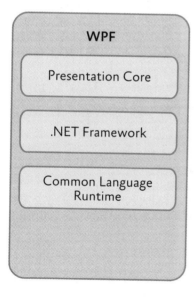
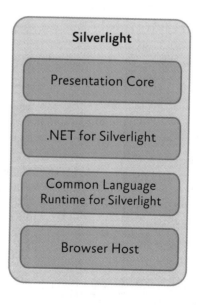

Differences Between Silverlight and WPF

To keep Silverlight small and lightweight, some WPF and .NET Framework features are not available in Silverlight. Because of this, there can be subtle—and not so subtle—differences you should carefully consider when moving an application between Silverlight and WPF or when building an application that targets both WPF and Silverlight. This section describes some of the major differences that the patterns & practices team encountered during Prism development. These differences relate to Silverlight 4 and WPF 4.0, the current versions at the time of this writing.

Resources

Resources are simple collections of key-value pairs that can store almost any element (strings, brushes, styles, data sources, and many others). Resources can be associated with almost any element class that exposes a **Resources** property of type **ResourceDictionary**.

Resources can contain static or dynamic content. Dynamic content can be changed at any time, and consumers of the resource will be updated automatically. However, in Silverlight, dynamic resource references are not supported; therefore, only static resource references are available. WPF does support dynamic resource references.

Triggers

Triggers allow designers to define the visual behavior of a control by declaratively specifying how its properties change in response to events or property changes, such as highlighting a button when it is clicked. Typically, triggers are fired when a property of a control changes and results in one or more other properties of that control also change. Triggers are defined inside a style and can be applied to any object of the specified target type.

Silverlight does not support triggers in **Styles**, **ControlTemplates**, or **DataTemplates** (the **Triggers** collection does not exist in these elements). However, you can achieve similar behavior by using the Silverlight Visual State Manager (VSM) to define interactive control templates. In VSM, the visual behavior of a control, including any animations and transitions, are defined in the control template. This can be easily done by using Expression Blend 4. However, be aware that the XAML file will get more complex and that control templates built for Silverlight are not yet compatible with WPF.

The Expression Blend SDK provides Expression Blend behaviors for animation and visual state management that can be used to apply a consist look and feel between WPF and Silverlight UIs.

Data Binding

Both WPF and Silverlight provide data binding support. The following are the main differences between Silverlight and WPF data binding:

• In Silverlight, there is no **OneWayToSource** data flow mode.

- In Silverlight, you cannot bind directly to XML data. A possible workaround for this is to convert the XML to CLR objects, and then bind to the CLR object.
- In Silverlight, there is no **XMLDataProvider** class.
- In Silverlight, there is no **DataTemplateSelector** class. In WPF, this class provides a way to choose a **DataTemplate** based on the data object and the data-bound element. However, to help support certain MVVM scenarios, Prism offers similar functionality for Silverlight in its **DataTemplateSelector** class.

Commanding

The following are the differences between Silverlight and WPF regarding commanding:

- Routed commands are not available in Silverlight. However, the **ICommand** interface is available in Silverlight, allowing developers to create their own custom commands. The Prism Library provides the **DelegateCommand** and **Composite Command** classes to simplify command implementation.
- In WPF, controls can be hooked up to commands through their **Command** property. By doing this, developers can declaratively associate controls and commands. This also means that a control can interact with a command so that it can invoke the command and have its enabled status automatically updated. In Silverlight, several controls support the **Command** property, but not as many as in WPF. For Silverlight controls that do not offer **Command** properties, consider using Expression Blend behaviors to invoke the command based on triggers.
- There is no input gesture or input binding support in Silverlight.

Miscellaneous

The following are some miscellaneous differences between Silverlight and WPF:

- In Silverlight, the **UIElement** class has an internal constructor; therefore, you cannot create a control that inherits from it.
- In Silverlight, there is no **x:Type** markup extension support or support for custom markup extensions.
- In Silverlight, there is no **x:Static** markup extension support or support for custom markup extensions. In Silverlight, items added to a **TabControl** control are not automatically wrapped inside a **TabItem** type, as is the case with WPF.
- All Silverlight network calls must be asynchronous.
- Silverlight networking, except for trusted out-of-browser applications, respect server-client access policies for servers outside the site of origin.

More Information

You can download Project Linker from Visual Studio Gallery or open Visual Studio, click **Tools**, point to **Extension Manager**, click **Online Gallery**, and search for "Project Linker."

For more information about structuring your assemblies to take advantage of the binary compatibility support between Silverlight and WPF, see the CLR Team Blog post, "Sharing Silverlight Assemblies with .NET Apps":

http://blogs.msdn.com/b/clrteam/archive/2009/12/01/sharing-silverlight-assemblies-with-net-apps.aspx.

For more information about WPF architecture, see "WPF Architecture" on MSDN:

http://msdn.microsoft.com/en-us/library/ms750441.aspx.

For more information about Silverlight architecture, see "Silverlight Architecture" on MSDN:

http://msdn.microsoft.com/en-us/library/bb404713(VS.95).aspx.

For a summary of the differences between WPF and Silverlight, see "WPF Compatibility" on MSDN:

http://msdn.microsoft.com/en-us/library/cc903925(VS.95).aspx.

For more information about the Visual State Manager and how it works in creating controls, see the following MSDN articles about creating customizable controls:

- http://msdn.microsoft.com/en-us/library/cc278064(vs.95).aspx. (for Silverlight)

- http://msdn.microsoft.com/en-us/library/ee330302.aspx. (for WPF in .NET Framework 4)

For more information about creating an application with elevated trust, see "Trusted Applications" on MSDN:

http://msdn.microsoft.com/en-us/library/ee721083(VS.95).aspx.

To access web resources more easily, see the online version of the bibliography on MSDN:

http://msdn.microsoft.com/en-us/library/gg405487(PandP.40).aspx.

11 Deploying Prism Applications

To successfully move a Prism application into production, you need to plan for deployment as part of the design process. This chapter covers the considerations and actions you need to perform to prepare your application for deployment and the actions you need to take to get the application in the user's hands.

Silverlight and Windows Presentation Foundation (WPF) have two very different hosting environments; therefore, the deployment considerations differ depending on whether you are building a Silverlight Prism application or a WPF Prism application.

Deploying Silverlight Prism Applications

Silverlight applications are delivered as .xap files via an HTTP request from a browser. A .xap file is really just a .zip file with a different file name extension and certain expectations about its content. A .xap file contains a set of application assemblies, an application manifest Extensible Application Markup Language (XAML) file that describes the package, and possibly additional resource files that the application uses. The .xap file is downloaded by the Silverlight plug-in hosted in a web page. After the Silverlight plug-in is downloaded, it activates the application and runs it within the context of a web page.

Note: *Even if you plan for your Silverlight application to run outside of a browser, the user will first need to use a browser to access the application's hosting page. After that, the user has the option of installing the application for out-of-browser use.*

As a result, the deployment of a Silverlight Prism application is mostly a matter of placing your .xap files in the right place on a web server so that the hosting page can download and run them.

PACKAGING PRISM MODULES AS .XAP FILES

As discussed in Chapter 4, "Modular Application Development," you can package application modules in multiple ways, including having multiple modules in a single .xap file or having a single .xap file act as a container for a single module. This decision should be based on whether multiple modules need to be downloaded at the same time because of dependencies between them or the way in which the application will be used, or whether the modules are logically independent. Packaging each module in its own .xap file can be a little cleaner from a maintenance and deployment perspective, because each module .xap file becomes a separate unit of deployment that can be versioned independently and added to or removed from the application by a simple change to the module catalog.

As an example, consider the architecture of the Stock Trader Reference Implementation (Stock Trader RI). It consists of the shell application and four modules: position, watch, market, and news. Because the application was designed so that all those features are available when the application starts, the modules of the Stock Trader RI are all added programmatically using the referenced types of the module classes. The Stock Trader RI shell application project has references to all the module assemblies as class libraries, and the modules are loaded through the **ModuleCatalog.AddModule** method in the bootstrapper during application startup. In this case, there is only a single .xap file built by the StockTraderRI.Silverlight shell application project, and it contains the shell, the four modules, and the shared infrastructure class library, as shown in the following illustration. To deploy the Stock Trader RI application, you simply place the .xap file on your web server and set up the source parameter tag of your Silverlight plug-in object tag in the hosting page to point to that .xap file (typically in a \ClientBin subfolder of your site, by using an ASP.NET web application hosting project template).

Stock Trader RI .xap structure

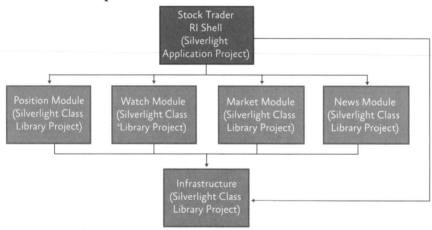

Alternatively, if the Stock Trader RI modules were more loosely coupled in terms of when they needed to be loaded, they could have been developed as Silverlight application projects and placed in individual .xap files. If you used that approach, the deployment architecture would more closely resemble the following illustration. After you break the modules into their own .xap files, you can choose to delay the loading of some of the modules, if appropriate, based on the application functionality. You would typically use a ModuleCatalog.xaml file packaged as part of the shell .xap file to determine what modules the application is composed of, what their dependencies are, and what their loading characteristics are (on-demand or not).

In the following illustration, the shell and each of the modules has a reference to the infrastructure assembly as a shared class library. If you leave the default settings on those references, you will end up with a separate copy of the library in each of the individual .xap files, which adds unnecessary download size and bandwidth utilization to the application.

Note: *If you plan to have your users install the application outside of the browser and you expect to deploy updates to your application after it is deployed, you will need to place all the modules in a single .xap file. The* **Application.CheckAndDownload UpdateAsync** *method will only update the main .xap file that the application was launched from.*

Modified Stock Trader RI .xap structure

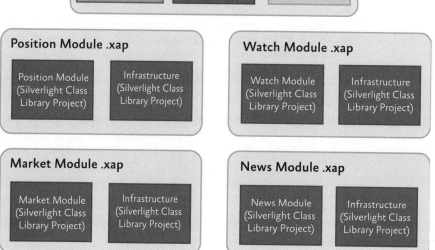

REDUCING THE DOWNLOAD SIZE OF MODULE .XAP FILES

To address the duplication of shared class libraries in multiple module Prism application .xap files, you have a couple of options. The first is to include the shared library in the shell application .xap file, as it will be by default when you add the reference. Then, in each of the modules that also uses the reference, set the **Copy Local** property on the reference to **false**. This causes the referenced assembly to be excluded from the compiled .xap file for that module. However, at run time, the class library provided by the shell application .xap file will also be available to the modules.

The second approach is to use application library caching in Silverlight. To use this feature, you open the Silverlight project properties for the project, and select the **Reduce XAP size by using application library caching** check box. When you do this, any referenced assemblies that have the appropriate metadata files collocated with them will not be included in the .xap file. Instead, these assemblies will be placed in a separate .zip file, and the .zip file will be referenced by the .xap file's ApplicationManifest.xaml file as an external part. The signed Silverlight Prism Library binaries, as well as the libraries from the Silverlight SDK and the Silverlight Toolkit, have the required metadata files to use this feature. To use this functionality in your own shared assemblies, you need to provide a metadata file, as described in the topic, "How to: Use Application Library Caching" on MSDN.

PREPARING A WEB SERVER TO HOST SILVERLIGHT APPLICATIONS

Silverlight applications can be hosted on most types of web servers, such as Internet Information Services (IIS) or Apache. Typically, however, a web server is configured to serve only a few well-known file name extensions. To allow Silverlight applications to be served from your web server, you have to allow the MIME types in the following table to be served.

Extension	MIME type
.xaml	application/xaml+xml
.xap	application/x-silverlight-app

DEPLOYING THE APPLICATION

To deploy a Silverlight application and the modules that are remotely loaded, you have to make the .xap files accessible on the web server. There are several ways to accomplish this:

- You can manually copy all the .xap files to a public folder on the web server.

- You can include the Silverlight .xap files in a web project or website and publish them from Microsoft Visual Studio. To do this with a web application project, the project must be part of the same solution as the Silverlight projects that create the .xap files. You then add the Silverlight projects to the **Silverlight Applications** tab in the web project settings, as shown in the following illustration. A copy of the .xap files from the included Silverlight projects will be placed in a \ClientBin subfolder of the published site. These files are synchronized in the web project each time you build.

Adding the remote modules as Silverlight applications

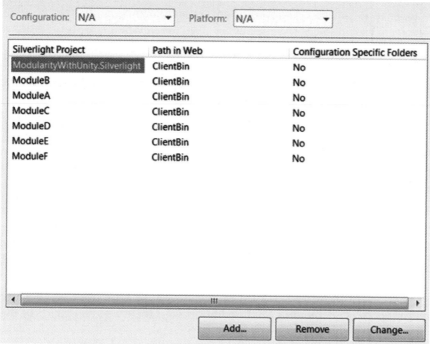

Note: *To avoid cross-domain call issues, the remote modules' .xap files should be located on the same domain as the main application. When deployed in this way, the* **Ref** *property on the* **ModuleCatalog** *should be a Uniform Resource Identifier (URI) relative to the main .xap file location on the web server.*

In addition to publishing or locating the .xap files in the hosting website, the hosting web page must refer to the shell application .xap file in its object tag source parameter. Because the hosting page should be part of the same site that the .xap files are placed in for cross-domain reasons, the path specified in the host page should be a relative path, as shown in the following code example.

```XAML
<object data="data:application/x-silverlight-2," type="application/x-silverlight-2"
width="100%" height="100%">
    <param name="source" value="ClientBin/ModularityWithUnity.Silverlight.xap"/>
        ...
</object>
```

Deploying WPF Prism Applications

A WPF Prism application can be composed of an executable and any number of additional DLLs. The main executable is the shell application project. Some of the additional DLLs will be the application modules. There may be additional DLLs that are shared assemblies used by the shell and application modules. In addition, you might have a set of resource or content files that get deployed along with the application.

To deploy a WPF Prism application, you have three choices:
- XCopy deployment
- ClickOnce deployment
- Windows Installer deployment

XCopy deployment is a general term for manual deployment through some sort of file copy operation, which may or may not include the use of the XCOPY command-line tool. If you choose to deploy the application in this way, it is up to you to manually package the files and move them to the target computer. The application should be ready to run as long as the expected folder structure and relative locations of the shell application executable, the module DLLs, and the content files are maintained.

In most situations, you will want to use a more automatic means of deployment to ensure that components are placed in the correct location and that the user has easy access to the application. To facilitate this type of installation, you can use ClickOnce or Windows Installer (.msi files), depending on the additional installation requirements of the application.

The reasons for choosing ClickOnce or Windows Installer are often misunderstood. ClickOnce is not intended to be a one-size-fits-all deployment technology. It is intended for applications that need a low-impact installation on a client computer. If your application needs to make computer-wide changes when it is installed—for example, to install drivers, integrate with other applications, install services and other things that are outside the scope of running an executable—ClickOnce is probably not an appropriate deployment choice. However, if you have a lightweight installation on the client computer and you want to benefit from network deployment and updates of your WPF application, ClickOnce can be a great choice.

To create a Windows Installer deployment package (.msi file) for your application, you have a variety of choices, including Visual Studio Setup projects, Windows Installer XML (WiX) projects, or numerous third-party installer creation products.

DEPLOYING WPF PRISM APPLICATION WITH CLICKONCE

ClickOnce is a Windows Presentation Foundation (WPF) or Windows Forms deployment mechanism that has been part of the .NET Framework since version 2.0. ClickOnce enables automatic deployment and update of WPF applications over the network from a deployment server. WPF Prism applications can use ClickOnce to get the shell, modules, and any other dependencies deployed on the client computer. The main challenge with Prism applications is that the Visual Studio publishing process for ClickOnce does not automatically include dynamically loaded modules in the published application.

Deploying a WPF application with ClickOnce is a two-step process. First, you have to publish the application from Visual Studio, and then you can deploy it on client computers. Publishing the application generates two manifests (a deployment manifest and an application manifest), and it copies the application files to a publish directory. The publish folder can then be moved to another server (that might not be directly accessible from the developer computer) to make the published application accessible to client computers from a known location and URL. Deploying an application on a client computer simply requires providing a URL or link that the user can navigate to. The URL points to the deployment manifest on the publishing deployment server. When that URL is loaded in the browser, ClickOnce on the client computer downloads the manifests and the application files specified by the manifests. After the files are downloaded and stored in the user profile, ClickOnce starts the application. If subsequent updates are published on the deployment server, ClickOnce can automatically detect those updates, download, and apply them. ClickOnce also provides settings that allow you to detect and apply updates on demand or in the background after the application starts.

Typically, when you publish a WPF Prism application that has dynamically loaded modules, the shell project will not have project references to the dynamically loaded modules. As a result, the published ClickOnce application manifest will not include those module files, and if you deploy the application using ClickOnce, the client computer will not receive the module files. To address this, you must modify the application manifest to include the module files that are not referenced by the shell application project.

ClickOnce Publishing Process

You can publish ClickOnce applications from Visual Studio 2010 by using a .NET Framework SDK tool named the Manifest Generating and Editing tool (Mage) or a custom tool that uses the ClickOnce publishing APIs. Visual Studio exposes most of the capabilities needed for ClickOnce publishing. However, Visual Studio might not be available to IT administrators who manage ClickOnce deployments on the server. Mage is designed to address most common administrative tasks for ClickOnce. It is a lightweight Windows-based .NET Framework application that administrators can use. However, Mage requires many detailed steps, which must be performed in the correct order, to successfully complete common tasks such as modifying the application files listed in the application manifest. To make these tasks simpler, a custom utility is needed.

The Manifest Manager Utility sample utility demonstrates how to use the ClickOnce publishing API to manage deployment and application manifests in a simpler way. This utility is used for updating application manifest file lists and deployment manifest settings in a single user interface (UI), and its use for deploying and updating Prism applications is described in later sections in this chapter. The Manifest Manager Utility uses APIs exposed in the **Microsoft.Build.Tasks.Deployment** namespace to load, manipulate, and save modified manifest files for a ClickOnce deployment. You can download the Manifest Manager Utility from the Prism community site on CodePlex at http://compositewpf. codeplex.com/releases/view/14771. To learn the specific steps involved in publishing and updating a WPF Prism application that uses dynamic module loading, see the "WPF Prism Deployment Hands-On Lab: Publishing and Updating with ClickOnce" on MSDN.

The following illustration shows the typical structure for a ClickOnce application publication, based on the way Visual Studio generates the deployment folders when you publish an application with ClickOnce. It includes a root folder for the application, which contains the default deployment manifest (.application file). The default deployment manifest usually points to the most recently published version when generated by Visual Studio, but it can be changed to point to whichever version the administrator chooses. The root folder also contains the Setup.exe bootstrapper, which allows you to deploy prerequisites for your application that might require an installer or executable to run before you use ClickOnce to deploy the application. There is a subfolder for the application-specific files, under which you have a separate subfolder for each version that you publish. The publish version is a separate project setting and entry in the deployment manifest file for versioning the application deployment as a whole, as opposed to the individual assembly versions of the assemblies that the application contains. The publish version is used by ClickOnce to determine when there is an update available for a client that has already installed a ClickOnce application.

ClickOnce publish folder structure

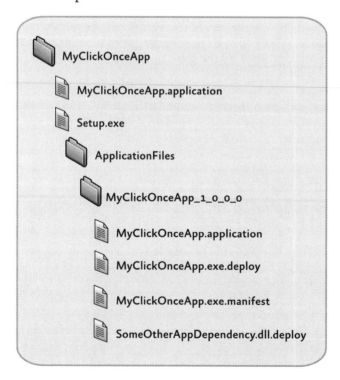

Under each publish version's application files folder, you have another copy of the deployment manifest (.application file) that can be used to deploy specific versions on a client computer, or it can be copied to the root folder to cause a server-side rollback to a previous version. The application executable, in addition to any dependent libraries (such as Prism module assemblies) and resource files, will also be in this folder and will be automatically suffixed by a .deploy file name extension when published by Visual Studio. This is done to simplify the file extension mappings on the publishing web server so that you don't have to allow downloads of .dll, .exe, and a myriad of other potential file types that the application is composed of.

The application manifest (.exe.manifest) file is also contained in this folder and is referenced by the deployment manifest. It contains the list of files the application is composed of with hash values per file to assist in change detection; it also contains a list of permissions required by the application to run because ClickOnce can start applications in a partial trust AppDomain if desired.

If you use Mage or a custom tool to manually generate or update a ClickOnce application publication, you are not constrained by this folder and file structure. However, any ClickOnce publication must include the following:

- A deployment manifest that points to the application manifest through an embedded code base URL.

- An application manifest that contains relative paths to each of the application files. These files must reside in the same folder that the application manifest resides in, or in a subfolder in that folder.

- The application files themselves, usually with a .deploy file name extension appended to the file name to simplify mapping these files to MIME types on the deployment server. ClickOnce automatically strips off the .deploy file name extension on the client side after the file is downloaded.

ClickOnce Deployment and Update Process

The actual deployment of the application on a client via ClickOnce is almost always initiated by providing a URL or hyperlink to the deployment manifest of the published application on the deployment server. The user clicks the hyperlink or enters the address in a browser, and the ClickOnce deployment process is invoked. After the manifest and application files are downloaded to the client computer, the application starts. There are ClickOnce options that allow you to install the application during the initial deployment for offline use, or you can require the user to start the application by using the link or URL every time. When you publish a new version of the application on the deployment server, ClickOnce can automatically or manually check for updates and download and apply the updates for the next time the application launches.

More Information

To learn how to use application library caching in Silverlight, see "How to: Use Application Library Caching" on MSDN:

http://msdn.microsoft.com/en-us/library/dd833069(VS.95).aspx.

To download the Manifest Manager Utility from the Prism community site on CodePlex at http://compositewpf.codeplex.com/releases/view/14771.

To learn the specific steps involved in publishing and updating a WPF Prism application that uses dynamic module loading, see the "WPF Prism Deployment Hands-On Lab: Publishing and Updating with ClickOnce" on MSDN:

http://msdn.microsoft.com/en-us/library/gg405497(PandP.40).aspx.

To access web resources more easily, see the online version of the bibliography on MSDN:

http://msdn.microsoft.com/en-us/library/gg405487(PandP.40).aspx.

Appendix A   Glossary

This glossary includes definitions of important terms that appear in the Prism documentation.

bootstrapper. The class responsible for the initialization of an application built with the Prism Library.

command. A loosely coupled way to handle user interface (UI) actions. Commands bind a UI gesture to the logic that performs the action.

composite application. An application that is composed of a number of discrete and independent modules. These components are integrated in a host environment to form a single, seamless application.

composite command. A command that has multiple child commands.

container. A layer of abstraction for the creation of objects. Dependency injection containers can reduce the dependency coupling between objects by providing the facility to instantiate instances of classes and manage their lifetime based on the configuration of the container.

DelegateCommand. A class that supports delegating command-handling logic to selected methods instead of requiring a handler in the code-behind file. It uses .NET Framework delegates as the method of invoking a target handling method.

EventAggregator. A service that is primarily a container for events. It allows publishers and subscribers to be decoupled so that they can evolve independently. This decoupling is useful in modular applications because new modules can be added that respond to events defined by the shell or other modules.

modularity. The ability to create complex applications from discrete functional units named *modules*. When you develop in a modularized fashion, you structure the application into separate modules that can be individually developed, tested, and deployed by different teams. It also helps you address separation of concerns by keeping a clean separation between the UI and business functionality.

model. A structure that encapsulates the application's business logic and data.

module. A logical unit of separation in the application.

ModuleCatalog. A list that defines the modules that the end user needs to run the application. The module catalog knows where the modules are located and the module's dependencies.

ModuleManager. The main class that manages the process of validating the module catalog, retrieving modules if they are remote, loading the modules into the application domain, and invoking the module's **Initialize** method.

module management phases. The phases that lead to a module being initialized. These phases are module discovery, module loading, and module initialization.

multi-targeted code. Code that uses the same (or nearly the same) code base to target two different platforms. This allows binaries targeting two different technologies to be produced while keeping the code as much the same as possible. The technologies that Prism helps you multi-target are Windows Presentation Foundation (WPF) and Silverlight.

navigation. The process by which the application coordinates changes to its UI as a result of user interaction with the application, or as a result of internal application state changes.

presenter-first composition. A composition approach in which the presenter is logically created first, followed by the view.

on-demand module. A module that is retrieved and initialized only when it is explicitly requested by the application.

region. A named location that you can use to define where a view will appear. Modules can locate and add content to a region in the layout without knowing exactly how and where the region is displayed. This allows the appearance and layout to change without affecting the modules that add content to the layout.

RegionContext. A technique that can be used to share context between a parent view and child views that are hosted in a region. The **RegionContext** can be set through code or by using data binding XAML.

RegionManager. The class responsible for maintaining a collection of regions and creating new regions for controls. The **RegionManager** finds an adapter mapped to a WPF or Silverlight control and associates a new region to that control. The **RegionManager** also supplies the attached property that can be used for simple region creation from XAML.

Separated Presentation pattern. The design pattern used to implement views. This pattern separates presentation and business logic from the UI. Using a separated presentation allows presentation and business logic to be tested independently of the UI, makes it easier to maintain code, and increases reuse opportunities.

shell. The location in which the primary UI content is contained; typically, the main window of a WPF application or the top-level **UserControl** of a Silverlight application.

scoped region. Regions that belong to a particular region scope. The region scope is delimited by a parent view and includes all the child views of the parent view.

service. An entity that uses an interface to provide functionality to other modules in a loosely coupled way. A service is often a singleton.

state-based navigation. Navigation accomplished by using state changes to existing controls in the visual tree.

UI composition. The act of building an interface by composing it from discrete views at run time, often from separate modules.

view. The main unit of UI construction in a composite UI application. The view encapsulates the UI and UI logic that you would like to keep as decoupled as possible from other parts of the application. You can define a view as a user control, data template, or even a custom control.

view-based navigation. Navigation accomplished by adding or removing elements from the visual tree.

view-first composition. A composition approach in which the view is logically created first, followed by the view model or presenter on which it depends.

view discovery. A way to add, show, or remove views in a region by associating the type of a view with a region name. Whenever a region with that name displays, the registered views will be created automatically, and then added to the region.

view injection. A way to add, show, or remove views in a region by adding or removing instances of a view to a region. The code interacting with the region does not have direct knowledge of how the region will handle displaying the view.

view model. An entity that encapsulates the presentation logic and state for the view. It is responsible for coordinating the view's interaction with any required model classes.

Appendix B

Patterns in the Prism Library

When you build applications, you typically encounter or employ patterns. In the Prism Library and example reference implementations, the guidance demonstrates some patterns that are briefly discussed in this appendix. The following illustration shows a typical composite application architecture using the Prism Library and some of the common patterns. A simpler Prism application would likely use some of these patterns, but not necessarily all of them.

Sample composite application architecture with common patterns

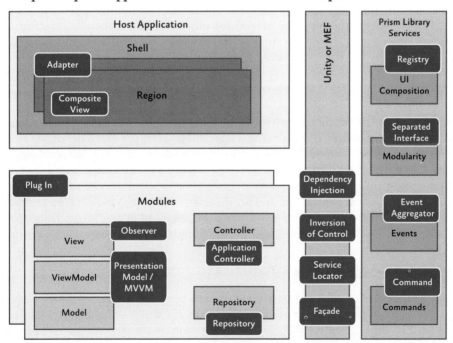

This appendix includes a brief overview of the patterns in alphabetical order and provides pointers to where you can see an example of each pattern in the Prism code.

Adapter

The Adapter pattern, as the name implies, adapts the interface of one class to match the interface expected by another class. In the Prism Library, the Adapter pattern is used to adapt regions to the Windows Presentation Foundation (WPF) or Silverlight **Items Control**, **ContentControl**, and **Selector**. To see the Adapters pattern applied, see the file ItemsControlRegionAdapter.cs in the Prism Library.

Application Controller Pattern

The Application Controller pattern allows you to separate the responsibility of creating and displaying views into a controller class. This kind of controller is a little different than the controller in an application that uses the Model-View-Controller (MVC) pattern. The application controller's responsibility is to encapsulate the control of view presentation. It takes care of instantiating views by placing them in the appropriate container in the user interface (UI), switching between views that share the same container, and sometimes coordinating communication between views or view models. Even though the name of the pattern is Application Controller, controllers are often scoped to a subset of an application, such as a module controller in a Prism application or a controller that spans a set of related views. As a result, you will often have more than one controller in a Prism application. For an example implementation of this pattern, see the **OrdersController** class in the Stock Trader Reference Implementation (Stock Trader RI).

Command Pattern

The Command pattern is a design pattern in which objects are used to represent actions. A command object encapsulates an action and its parameters. This allows a decoupling of the invoker of the command and the handlers of the command. The Prism Library provides a **CompositeCommand** that allows combining of multiple **ICommand** items and a **DelegateCommand** that allows a ViewModel or controller to provide an **ICommand** that connects to local methods for execution and notification of ability to execute. To see the usage of the **CompositeCommand** and the **DelegateCommand** in the Stock Trader RI, see the files StockTraderRICommands.cs and OrderDetailsViewModel.cs.

Composite and Composite View

At the heart of a composite application is the ability to combine individual views into a composite view. Frequently, the composing view defines a layout for the child views. For example, the shell of the application may define a navigation area and content area to host child views at run time, as shown in the following illustration.

Composition example

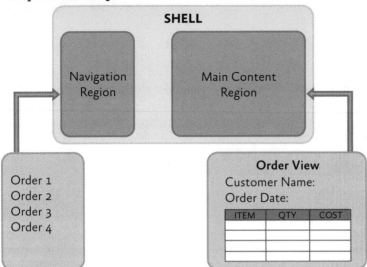

In the Stock Trader RI, this is demonstrated by the use of regions in the shell. The shell defines regions that modules locate and add views to during the initialization process. For examples of defining regions, see the Shell.xaml file.

Composite views do not have to be dynamically composed, as is the case with Prism regions. A composite view can also just be a view that is built up of several other child views that are statically composed through the UI definition. An example of this is child user controls that are declared in the Extensible Application Markup Language (XAML).

Dependency Injection Pattern

The Dependency Injection pattern is a specialized version of the Inversion of Control pattern (described later in this appendix) in which the concern being inverted is the process of obtaining the needed dependency. Dependency Injection is used throughout the Stock Trader RI and the Prism Library. When using a container, the container is responsible for construction, instead of the consuming class. During object construction, the dependency injection container resolves any external dependencies. Because of this, the concrete implementation of the dependencies can be changed more readily as the system evolves. Because of its looser coupling, this pattern better supports testability and growth of a system over time. The Stock Trader RI uses the Managed Extensibility Framework (MEF) to help manage dependencies between components. However, the Prism Library itself is not tied to a specific dependency injection container; you are free to choose whichever dependency injection container you want, but you must provide an adapter that implements the **IServiceLocator** interface. The Prism Library provides adapters for both the MEF and Unity Application Block (Unity).

To see an example of a component with its dependencies resolved by injection in the Stock Trader RI, see the constructor in the NewsController.cs file. For examples using Unity, see the **ModuleInit** class in the UI Composition QuickStart.

Event Aggregator Pattern

The Event Aggregator pattern channels events from multiple objects through a single object to simplify registration for clients. In the Prism Library, a variation of the Event Aggregator pattern allows multiple objects to locate and publish or subscribe to events. To see the **EventAggregator** and the events it manages, see **EventAggregator** and the **CompositePresentationEvent** in the Prism Library. To see the usage of the **Event Aggregator** in the Stock Trader RI, see the file WatchListViewModel.cs.

Façade Pattern

The Façade pattern simplifies a more complex interface, or set of interfaces, to ease their use or to isolate access to those interfaces. The Prism Library provides façades for the container and the logging services to help isolate the library from changes in those services. This allows the consumer of the library to provide its own services that will work with the Prism Library. The **IServiceLocator** and **ILoggerFacade** interfaces define the façade interfaces the Prism Library expects when it communicates with a container or logging service.

Inversion of Control Pattern

The Inversion of Control (IoC) pattern is often used to enable extensibility in a class or framework. For example, a class designed with an eventing model at certain points of execution inverts control by allowing event listeners to take action when the event is invoked.

Two forms of the IoC pattern demonstrated in the Prism Library and Stock Trader RI include dependency injection and the Template Method pattern. Dependency injection is described earlier. In the Template Method pattern, a base class provides a recipe, or process, that calls virtual or abstract methods. Because of this, an inherited class can override appropriate methods to enable the behavior required. In the Prism Library, this is shown in the **UnityServiceLocatorAdapter** class. To see another example of using the Template Method pattern, see the file StockTraderRIBootstrapper.cs in the Stock Trader RI.

Observer Pattern

The Observer pattern seeks to decouple those interested in an object's state change from the changing object. In the .NET Framework, this is often seen through events. Prism demonstrates a variation of the Observer pattern to separate the request for interaction with the user from the actual chosen interaction. This is done through an **Interaction Request** object that is often offered by a view model in the Model-View-ViewModel (MVVM) pattern.

This **InteractionRequest** is an object that encapsulates an event monitored by the view. When the view receives an interaction request, it can choose how to handle the interaction. A view may decide to display a modal window to provide feedback to the user, or it may display an unobtrusive notification without interrupting the user's workflow. In WPF and Silverlight, offering this request as an object provides a way to bind data to the request and to specify the response without requiring a code-behind file for the view.

Presentation Model Pattern

Presentation Model is one of several UI patterns that focus on keeping the logic for the presentation separate from the visual representation. This is done to separate the concerns of visual presentation from that of visual logic, which helps improve maintainability and testability. Related UI patterns include Model-View-Controller (MVC) and Model-View-Presenter (MVP). The Model-View-ViewModel (MVVM) approach, demonstrated in the Prism's Stock Trader RI and Model-View-ViewModel Reference Implementation (MVVM RI), is a specific implementation variant of the Presentation Model pattern.

The Prism Library itself is intended to be neutral with respect to choice of separated UI patterns. You can be successful with any of the patterns, although considering the facilities in WPF and Silverlight for data binding, commands, and behaviors, the MVVM pattern is the recommended approach and the Prism guidance provides documentation and samples to get you started using MVVM. To see examples of MVVM in the MVVM RI, see the files QuestionnaireView.xaml, QuestionnaireView.xaml.cs, and Questionnaire-ViewModel.cs.

Registry Pattern

The Registry pattern specifies an approach to locating one or more objects from a well-known object. The Prism Library applies the Registry pattern when associating view types to a region. The **IRegionViewRegistry** interface and **RegionViewRegistry** class define a registry used to associate region names to the view types created when those regions are loaded. This registry is used in the ModuleInit.cs file in the UI Composition QuickStart.

Repository Pattern

A repository allows you to separate how you acquire data for an application from the code that needs the data. The repository represents a collection of domain objects that the application code can consume without needing to be coupled to the specific mechanism that retrieves those objects. The domain objects are part of the model of the application, and by obtaining those objects through a repository, the repository retrieval and update strategy can be changed without affecting the rest of the application. Additionally, the repository interface becomes an easy dependency to substitute for the purposes of unit testing. To see an example of this in code, see the QuestionnaireRepository.cs file in the MVVM RI.

Separated Interface and Plug-In

The ability to locate and load modules at run time opens greater opportunities for parallel development, expands module deployment choices, and encourages a more loosely coupled architecture. The following patterns enable this ability:

- **Separated Interface**. This pattern reduces coupling by placing the interface definition in a separate package from the implementation. When you use Prism with Unity, each module implements the **IModule** interface. For an example of implementing a module in the UI Composition QuickStart, see the file ModuleInit.cs.

- **Plug-In**. This pattern allows the concrete implementation of a class to be determined at run time to avoid requiring recompilation when a different concrete implementation is used or because of changes in the concrete implementation. n the Prism Library, this is handled through the **DirectoryModuleCatalog**, **ConfigurationModuleCatalog**, and the **ModuleInitializer,** which work together to locate and initialize **IModule** plug-ins. For examples of supporting plug-ins, see the files DirectoryModuleCatalog.cs, ConfigurationModuleCatalog.cs, and ModuleInitializer.cs in the Prism Library.

  Note: *MEF was designed to support the plug-in model, allowing components to declaratively export and import concrete implementations.*

Service Locator Pattern

The Service Locator pattern solves the same problems that the Dependency Injection pattern solves, but it uses a different approach. It allows classes to locate specific services that they are interested in without needing to know what implements the service. This is often used as an alternative to dependency injection, but there are times when a class will need to use service location instead of dependency injection, such as when it needs to resolve multiple implementers of a service. In the Prism Library, this can be seen when the **ModuleInitializer** service resolves individual **IModules**. For an example of using the **UnityContainer** to locate a service in the UI Composition QuickStart, see the file ModuleInit.cs.

More Information

The following are references and links to the patterns found in the Stock Trader RI and in the Prism Library:

- Composite pattern in Chapter 4, "Structural Patterns," in *Design Patterns: Elements of Reusable Object-Oriented Software* (1)
- Adapter pattern in Chapter 4, "Structural Patterns," in *Design Patterns: Elements of Reusable Object-Oriented Software* (1)
- Façade pattern in Chapter 4, "Structural Patterns," in *Design Patterns: Elements of Reusable Object-Oriented Software* (1)
- Template Method pattern in Chapter 5, "Behavioral Patterns," in *Design Patterns: Elements of Reusable Object-Oriented Software* (1)
- Observer pattern in Chapter 5, "Behavioral Patterns," in *Design Patterns: Elements of Reusable Object-Oriented Software* (1)
- "Exploring the Observer Design Pattern" on MSDN: http://msdn.microsoft.com/en-us/library/Ee817669(pandp.10).aspx.
- Repository pattern in *Patterns of Enterprise Application Architecture* by Martin Fowler or the abbreviated version on his website: http://www.martinfowler.com/eaaCatalog/repository.html.
- Inversion of Control containers and the Dependency Injection pattern on Martin Fowler's website: http://www.martinfowler.com/articles/injection.html.
- Plugin pattern on Martin Fowler's website: http://www.martinfowler.com/eaaCatalog/plugin.html.
- Registry pattern on Martin Fowler's website: http://martinfowler.com/eaaCatalog/registry.html.
- Presentation Model pattern on Martin Fowler's website: http://www.martinfowler.com/eaaDev/PresentationModel.html.
- Event Aggregator pattern on Martin Fowler's website: http://www.martinfowler.com/eaaDev/EventAggregator.html.
- Separated Interface pattern on Martin Fowler's website: http://www.martinfowler.com/eaaCatalog/separatedInterface.html.
- MVC and MVP variants on Martin Fowler's website: http://martinfowler.com/eaaDev/uiArchs.html.
- "Design Patterns: Dependency Injection" by Griffin Caprio on MSDN: http://msdn.microsoft.com/en-us/magazine/cc163739.aspx.
- Model-View-ViewModel pattern on John Gossman's blog: http://blogs.msdn.com/johngossman/archive/2005/10/08/478683.aspx.

For more information about the Unity Application Block, see "Unity Application Block" on MSDN:

http://www.msdn.com/unity.

To access web resources more easily, see the online version of the bibliography on MSDN: http://msdn.microsoft.com/en-us/library/gg405487(PandP.40).aspx.

(1) Gamma, Erich, Richard Helm, Ralph Johnson, and John Vlissides.
Design Patterns: Elements of Reusable Object-Oriented Software.
Addison-Wesley Professional, 1995.

Appendix C   Prism Library

The Prism Library, formerly named the Composite Application Library, helps architects and developers create applications for Windows Presentation Foundation (WPF), Silverlight, and Windows Phone 7. The Prism Library can support those who want to build a number of application styles with WPF or Silverlight, but it is was primarily constructed for applications composed of discrete, functionally complete pieces that work together to create a single, integrated user interface (UI), often referred to as a composite application. The Prism Library uses proven design patterns to accelerate the development of applications.

The Prism Library is primarily designed to help architects and developers accomplish the following:

- Build clients composed of independent, yet cooperating, modules or pieces.
- Separate the concerns of module builders from the concerns of the shell developer. By doing this, business units can concentrate on developing domain-specific modules instead of the WPF or Silverlight architecture.
- Separate the concerns of presentation, presentation logic, and application model through support for presentation model patterns such as Model-View-ViewModel (MVVM).
- Use an architectural infrastructure to produce a consistent and high quality integrated application.
- Build applications that target both WPF and Silverlight.

When building your application with the Prism Library, you can use the Unity Extensions for the Prism Library and the Unity Application Block (Unity) or the Managed Extensibility Framework (MEF) Extensions for the Prism Library and MEF. These are built on the .NET Framework 4 for WPF or the .NET Framework for Silverlight 4, as shown in the following illustration.

Composite application package

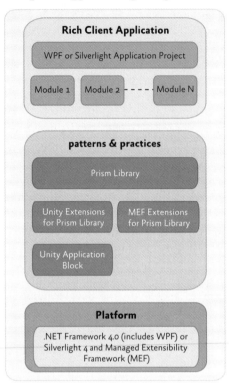

The Prism Library addresses common requirements for building both composite and non-composite applications on the WPF and Silverlight platforms. As a whole, the Prism Library accelerates development by providing the services and components to address these needs.

The Prism Library ships both as signed binaries to allow you to take advantage of Prism immediately without the need to compile, and as source in case you want to make modifications or just see how it works.

Registering with Visual Studio 2010

Because the Prism library is delivered as a self-extracting executable file, the library assemblies do not automatically register with the Visual Studio 2010 **Add References** dialog box. If you want to register the assemblies with the **Add References** dialog box, you can run the RegisterPrismBinaries.bat file located where Prism was unpackaged, as shown here.

RegisterPrismBinaries.bat

If you want to unregister these, specify /u, as shown here.

RegisterPrismBinaries.bat /u

Organization of the Prism Library

The Prism Library can be used in a WPF, Silverlight, or Windows Phone 7 application. There are Prism binaries for desktop, Silverlight, and Windows Phone in the Bin folder where Prism is installed. The binaries in the Desktop folder target WPF.

The Prism Library targeted for desktop applications consists of four assemblies:

- **Microsoft.Practices.Prism**. This assembly contains interfaces and components to help build composite applications. These components include the **EventAggregator**, **ModuleManager**, **ModuleCatalog**, and **Bootstrapper**. Additionally, this assembly contains components that relate to the presentation layer of the desktop application. These include **CompositeCommand**, **DelegateCommand**, **CompositePresentationEvent**, **RegionManager**, and **NotificationObject**.

- **Microsoft.Practices.Prism.Interactivity**. This assembly contains behaviors and actions for interactions with the UI based on Microsoft Expression Blend Behaviors (available in the Blend SDK), largely in support of the MVVM pattern. This includes **InteractionRequest**, **InteractionRequestTrigger**, **Confirmation**, and **Notification**.

- **Microsoft.Practices.Prism.UnityExtensions**. This assembly provides components for using the Unity Application Block (Unity) with the Prism Library. These components include **UnityBootstrapper** and **UnityServiceLocatorAdapter**.

- **Microsoft.Practices.Prism.MefExtensions**. This assembly provides components for using Managed Extensibility Framework (MEF) with the Prism Library. These components include **MefBootstrapper** and **MefServiceLocatorAdapter**.

The Prism Library targeted for Silverlight applications consists of four assemblies. The following describes additional functionality in each component specific to Silverlight:

- **Microsoft.Practices.Prism**. For Silverlight, this assembly includes classes that handle remote module loading, such as the **FileDownloader** and **XapModuleTypeLoader**. It also accounts for some behavioral differences in controls for regions with additional adapters and behaviors, such as **TabControlRegionAdapter** and **TabControlRegionSyncBehavior**.

- **Microsoft.Practices.Prism.Interactivity**. The Silverlight version contains **TriggerActions** to respond to **InteractionRequest**s, such as **ConfirmationChildWindow**, **NotificationChildWindow**, and **PopupChildWindowAction**.

- **Microsoft.Practices.Prism.UnityExtensions**. This assembly provides components to use Unity for Silverlight with the Prism Library. These components include **UnityBootstrapper** and **UnitServiceLocatorAdapter**.

- **Microsoft.Practices.Prism.MefExtensions**. This assembly provides components to use MEF with the Prism Library. These components include **MefBootstrapper** and **MefServiceLocatorAdapter**.

The Prism Library targeted for Windows Phone 7 applications consists of a functional subset from the Prism Library and additional phone-specific features. The Phone Library consists of two assemblies:

- **Microsoft.Practices.Prism**. This contains the components for commanding, including **DelegateCommand**; components to support view models, including **NotificationObject** and **DataTemplateSelector**; and components to support event aggregation, including **EventAggregator** and **CompositePresentationEvent**.
- **Microsoft.Practices.Prism.Interactivity**. This assembly also includes phone-specific behaviors, including **ApplicationBarButtonCommand**, **ApplicationBar ButtonNavigation**, **UpdatePasswordBindingOnPropertyChanged**, **Message BoxRequestTrigger**, and **ToastRequestTrigger**.

The Prism Library Source

The source for the Prism Library can be found in the PrismLibrary folder in which Prism is installed. The versions for the Desktop, Silverlight, and Windows Phone appear in their own folders. The source code in the Desktop folder targets WPF.

There is a Visual Studio 2010 project for each of the assemblies listed earlier, in addition to projects for test assemblies. Because each platform has very similar functionality, these projects work from a shared code-base. The primary source for the code base is in the Desktop folder. The Silverlight and phone projects have links to source files in the Desktop folder. Platform-specific source files are under the platform-specific branches. For example, the **TabControlRegionAdapter** is only available in the Silverlight version of the Prism Library source.

> **Note:** *The Prism Library project and project folder names do not match their compiled assembly names for maximum path length reasons. The convention is that the project names have "Microsoft.Practices" removed from them.*

Modifying the Library

If you want to modify the Prism Library, you can replace the signed binaries (in the Bin folder) with your own version of the binaries. To accomplish this, run the UpdatePrism Libraries.bat file. This will compile the Prism Library projects and copy the output to the appropriate place in the Bin folder, as shown here.

UpdatePrismBinaries.bat

Be default, this will only build the Desktop and Silverlight projects and copy their output. If you want to also build and copy the phone project, add the **IncludePhone** option to the batch command, as shown here.

UpdatePrismBinaries.bat /IncludePhone

Note: *When you run these commands, they will overwrite the signed binaries delivered originally with the Prism Library. If you accidentally overwrite these files, you can recover them only by again extracting Prism from the self-extracting executable file.*

Running the Tests

If you modify the Prism Library and want to verify that existing functionality is not broken, execute the unit tests for the projects. To run all the desktop unit tests in the solution file PrismLibrary.sln, on the **Test** menu, point to **Run**, and then click **All Tests in Solution**.

Executing all the Silverlight tests is a bit more difficult. Each Silverlight test project is an individual Silverlight application and, as such, must be run independently.

To run a Silverlight test

1. Right-click the desired test project in Solution Explorer, and then click **Set as Startup Project**.

2. On the **Debug** menu, point to **Start Without Debugging.**

More Information

Prism's community site is http://www.codeplex.com/Prism.
For more information about Unity, see the following:
- "Unity Application Block" on MSDN:
  http://www.msdn.com/unity.

- Unity community site on CodePlex:
  http://www.codeplex.com/unity.

  For more information about MEF, see the following:
- "Managed Extensibility Framework Overview" on MSDN:
  http://msdn.microsoft.com/en-us/library/dd460648.aspx.

- MEF community site on CodePlex:
  http://mef.codeplex.com/.

For more information about the service locator, see the Common Service Locator on CodePlex:
http://commonservicelocator.codeplex.com/.
For more information about using Prism on Windows Phone 7, see the Windows Phone 7 Developer Guide community site on CodePlex :
http://wp7guide.codeplex.com/.
To access web resources more easily, see the online version of the bibliography on MSDN at:
http://msdn.microsoft.com/en-us/library/gg405487(PandP.40).aspx.

Index